ANGLISTIK UND ENGLISCHUNTERRICHT

Herausgegeben von
Gabriele Linke
Holger Rossow
Merle Tönnies

Band 79

KORNELIA FREITAG
BRIAN REED (Eds.)

Modern American Poetry

Points of Access

Universitätsverlag
WINTER
Heidelberg

Bibliografische Information der Deutschen Nationalbibliothek
Die Deutsche Nationalbibliothek verzeichnet diese Publikation
in der Deutschen Nationalbibliografie;
detaillierte bibliografische Daten sind im Internet
über *http://dnb.d-nb.de* abrufbar.

Herausgeber:
Prof. Dr. Gabriele Linke
PD Dr. Holger Rossow
Prof. Dr. Merle Tönnies

ISBN 978-3-8253-6169-3
ISSN 0344-8266

Dieses Werk einschließlich aller seiner Teile ist urheberrechtlich geschützt. Jede Verwertung außerhalb der engen Grenzen des Urheberrechtsgesetzes ist ohne Zustimmung des Verlages unzulässig und strafbar. Das gilt insbesondere für Vervielfältigungen, Übersetzungen, Mikroverfilmungen und die Einspeicherung und Verarbeitung in elektronischen Systemen.

© 2013 Universitätsverlag Winter GmbH Heidelberg
Imprimé en Allemagne · Printed in Germany
Druck: Memminger MedienCentrum, 87700 Memmingen

Gedruckt auf umweltfreundlichem, chlorfrei gebleichtem
und alterungsbeständigem Papier

Den Verlag erreichen Sie im Internet unter:
www.winter-verlag.de

Contents

Kornelia Freitag and Brian M. Reed
   Introduction: How to Read 7

Lisa Simon
   Teaching War Poetry:
   A Dialogue Between the Grit and the Glory............................ 17

Sabine Sielke
   To "Dwell in Possibility":
   On the Challenges and Rewards of Teaching and Studying
   Emily Dickinson 37

Susanne Rohr
   On Being in Love with the World:
   Gertrude Stein's *Tender Buttons* 59

Wolfgang Wicht
   "Language is made out of concrete things":
   The Imagist Movement and the Beginning of Anglo-American
   Modernism... 79

Brian M. Reed
   Confessional Poetry: Staging the Self 99

Heinz Ickstadt
   Frank O'Hara and the "New York School":
   Poetry and Painting in the 1950s 115

David Huntsperger
   Postmodern Poetic Form in the Classroom............................. 139

Walter Grünzweig and Julia Sattler
   People's Poetry:
   Translation as a Collective Experience................................... 157

Kornelia Freitag
  Contemporary Indian-American Poetry:
  At the Crossroads of Cultures 175

Martina Pfeiler
  No Rules But in Schools?:
  Teaching and Learning from Slam Poetry 195

Kornelia Freitag (Bochum) and Brian M. Reed (Seattle)

Introduction: How to Read

> That one being one teaching is one teaching some one everything.
>
> Gertrude Stein

Terry Eagleton begins *How to Read a Poem* (2007) by complaining that the young men and women in his classes habitually ignore how poems are written and instead jump to shaky, reductive conclusions about what they "mean." They seem to believe that "[p]aying attention to form [...] means saying whether the poem is written in iambic pentameters, or whether it rhymes," but, as he points out, "saying what the poem means, and then tagging on a couple sentences about its metre or rhyme scheme, is not exactly engaging questions of form." Language is not "a kind of disposable cellophane in which the ideas come ready-wrapped." For example, one interprets the same facts differently depending on whether a writer's tone is "shrill or sardonic, mournful or nonchalant, mawkish or truculent, irascible or histrionic" (2).

Marjorie Perloff makes a similar argument in the introduction to *Differential Poetics: Poetry, Poetics, Pedagogy* (2004). She laments her students' tendency to offer "bizarre" readings of lyrics that expose fundamental misunderstandings of textual specifics (xii). She, too, recommends heightened attention to the selection, ordering, and placement of words in a poem as an antidote to hasty (mis)interpretation. She advises readers to learn to "discriminate *difference*," that is, to perceive and appreciate the shifts in meaning that follow from even the slightest variations in sound patterns, grammatical syntax, and page layout (xxvi; her emphasis).

Eagleton and Perloff are eminent, influential critics who more typically take on sophisticated intellectual topics such as the origins of modernism and the fate of the humanities. Veteran readers of poetry might find it somewhat surprising to discover them writing polemics on behalf of what can sound like close reading techniques that used to be taught in English 101. What has happened? In the twenty-first century, are the very basics of poetry interpretation truly in need of delineation, defense, and modeling?

A rash of recent publications offering professors pragmatic advice about how to teach verse certainly suggests so, among them Paula Bennett, Karen Kilcup, and Philipp Schweighauser's *Teaching Nineteenth Century American Poetry* (2007); Peter Middleton and Nicki Marsh's *Teaching Modernist Poetry* (2010); Joan Retallack and Juliana Spahr's *Poetry and Pedagogy: The Challenge of the Contemporary* (2006); and Joshua Maria Wilkinson's *Poets on Teaching: A Sourcebook* (2010). The MLA Bibliography, too, will confirm that poetry instruction is currently a lively area of scholarly inquiry. Searching the database using the keywords "poetry and teaching" will turn up over one thousand books, book chapters, and articles published since 2000. The keywords "poetry and pedagogy" will yield another 156 entries dating from between 2000 and 2009.

The same two database searches will also reveal another important fact, after the total number of hits (roughly three thousand) are broken down by decade:

	Search String "Poetry and Teaching"	Search String "Poetry and Pedagogy"
1920-1929	59	0
1930-1939	75	0
1940-1949	64	0
1950-1959	101	0
1960-1969	164	0
1970-1979	181	1
1980-1989	397	20
1990-1999	628	42
2000-2009	982	156

While these simple keyword searches do raise many questions, definitional and otherwise, nonetheless, the overall tendency is unmistakable. Eagleton and Perloff are belatedly joining a fifty-year-old conversation. Starting in the 1950s, every decade has seen a substantial increase in the total number of scholarly publications concerning *die Didaktik der Dichtung*. This trend, moreover, is not simply a result of an increase in academic publication in general. If one looks up "poetry and meter" and "poetry and prosody," for instance, one will find that those subjects reached their peaks in the 1980s and have fallen steadily ever since. Academics seem increasingly driven to discuss what kinds of education help people become "poetry-literate" (Middleton 332).

A long list of causes – cultural, economic, political, vocational, and institutional – have surely contributed to this half-century of steadily intensifying investment in poetry and pedagogy. One key factor, though, has doubtless been the swiftly escalating number of creative writing programs in the United States since World War II. Although this phenomenon's origins date back to the 1880s, the idea of "having practitioners of that art teach that art" only began to gain widespread respectability in academic circles around 1950. By 1967 enough "accomplished authors" had been hired by colleges and universities to teach creative writing that they were able to found a national umbrella organization, the Associated Writing Programs (AWP) (Fenza). Since then, the credentialization of creative writers has mushroomed into "an enterprise that now numbers some 350 institutional participants and continues to grow" (McGurl xii). And insofar as creative writing as a discipline places at its center not the "conservation" of literature but its production, one outcome has been the proliferation of publications that provide advice – and analyze and speculate – about how poetry writing is best taught (Fenza). How should a teacher conduct a workshop? Should she present herself as a role model, a facilitator, or an editor? Can she ever hope to pass on to students the ineffable *je ne sais quoi* that distinguishes true genius from hackwork? Classics in this vein include Kim Addonizio's *The Poet's Companion* (1997), Richard Hugo's *The Triggering Town* (1979), and Mary Oliver's *A Poetry Handbook* (1994).

While the question of the workshop and the problem of how to teach poetry composition to students who want to become poets themselves do feature prominently in recent publications such as Middleton and Marsh's *Teaching Modernist Poetry*, Retallack and Spahr's *Poetry and Pedagogy*, and Wilkinson's *Poets on Teaching*, the contributors to those works also overwhelmingly share Eagleton's and Perloff's concern that most of today's students – far from wanting to write it – appear to lack the tools, experiences, and concepts necessary to *read* poetry. Does this mean that – except among aspiring poets – "poetry literacy" in general has been declining? There might be something to this thesis, as the status of poetry seems to have dropped over the last decades. As Joseph Harrington has argued, "in U.S. criticism from the 1950s to the present, the emerging field of 'American literature' has come to be defined preeminently by prose narrative" (508). *The Marginalization of Poetry* (Bob Perelman's 1996 book title) in academic and public discourse has led to more or less heated debates which culminated in dramatic declarations of the *Death of Poetry* (part of a 1993 book title by Vernon Shetley), the question "Who Killed Poetry" (Joseph Epstein 1988), and battle cries like "Death to the Death of Poetry" (Donald Hall 1992). Yet while Hall, Epstein, and Shetley centered their lamentations narrowly on poets, their texts, and national reading preferences, Harrington argues convincingly that "the exclusion of American poetry from 'American literature' and the identification of the latter with prose narrative has more to do with institutional history than with any inherent generic or national characteristics" (510). Somewhat along the same lines, Alan Golding has observed that one reason for the "intellectual narrowness" of preferring prose to poetry is the widespread assumption that "prose forms (usually fiction) [...] have a superficially more 'direct' connection to social and historical reality" (xiii).

And the study of poetry itself, which – death warrants notwithstanding – of course has never ceased, has also been influenced by "institutional history" (Harrington). Hence, a further frame that can help one think about developments and changes in post-World War II interest in poetry and pedagogy is the history of poetry study as a profession in the United States. According to Gerald Graff, the 1950s and 1960s, the years when, according to Table 1, the publication of scholarship on the teaching of poetry began to take off, were a time of "routinization of criticism" (240). A bundle of analytic and pedagogical practices loosely and somewhat misleadingly called "New Criticism" – promoting "close reading" of "respectable poetry" to cherish the "ordered" ambiguity created by "great" writers (Richards 203) – became ubiquitous and normative. But by the late 1960s and early 1970s, as Nicholas Birns's *Theory after Theory* (2010) narrates, students and professors began vigorously challenging that orthodoxy, and the subsequent decades have been marked by a series of successive "waves" and "turns," as different approaches, theories, and methodologies gained currency and fell out of favor. The challenge of feminism, the vogue for poststructuralist philosophy, the popularization of postcolonial critique, the provocation of queer theory, the impact of cultural studies, and the emergence of a variety of neo-formalisms: Table 1 suggests that academic interest in the teaching of poetry continued its smooth upward ascent during each leg of this pass-the-baton narrative.

One can intuitively grasp why this might be the case. Over time, as critics repeatedly revisited the same corpus of poets, they discovered new and productive routes into their writings. New canons and kinds of poetry began to be studied, too, which in turn led to the re-evaluation of long cherished aesthetic, cultural, and moral norms. Different varieties of close reading were devised to enable pursuit of distinct ends, and the connections between poetic language and many other types of discourse were identified and analyzed. Under such circumstances, is it any surprise that confusion and disagreement might arise over – and that people might seek guidance concerning – what constitutes basic, intermediate, and advanced knowledge and skills? Today, as Marsh puts it in the introduction to *Teaching Modernist Poetry*, specialists in modern and contemporary verse who want their students to benefit from the many breakthroughs and advances of the last half century have to take an "overwhelming array of new methodologies, resources, and knowledge" and adapt them to the "practical exigencies of a pedagogy that is attempting to encourage ten, twenty, or even two hundred students to confidently approach a poem that appears to resist a singular reading" (3). How can one ever hope to carry out such a daunting task?

But – isn't it worth a try? For all its apparent marginalization within the academy, the publishing industry, and popular culture, poetry nonetheless remains a vibrant, variegated art form in the United States. A series of recent high-profile anthologies – among them Reginald Shepherd's *Lyric Postmodernisms* (2008), Cole Swensen and David St. John's *American Hybrid* (2009), and Kenneth Goldsmith and Craig Dworkin's *Against Expression* (2011) – testify to the continuing ingenuity and ambition of American poets. And those poets also continue to publish a great deal. The Poets House in New York City, "which aspires to acquire every book of poetry published in America, excluding vanity press publications [...] shelved over 20,000 volumes from between the years 1993 and 2006" (Dworkin 8). Verse is positively thriving online, too. There are popular portal sites such as Poetryfoundation.org, Poets.org, and PennSound; poetry-focused e-zines such as *Eoagh*, *Jacket2*, and *Rain Taxi*; and innumerable blogs, most famously Ron Silliman's, which exceeded two million total hits in 2009. Older poetry has benefited as well as new. On YouTube.com, for instance, one will find that a recording of T.S. Eliot reading "The Waste Land" has been downloaded over 180,000 times. Allen Ginsberg reading the first part of "Howl" clocks in at around 212,000 downloads. Sylvia Plath reading "Daddy" over half a million. Today's youth might not be ideally prepared to grapple with the many interpretive difficulties that modern poetry often poses, but there is a whole world of it out there to discover, and a surprising number of students are already aware of its wonders and, when given the chance, are eager to learn more.

The present volume – *Modern American Poetry: Points of Access* – assembles ten essays that offer "reports from the front lines." These pieces distill and share tips, facts, arguments, interpretations, and techniques that a range of different German and American scholars think to be helpful and have previously tried out in classroom situations. Some of the essays have a personal and meditative tone. Others are more objective and strive to pass along a summary of what a person would need to know to teach a subject properly. Regardless, all the participating scholars share a single goal: to provide interested readers and especially instructors with insight into how aspects of an exciting, chaotic, contested field of study can be transformed into lessons that are enlightening and, ideally, enjoyable.

At issue, again and again, is the problem that vexes Eagleton and Perloff, namely, how to persuade students to perceive and wrestle with the linguistic and material specificity of poetry as an indispensable part of making a responsible, supportable statement about "what it says." This insistence on the quiddity of language, on its sensuous, tangible, and stubborn *thereness*, is more than a recurrent theme. These critics ascribe value to it, aesthetic and otherwise, and, each according to his or her own lights, seek to persuade readers of the rewards of exploring its marvels, intricacies, and urgencies. After a generation of challenges to New Criticism from every quarter, this shared investment in poetry as patterned, resonant language represents a hard-won but significant consensus about how and why one reads – and teaches – poetry.

Three of the essays – Sabine Sielke's "To 'Dwell in Possibility': On the Challenges and Rewards of Teaching and Studying Emily Dickinson," Susanne Rohr's "On Being in Love With the World: Gertrude Stein's *Tender Buttons*," and Heinz Ickstadt's "Frank O'Hara and the 'New York School': Poetry and Painting in the 1950s" – concentrate on individual poets. They showcase a variety of ways of approaching works that often perplex beginning readers, and they point to contexts that can enrich and ease students' first exposure to these poets' artistry. Sielke examines Dickinson's place in contemporary American popular culture, Rohr places Stein within what she calls the "upheavals of modernism," and Ickstadt examines O'Hara's involvement with the New York arts scene.

An additional three essays – Wolfgang Wicht's "'Language is Made Out of Concrete Things': The Imagist Movement and the Beginning of Anglo-American Modernism," Brian M. Reed's "Confessional Poetry: Staging the Self," and Kornelia Freitag's "Contemporary Indian-American Poetry: At the Crossroads of Cultures" – look at groups of writers, providing abundant opportunities for comparison as well as for meditations on the relationship between literary composition and the social milieu in which it takes place. Wicht surveys the origins and character of Imagism, both as a movement and as a set of prescriptions about good versecraft that catalyzed the modernist revolution in literature. He spotlights the contributions of Ezra Pound, F.S. Flint, T.E. Hulme, and H.D. Reed describes the origins of the literary-historical term *confessional poetry* in the mannered, highly theatrical writing styles of mid-twentieth-century poets such as Robert Lowell and Sylvia Plath. Freitag discusses several contemporary Indian-American poets, including R.K. Ramanujan, Meena Alexander, Prageeta Sharma, and Srikanth Reddy, and she examines the role played in their work by such themes as immigration, diaspora, and exile.

The final four essays each tackle a particularly thorny pedagogical question. Drawing on poetry from the American Revolution, Civil War, and World War I, Lisa Simon's "Teaching War Poetry: A Dialogue Between the Grit and the Glory" demonstrates that one can conscientiously and effectively introduce politically and emotionally troubling material into the literature classroom. In "Postmodern Poetic Form in the Classroom" David

Huntsperger surveys several varieties of the tricky, eccentric, experimental post-World War II verse that are collectively called "postmodern," and he explores ways of making them accessible to readers who might otherwise consider them off-putting or unintelligible. Martina Pfeiler rehearses in her contribution "No Rules But in Schools?: Teaching and Learning from Slam Poetry" the history of "slam poetry," and she offers formal and sociohistorical approaches to an exciting body of oral literature that has rarely been studied with the care that it deserves. Lastly, Walter Grünzweig and Julia Sattler share details concerning two translation initiatives at Technische Universität Dortmund. They suggest in "People's Poetry: Translation as a Collective Experience" that small groups working together to translate modern American poetry into German can provide an invaluable lesson in what Perloff calls "discriminat[ing] difference" (xxvi). These groups must wrestle with fine nuances of meaning, and they must think through how to balance syntactical and referential fidelity to a source text with a deeper faithfulness to its style and spirit.

The essays in *Modern American Poetry: Points of Access* are organized roughly chronologically, beginning with Simon on nineteenth-century poets such as Joel Barlow, Herman Melville, and Walt Whitman and ending with Pfeiler on Zora Howard, a contemporary performance poet and the author of the slam poem "Biracial Hair." This collection provides examples of how to teach Civil War-era, modernist, late modernist, and postmodern verse. It features both well-known authors – like Whitman, Dickinson, Stein, Pound, O'Hara, and Plath – and writers who might be less famous but are today considered important figures within the expanded multicultural American poetry canon – Agha Shahid Ali, Lyn Hejinian, June Jordan, and Zora Howard. Poet-scholar Charles Bernstein has written, "[t]he point is not that all poetic study needs to be fun, but that thematic and formal analysis needs to be connected with the experiential dimension of the poem" (47). As should be clear, this collection means to open manifold routes to poetic experiences. Encountering the poems and authors that are discussed here, students will have the chance to lose themselves in the warp and woof of artfully arranged language. May they come to agree with Audre Lorde: "Poetry makes something happen, indeed. It makes you happen. It makes your living happen […]. A poet is by definition a teacher also" (184).

Bibliography

Bernstein, Charles. *Attack of the Difficult Poems: Essays and Inventions.* Chicago, IL: University of Chicago Press, 2011.

Dworkin, Craig. "Seja Marginal." *The Consequence of Innovation: 21st Century Poetics.* Ed. Craig Dworkin. New York, NY: Roof Books, 2008. 7-24.

Eagleton, Terry. *How to Read a Poem.* Oxford: Blackwell-Wiley, 2007.

Epstein, Joseph. "Who Killed Poetry?" *Commentary* 86.2 (August 1988): 13-20.

Fenza, David. "About AWP: The Growth of Creative Writing Programs." *Association of Writers & Writing Programs.* Available at http://www.awpwriter.org/aboutawp/index.htm. Last accessed 11 Sept. 2011.

Golding, Alan. *From Outlaw to Classic: Canons in American Poetry.* Madison, WI: University of Wisconsin Press, 1995.

Graff, Gerald. *Professing Literature: An Institutional History.* Rev. ed. Chicago, IL: University of Chicago Press, 2007.

Hall, Donald. "Death to the Death of Poetry." *Harpers Magazine* 279 (September 1992): 72-76.

Harrington, Joseph. "Why American Poetry Is Not American Literature." *American Literary History* 8.3 (Fall 1996): 497-515.

Lorde, Audre. *I Am Your Sister: Collected and Unpublished Writings.* Ed. Rudolph P. Bird, Johnetta Betsch Cole, and Beverly Guy-Sheftall. New York, NY: Oxford University Press, 2009.

Marsh, Nicki. "Introduction: Poetry and Pedagogy." *Teaching Modernist Poetry.* Ed. Peter Middleton and Nicki Marsh. New York, NY: Palgrave, 2010. 1-9.

McGurl, Mark. *The Program Era: Postwar Fiction and the Rise of Creative Writing.* Cambridge, MA: Harvard University Press, 2009.

Middleton, Peter. "The Contemporary Poetry Reading." *Close Listening: Poetry and the Performed Word.* Ed. Charles Bernstein. New York, NY: Oxford University Press, 1998. 262-299.

Perelman, Bob. *The Marginalization of Poetry: Language Writing and Literary History.* Princeton, NJ: Princeton University Press, 1996.

Perloff, Marjorie. *Differentials: Poetry, Poetics, Pedagogy.* Tuscaloosa, AL: University of Alabama Press, 2004.

Richards, I. A. *Practical Criticism.* Repr. London: Routledge, 1964.

Shetley, Vernon. *After the Death of Poetry: Poet and Audience in Contemporary America.* Durham, NC: Duke University Press, 1993.

Lisa Simon (Missoula, Montana)

Teaching War Poetry:
A Dialogue Between the Grit and the Glory

Poems about war date back to our earliest literature, and yet they are still being written in earnest today. The subject holds the gravitas of time-honored tradition at the same time it is continuously renewed by the energy and immediacy of current events. Yet the subject of war is too often taught as if it were one or another – historical or current. Literature often views the past in epochs, which inadvertently overlooks a crucial element in the study of war poetry – its dialogue across time. This dialogue within the poetry has great potential for generating dynamic discussion about the conflicts implicit in war itself, and about how literature helps us – and has always helped us – understand what it is to be human.

Good poems find ways to express conflicting ideas simultaneously, and war poems in particular convey the often deeply conflicted values of a culture. On one hand positive human qualities are routinely acknowledged and honored in the poetry of war: great human strength, bravery and grace; arguments for justice, liberty and the autonomy of a nation. The good is often also celebrated in the ingenuity of war strategy and the power of new technologies of warfare – guns, airplanes, submarines, even biological weaponry. On the other side of the coin, of course, is the violence and carnage on the battlefield, the suffering of soldiers and the widespread grief caused to families and cultures by massive losses of human life. Good poems tend to demonstrate a spectrum of thought; they find ways to both honour courage and show regret for loss. And poets always have been, as James Anderson Winn points out, great teachers of complexity and doubleness (8). Poets have long practiced what John Keats called "Negative Capability" – the capacity to acknowledge, even live with, inherent contradictions without any "irritable reaching" toward univocal truth (41-42).

Teaching war poetry then is a particular and delicate challenge and one much needed in today's world. Poets deepen our understanding of the experiences of the battlefield; they temper the claims of grandeur; they can make us see and feel the lives behind the abstractions, expose military euphemisms like "collateral damage" and "rendition" to the tragedy of individual lives again. They show us over and over that even so-called good wars are rife with suffering and scarring, both physical and psychological. So while it is generally acknowledged that literature has dealt with war since Homer's *Iliad* the fact that poets have been writing *back* to Homer and to each other has received less attention. But it is here where the most earnest dialogue takes place. Poets examine what it is to go to war – to believe in national causes, to suffer, to survive, and to wish one had not. We can deepen our understanding about armed conflict from these teachers as we take the poetry of war into our classrooms.

Using just American sources, primarily from three wars – the American Revolutionary War, the American Civil War and World War I – I'll be tracing an evolution of thought and its depiction in poetry down to the twenty-first century. At the start of this evolution, poets generally align themselves with "the fight," presenting panoramic, even bird's-eye views of war that barely consider the actual conditions of combat. A few generations later, however, we see poets complicating this one-sided view, moving to a more complex position of critique. America's Civil War poets negotiate the "good" of war as depicted by their predecessors while introducing the gritty and unflinching realism of the battlefield and the physical suffering of soldiers. By the early twentieth century, we see poets taking up war's effects on individual psychology. Since World War I, in a theater where millions waited to die in putrid trenches – by gunfire, suicide, gas, frost or by drowning in the mud itself – poets have been preoccupied with expressing through language the mind's response to prolonged exposure to violence – how it breaks down and how it fortifies itself against the inevitable horrors of war. Even as new poets deepen our understanding of martial conflict, they use poetry of the past to guide the way. My goal in teaching war poetry is to give students these seemingly simple but accruing concepts to take with them in their own negotiations of ideas about war.

1. Early American War Poetry

America's Revolutionary War was the product of Enlightenment philosophical and intellectual discourses of democracy. America was imagined as a place that could resist the tyranny of monarchs and despots, where citizens could reasonably choose leaders who would govern under agreed-upon rules of law. Enlightenment thinkers often regarded war as *necessary*, a way to purge corruption, to purify the oppressive heads of state and truly begin a new way of life. The preponderance of idealism in this new national venture allowed early poets to focus on the righteous cause and to downplay the loss of human lives. Most of the era's war poems extol the power and glory of war. In one such poem, *The Columbiad* (1807) by Joel Barlow, the bloodshed and fighting are subordinate to the atmosphere and spectacle of war:

> Now roll like winged storms the solid lines,
> The clarion thunders and the battle joins,
> Thick flames in vollied flashes load the air,
> And echoing mountains give the noise of war;
> Sulphureous clouds rise reddening round the height,
> And veil the skies, and wrap the sounding fight. (198-99)

Barlow eyes war from a lofty distance and pays attention to the sights and sounds as if they were merely powerful occurrences within the natural world. Like many Enlightenment-era authors, he chooses the metaphor of a mountain's erupting volcano to depict war (Fuller 5); that is, he sees battle as a force that begins with a rumbling and then demonstrates a fiery power that, importantly for a fledgling America, forges new ground. Lacking in this period of poetry are the experiences of individual soldiers. Poets primarily depict the visual spectacle as in the "vollied flashes," and how the "clouds rise reddening round the height," but we remain remote from the actual "sounding fight." The "noise of war" is cast as an environmental phenomenon within the larger framework of "echoing mountains."

This focus on war's visual aesthetic – its capacity to purge with literal fire via bombs, firearms, and cannons – is known as the *military sublime*. Like more traditional uses of the term sublime, it denotes an apex of aesthetic experience while connoting a potential for destruction. It emphasizes the excitement, noise, and chaos of battle that Homer called "the wild joy of war" (qtd. in Fuller 105).

The military sublime is apparent in the poem "Defence of Fort McHenry" (1814), composed during the War of 1812. This war, like the Revolutionary, was fought against Britain and is often called America's *second* war of independence. The poem and its back-story are well known to Americans. The inspiring event takes place during a tense period when the British were attacking ports all along the Eastern seaboard. Under a flag of truce, a small emissary for the United States – including John Stuart Skinner, a diplomat, and the poem's author, Francis Scott Key – boarded a British battleship to arrange for the release of a prisoner, Dr. William Beanes. These negotiations were successful, but the British feared that if they let the Americans return too soon they would alert their side to an impending attack on Fort McHenry in Baltimore. The British chose to detain them until morning. During the heavy bombardment that continued throughout the night, the captive party anxiously watched the fort's shoreline. As daylight broke they searched for any sign that the British had been defeated. At last the smoke cleared and they saw the American flag, tattered and blackened, still flying over the fort. That image became a rousing symbol of defiance and courage for the new democracy. And the poem penned by Francis Scott Key would eventually become America's national anthem. In this first stanza, the anxious inquiry is focused on the blazing sky above the hostile combat:

> O! say, can you see, by the dawn's early light,
> What so proudly we hail'd at the twilight's last gleaming,
> Whose broad stripes and bright stars through the perilous fight,
> O'er the ramparts we watch'd, were so gallantly streaming?
>   And the rockets' red glare, the bombs bursting in air,
>   Gave proof through the night that our flag was still there –
>   O, say, does that star-spangled banner yet wave
>   O'er the land of the free, and the home of the brave? (18-19)

Like Barlow, Key trains the poem's gaze on the awesome visual spectacle. He depicts the "rockets' red glare, the bombs bursting in air" more like a delightful fireworks display than a lethal, devastating shelling. The flag, that "star-spangled banner" (as the poem was eventually renamed), attracts attention away from the human beings who died in order for it to fly. These lives are presumed to have been given with dignity and taken with honor, a point later poets will question. But here, soldiers are largely anonymous and invisible heroes who pay the ultimate price for "the land of the free, and the home of the brave." This is familiar and enticing language, and it is precisely what needs to be complicated by pointing out what it excludes: namely the human experience of war. Did, in fact, the soldiers die with dignity and honor? Is soldiering always, by definition, heroic?

If we answer yes to those questions, we have to wonder then why the imagery of war poetry is so often fixed in an imaginary or romanticized past of medieval knights or ancient Greek heroes. Can't it be noble within the context of its own time, its own reality? We see Key display this romanticizing impulse when he describes the flag, as seen over the ramparts, in a personification of a chivalric knight, his "banner" "gallantly streaming." Key harkens to a past that imagines war as a romanticized knightly conquest in a medieval setting. This long-standing trope of war poetry denies the horrific levels of violence, corruption and mayhem that scholars tell us characterized the actual culture of knights. The poet's use of the military sublime and the imaginary past in this work deflect from the gore and loss of human lives in a way that is misleading at best. In the last stanza, Key does confess to the "war's desolation" on the ground, but his work largely keeps the reader's gaze above that grisly reality – both in its imagery and via its underlying idealism (19).

The poetry and songs of early America are steeped in patriotism, professing a greater good that might be achieved in a "free" society. These rousing calls for national solidarity, coupled with the attention to the visual aesthetics of war, are part of the complicated pleasure people derive from war poetry of this era. But most literary critics agree that the poetry of this period is not particularly good, largely because it is too simplistic. In the classroom, I use the poetry of this period to tease out my students' ideas about what is "good" about war – to get them to articulate their own feelings of patriotism and nationalism; their thirst for adventure and danger; their desire to be brave, to earn praise from their peers, loved ones and communities; and their interest in guns, machinery and war technology. I let class discussion digress into their enthusiasm for popular books and films that depict war. It's my belief that to truly prepare for the next stage, to truly feel the complicated, ethical quarrel always present in the discourse of war, the inherent seduction and thrills of warfare must be present in the classroom. I often bring in visuals, showing, for example, riveting clips from popular movies such as *Saving Private Ryan* (1998). I create strong visual, visceral experiences that usually fascinate students. While I have organized the class in different ways over the years, the right order of the lesson seems to be to pique their curiosity through the time-honored and deep cultural fascination with visual spectacle. I make sure they can identify uses of the military sublime (awesome visuals and sounds), romantic abstraction (a singular focus on "glory" and "honor"), euphemistic uses of personification (such as Key's knightly flag) and metaphor (such as Barlow's volcano as America) and the larger technique of casting modern battle onto a nostalgic and imagined past, usually ancient or chivalric. I don't lecture on the limits of these devices; rather, I allow them to discover these limitations for themselves in the next stage, when, historically, the poetry itself troubles these notions.

2. Civil War Poetry

Early American wars were justified as noble fights against tyranny, oppression and corruption, but the Civil War (1861-1865) was fought to prevent the dissolution of the union, to resolve by might what could not be resolved through diplomacy. America's high ideals were tested as a democracy that boasted *e pluribus unum* – out of many one – threatened to dissolve into two radically different factions when the southern region sought to secede. No one thought the war would last long, and they certainly never predicted the horrific levels of violence the war would usher into this young country's history.

An early response to that war, demonstrating an uneasy balance in the poetry of a new, rising sensibility, is Walt Whitman's "Beat, Beat, Drums" (1861). The title evokes the sounds typical of a military parade and suggests the visual spectacle we would expect from the Revolutionary War poems. But the drums and bugles of Whitman's poem herald more than the military sublime. As we read on we see the noise anticipating an abrupt interruption of the lives of everyday citizens:

> Beat! beat! drums! – blow! bugles! blow!
> Through the windows—through doors – burst like a ruthless force,
> Into the solemn church, and scatter the congregation,
> Into the school where the scholar is studying;
> Leave not the bridegroom quiet – no happiness must he now have with his bride,
> Nor the peaceful farmer any peace, ploughing his field or gathering his grain,
> So fierce you whirr and pound you drums – so shrill you bugles blow. (222)

The force of the military parade bursts through the landscape with a whirring and pounding comparable to the noise and visual spectacle we saw in *The Columbiad* and "Defence of Fort McHenry." Yet Whitman depicts the civic arena forcefully disrupted: a congregation of worshippers is scattered, a scholar leaves his study, a recently married couple is rent from one another, and a farmer – notice the poet emphasizes a *peaceful* farmer – is kept from the labour that sustains his family. The disruption of universities, churches, marriages, and agriculture signal the consequence of war tearing at the very fabric of society and finding its way into the nation's poetry.

The cost of the Civil War – in time, in national resources and in soldiers – was grossly underestimated by the orchestrators of the war and its supporters on both sides. The general population was so naive and full of illusions about the reality of war that at one early battle groups of civilians actually showed up as spectators to what they thought would be a scene of gentlemanly warfare comparable to the ones they had read and heard about. The historian Randall Fuller depicts the scene:

> What they saw instead was panic and confusion. Entire companies of men fled, some dazed and bloodstained, some screaming in pain. They ran from the battlefield as fast as they could, stunned by what they had just experienced in nearby fields and woods. The fear was contagious. Hearing hysterical soldiers shriek, "Turn back! Turn back! We are whipped!" the civilians fled in as hurried and disorganized a fashion as the disgraced Army of the Potomac. (29)

What many saw and what pierced the illusions of abstract glory and heroism was human suffering on a massive, previously unimaginable scale – soldiers by the thousands, bleeding, screaming, dying, calling out for help, and crying for the end of pain. A survivor recalls, "we saw for the first time the results of real war. It was a new sight probably to everyone in the regiment; the dead and wounded lying where they fell" (qtd. in Fuller 29). Whitman too would be changed. He recalled later: "The dream of humanity, the vaunted Union we thought so strong, so impregnable – lo! it seems already smash'd like a china plate" (qtd. in Fuller 30).

But if the grisly realities of early Civil War battles awakened the population to the human cost of war, the battle of Shiloh in Tennessee stunned the nation with a bloodletting beyond imagination. The once sleepy fields of Shiloh saw 100,000 soldiers fight in grisly combat over two days "with one in four killed, wounded, or taken prisoner. More young men were killed in a single day than had been killed in the previous year combined" (Fuller 100). When it was over, nearly 24,000 had died, some from fighting and some from an intense fire that swept through a patch of dense underbrush where medics were taking wounded soldiers to care for them. An eye-witness claimed that "the sights of that battlefield ought to cure anybody of war," and he described bodily carnage so thick it was impossible to walk through the field without stepping on bodies, living and dead. He further observed "[w]ounded men with mangled legs and arms and heads half shot off." They were tended by unsophisticated medical practitioners as "surgeons saw[ed] off legs and arms on outdoor tables" (qtd. in Fuller 54-55). Battlefield stories such as these chastened earlier notions that war could be considered merely in terms of grand or honorable abstractions. The discord between jingoistic battle calls and actual battlefield experiences forced the American culture to acknowledge the physical consequences of warfare in a way the Revolutionary War had not.

The shift in attitude is reflected in a short but culturally loaded poem by Herman Melville, "Shiloh: A Requiem" (1862). The poem begins in a mode that recalls its antecedents; it describes the atmospheric conditions over Shiloh's calm pastures which, before the battle, were only visited by those gathering to worship at the picturesque log church that stood at the edge. The speaker's gaze begins above the scene focused on a bird's flight:

> Skimming lightly, wheeling still,
> The swallows fly low
> Over the field in clouded days,
> The forest-field of Shiloh — (63)

Unlike the poems of Barlow and Key, Melville's poem shifts its gaze slowly from the air to the ground, allowing scenes of grievous human suffering to enter the pastoral setting.

> Over the field where April rain
> Solaced the parched ones stretched in pain
> Through the pause of night
> That followed the Sunday fight
> Around the church of Shiloh —
> The church so lone, the log-built one,
> That echoed to many a parting groan
> And natural prayer
> Of dying foemen mingled there — (63)

Melville cunningly employs the archaic word "foemen" to wind down his description of men on both sides dying together, whispering "natural prayer[s]" around the church. Just as the poem's airborne perspective harkens back to poems of the past, the word "foeman" in the last line of this stanza, as well as its recurrence in the next line, signals a connection to the larger discourse of literature about war. "Foemen" was not a word in contemporary circulation but rather served as a genre signifier for works seeped in Romantic chivalric fantasy. And there was no greater exemplar within that genre than Scottish writer Sir Walter Scott.

In fact, Scott, known as a historical novelist, was a favorite for Southern readers throughout the 19th century. But his flowery depictions of warfare made him a target for the very sharp barbs of the iconic American writer of the South, Samuel Clemens, better known as Mark Twain. Clemens accuses Scott of actually causing the war because the latter had "run the people mad, a couple of generations ago, with his medieval romances" (40). Scott's poetry, he continues, fomented a normalcy based on fake and dreamy premises by depicting

> the world in love with dreams and phantoms [...] with the sillinesses and emptinesses, sham grandeurs, sham gauds, and sham chivalries of a brainless and worthless long-vanished society. He did measureless

harm; more real and lasting harm, perhaps, than any other individual that ever wrote. (162)

Melville's repetition of the archaic "foemen" alludes to just these romanticized scenes of warfare. Scott peppers his *faux*-medieval romances with such archaic words in order to, perhaps ironically, add linguistic validity to an imaginary world in a fabled time where knights gallantly combat each other for the purity of maidens while spouting florid lines like "the stern joy which warriors feel / In foemen worthy of their steel" (*Lady of the Lake* 147).

The outrage of Melville's protest against romanticizing battlefield experiences emerges in the next lines between the jarring disharmony in depictions of "honourable" warfare and the irredeemable anguish of soldiers. The poem takes a dramatic turn and shows that, in the face of death, these young soldiers see the folly of quixotic depictions of warfare. Melville repeats the archaic "foemen" for emphasis:

> Foemen at morn, but friends at eve –
> Fame or country least their care:
> (What like a bullet can undeceive!) (63)

The poet suggests that these soldiers didn't come to battle as enemies; rather they came as "foemen," bearers of archaic and imagined notions of battle. Melville sardonically questions whether battle or self-deception is more to blame. In death these false notions fall away and the dying become friends and authentically human. As eyewitnesses noted, the fallen comforted each other regardless of the color of their uniforms. The lofty justifications for heroic battle – personal fame, the ideals of a country – became "least their care." Melville's torrid parenthetical line, which like a bullet pierces through otherwise soft and lumbering stanzas, alludes to one of Scott's most famous statements, "O what a tangled web we weave / When first we practice to deceive!" (*Marmion* 343). The focus on the material bullet, the raw lead artefact, exerts itself between this visual of suffering bodies and outmoded chivalric notions. In doing so, it "undeceives" a nation in love with chivalric battle. The practices of cultural deception, which include war cast in the military sublime, are disabused in that moment. Melville ends the poem in a deadened calm, moving the poetic gaze back into the atmosphere as the hillsides of Shiloh absorb the bodies and nature resumes her cycle. The birds flit by, unaware of the follies of mankind:

> But now they lie low,
> While over them the swallows skim
> And all is hushed at Shiloh. (63)

Ultimately the requiem that Melville pens for the battle of Shiloh is as much for these deceiving cultural practices as it is for the 24,000 dead. In the Civil War the battles of Gettysburg and Chickamauga lay ahead, and each would claim at least another 35,000 lives. Yet American literature had taken a historical turn toward realism in how it regarded, depicted and calculated warfare.

Near the end of the Civil War Walt Whitman published a firsthand account of his time aiding the wounded in a hospital in "The Wound Dresser" (1865). In this adjunct role helping wounded soldiers, he conveys a responsibility to record the corporeal reality of battle. His stanzas create a relentless, material litany of the ways that the human body can be broken. He stoically walks through the hospital as a "witness," "bearing bandages, water and sponge" as he tends "a crushed head," a "perforated shoulder" and a foot with a bullet wound that is "gnawing and putrid gangrene" (242-43). Although he is a non-combatant, Whitman assumes the role of a dutiful soldier – "I am faithful, I do not give out" – as he moves on to more wounds that come in rapid succession (243). The poet is very much aware that his poetic attention to the reality of these bodies changes the story told in poetry about war. He anticipates being asked some time in the future to tell the conventional romanticized stories of "armies so rapid so wondrous" and of "unsurpass'd heroes" (242). Whitman prefigures the haunting psychological effects of the next war when he responds that what he'll remember, what he cannot erase from his mind, are the broken bodies of young soldiers, their suffering, the relentless routine and the overwhelming feeling that mercy has been divinely administered when at last they die.

3. World War I Poetry

We have seen how the more simplistic poetry of the early American wars was complicated in subsequent wars with poets' attention to the corporeal experience of soldiers in the field, the ushering in of realism to counter the idealism of the earlier age. World War I poetry makes clear that even when soldiers survive and bodies heal their psychic wounds endure. This poetry demonstrates that this psychological trauma is not contained within the battlefield or with combatants; the debilitating effects on the entire culture last many years after the war has been lost or won.

The United States joined World War I in April of 1917, almost three years after the conflict began. By that late date, American citizens were already well-informed of the appalling atrocities of warfare fought from the trenches. Death tolls far exceeding those of Shiloh emerged at Somme, Verdun and Ypres, each of which saw upwards of 300,000 men killed. The new heavily mechanized modes of warfare – tanks, machine guns, submarines and poisonous gasses – increased the destructive power of not just armies but also individual soldiers. The mobility of automated machine guns made it possible for a single shooter to kill or wound ten or fifteen enemy soldiers in a matter of seconds. But such mass destruction on the battlefield did little to quash the idealism in war poetry. Yet although the idealism exists, as the war dragged on, we find it is almost always coupled with a darker tone that is sometimes sarcasm, sometimes irony and sometimes bold defiance. However it manifests, careful reading will show that the limited idealism typical of the Revolutionary timeframe no longer goes unchecked.

For instance, the soldier Hervey Allen fuses abstraction with gritty realism in the traditional form of a sonnet entitled "Soldier-Poet" (1917). It begins with the now familiar tactic of directing our gaze to the sky over the battlefield, yet our attention is drawn not to visual spectacle of military might but to "screaming eagles," a potent symbol of American military patriotism. An eagle alone might summon feelings of national pride, but the uneasy modifier "screaming" signals something is amiss. Like Whitman, this poet speaks as an individual witness as he contemplates a fallen French soldier:

> I think at first like us he did not see
> The goal to which the screaming eagles flew;
> For romance lured him, France, and chivalry;
> But Oh! Before the end he knew, he knew! (60)

The "goal" of the screaming eagles that many soldiers "did not see" was the inevitable death toll; the visual spectacle draws attention to what is happening in the sky, just like the volcanic clouds and the bombs bursting in air in earlier works. The true goal of war eludes soldiers who have been "lured" by the ideals of their countries and, once again, the outmoded and imaginary warfare of medieval chivalry. But note that this familiar trope is introduced within the context of the speaker's explicit recognition and prescience of what is to come. The moment of being "undeceived" begins in the first line. Even if some soldiers are vulnerable to the subterfuge of the military sublime, the "Soldier-Poet" of the title has absorbed the poetic lessons from his predecessors. Unlike the wounded men in "Shiloh" or the French solider, it will not take the poet's own death to "undeceive" him.

The French soldier's enchanted interest is directed toward a symbolic female figure whose image can be traced back to the Enlightenment and was made famous in monumental paintings of revolution such as "Liberty Leading the People" (1803) by French painter Eugène Delacroix. Allen depicts the soldier giving his all in a gesture of romantic love to this representation of liberty:

> And gave his first full love to Liberty,
> And met her face to face one lurid night
> While the guns boomed their shuddering minstrelsy
> And all the Argonne glowed with demon light. (60)

Despite a dawning awareness the young soldier goes toward the boom of the guns – the celebrated sound of glorious warfare – even as it morphs into an unmistakable threat, "shuddering minstrelsy" covered in "demon light." Allen modifies the archaic word for courtly medieval music, "minstrelsy," with "shuddering" to show that terms of chivalry no longer pass without a moribund sense of irony. Likewise, the figure of Liberty becomes an assemblage of all the archaic and imagined pasts that have enticed men to war in the Western world – chivalric, ancient Greek, and Enlightenment ideals:

> And Liberty herself came through the wood,
> And with her dear, boy lover kept the tryst;
> Clasped in her grand, Greek arms he understood
> Whose were the fatal lips that he had kissed –
> Lips that the soul of Youth as loved from old –
> Hot lips of Liberty that kiss men cold. (60)

Allen's clear-eyed understanding of the usual ruses of war propaganda demonstrates his engagement with the poetic lessons of the past. We see a more psychologically astute poet, aware of how culture, history and art act upon the imaginations of young people. The extent to which his familiarity works both against and in support of literary tradition creates the tension in the poem.

A good many poets from World War I subtly chip away at idealistic poetic tactics as Allen does in his sonnet, which depicts "love" and patriotism in disturbing ways. Poets also take the concept of "worthy sacrifice" common in the Revolutionary War and portray that sacrifice as a merciless and arbitrary waste of youthful lives. Two poems by female witnesses exemplify this shift and illustrate that once the discourse moves beyond the battlefield and into the realm of the psychological, war affects more than just soldiers in battle. Non-combatants suffer deep losses and traumas as well. Thus the reach of war extends past the lives lost and the social institutions affected and into the often unacknowledged suffering of women and families left behind. As the experience depicted in the poetry of war moves inward to psychology, its destructive capacity moves outward in society.

In her poem entitled "In the Stadium – Marshall Joffre Reviewing the Harvard Regiment, May 12, 1917," Amy Lowell captures the multi-layered social impact of war by exposing the rigidity of cultural roles in the arena of a parade at the culturally prestigious university of Harvard. The length of the title, along with the hyper-specificity of its setting, suggests once again the role of witness, the recorder of facts, in war poetry. Yet the poet depicts a new cynicism towards the war's orchestrators, and extends that cynicism to the ongoing naivety of the freshly enlisted young men, who it seems did not learn the lessons of wars past. The males in this parade seem stereotypical, the general decrepit and hypocritical and the young men earnest to the point of foolishness. We've seen them before, she says of the general: "They are all like this: / Napoleon, /

Hannibal, / Great Caesar even" (229). The only authentic poignancy comes from the outside speaker toward the young men who cannot see that they are like "bulwark[s] [...] heaped like sandbags / Against the German guns" (231). She continues:

> This is war:
> Boys flung into a breach
> Like shovelled earth
> And old men
> Broken,
> Driving rapidly before crowds of people
> In a glitter of silly decorations. (231)

The gaze of the poet shifts past the spectacle of the military sublime being showcased in the parade and ends on an image not seen much in the poetry of war, the women left behind. The poet conjures a graver personification than the female Liberty leading and depicts instead the figure of Life following behind and wailing as the persistent cycles of war continue:

> Life weeps,
> And shreds her garments
> to the blowing winds. (231)

Similarly, the abstract ideas of a "noble" sacrifice and heroic deaths are challenged in the war poetry of Mary Borden. As a nurse behind the front, in what was called "the forbidden zone," Borden observed battle and battle-related deaths *en masse*. Her poetry bears highly realistic and calm witness to the waste of war that is the underside of promised heroism. "The Song of the Mud" (1917) demonstrates how far from noble many wartime deaths actually are:

> This is the song of the mud — the obscene, the filthy, the putrid,
> The vast liquid grave of our armies.
> It has drowned our men.
> Its monstrous distended belly reeks with the undigested dead.
> Our men have gone into it, sinking slowly.
> And struggling and slowly disappearing.
> Our fine men, our brave, strong, young men (18)

The personification here is far from euphemistic; the poet presents us with a grotesque mud ogre swallowing the unsuspecting soldiers in undignified deaths that are incidental rather than central to the war effort. Most disturbing is her reference to the "undigested dead," those who are "struggling and slowly disappearing," perhaps still physically alive but existing in near-catatonic states of shell shock, nightmare and psychological terror. The poet ironically emphasizes the distance between what she witnesses and what the larger culture promises when it sends men off to war, often in patriotic song about our "fine men, our brave, strong, young men."

This psychology of war manifests as deep numbness and disillusion – to the point of nihilism – in T.S. Eliot's "The Hollow Men" (1925). Here the speaker's autonomy is completely subsumed by psychological trauma and cultural abandonment. He becomes a shell of a human, a stuffed man, without hope or meaning:

> We are the hollow men
> We are the stuffed men
> Leaning together
> Headpiece filled with straw. Alas!
> Our dried voices, when
> We whisper together
> Are quiet and meaningless
> As wind in dry grass
> Or rats' feet over broken glass
> In our dry cellar
>
> Shape without form, shade without colour,
> Paralysed force, gesture without motion (56)

It's hard not to imagine these bodies "leaning together" like those dying in the fields of Shiloh, whispering a "natural prayer" in their last moments. And as in Melville's "Shiloh," the natural world – wind, grass and rats – is taking better care of its life force than humans. But unlike most Civil War literature, the poetry of World War I dwells on the psychology of the soldier. We are not just watching it; we are feeling and experiencing the numbness, the regret, the loss of once vital lives. For instance, in Eliot's poem we hear the wishes of those about to die sent out toward those who have already "crossed":

> Those who have crossed
> With direct eyes, to death's other Kingdom
> Remember us – if at all – not as lost

> Violent souls, but only
> As the hollow men
> The stuffed men. (56)

The speaking persona doesn't want to be remembered as a soldier, as a "violent soul," but prefers to be thought of as "hollow," someone who did what he was told, perhaps like the French soldier in Allen's poem, someone stuffed with notions of war that were exposed as no longer credible. Eliot ends his poem with lines reminiscent of a children's nursery rhyme:

> *This is the way the world ends*
> *This is the way the world ends*
> *This is the way the world ends*
> *Not with a bang but a whimper.* (59, emphasis in original)

With such ironic interplay, the poet emphasizes both the nostalgia and utter nonsense that are bound together in this troubled but persistent mode of poetic discourse.

4. *War Poetry Beyond*

Military idealism, battlefield realism and psychological trauma are all subjects that have continued to complicate and create tension in poetry about American wars – those in Korea, Viet Nam and the Persian Gulf. I'll conclude by considering a recent poem; it is, like many I see coming out of the most recent wars, in dialogue with the poetry of America's earlier wars.

In "Here, Bullet" (2005) Brian Turner, himself a veteran, focuses readers' attention on the simplest material object of destruction, the bullet. The poet addresses the single bullet he considers meant for him, in the same way that Melville focuses on a single bullet in the aftermath of Shiloh. Where the earlier poet leads up to the topic obliquely, Turner begins with it brazenly. Melville's powerful line "what like a bullet can undeceive" criticizes jingoistic promises and romantic notions that soldiers could achieve noble deaths for "fame and country." Turner's poem, in contrast, holds no deception. In a clear-eyed response to what his country is asking of him, Turner addresses the undeceiving bullet with uncanny prescience. The poet unflinchingly accepts what the bullet will do to his body; he accepts what the material consequences of war are on the flesh. And in a calm and rational tone, he acknowledges that these conditions, these sacrifices of minds and bodies, have always been the terms of warfare. He calls to the bullet directly:

> If a body is what you want,
> then here is bone and gristle and flesh.
> Here is the clavicle-snapped wish,
> the aorta's opened valves, the leap
> thought makes at the synaptic gap.
> Here is the adrenaline rush you crave,
> that inexorable flight, that insane puncture
> into heat and blood. And I dare you to finish
> what you've started. Because here, Bullet,
> here is where I complete the word you bring
> hissing through the air, here is where I moan
> the barrel's cold esophagus, triggering
> my tongue's explosives for the rifling I have
> inside of me, each twist of the round
> spun deeper, because here, Bullet,
> here is where the world ends, every time. (13)

The relationship between bullet and flesh is uncomplicated. The war machine continues; it "wants a body" to do what it has historically done to bodies throughout America's now long history of war: destroy them. The poet trains his eye on that destruction without pity or quest for glory. The attention is no longer in the air or the ground, but is fixed on the physical. The speaker in Turner's poem is markedly different from the hollow men that Eliot envisioned lost in a nightmare of disillusion, disoriented religious symbols and impotent bodies. Turner's soldier holds no illusions. He does not call out to bugles or imaginary pasts; his relationship is just with his own mortality; his thoughts are only on the object designed to kill him.

Turner's poem echoes the war poetry of the past in significant ways. It parallels Melville's single bullet that undeceives a nation, repeats Whitman's litany of physically damaged body parts, and reprises Eliot's aversion to lofty abstractions and romantic diction. In Turner's poem, however, the world ends not with a whimper but with a bang, that is, not with psychological angst or despair but with a very material bullet, ripping its way through bodily systems – gristle and bone, aorta, clavicle. Furthermore, Turner insists it always has ended like this for soldiers. He asserts: "This is the way the world ends, every time." His last line defies Eliot's totalizing and defeated whimper. This soldier-poet takes on with full knowledge – not the war, not the cause, not the idealism, not the conventional role of males – but dying itself as the unambiguous job of a soldier. The veils of persuasion so often employed to cover up the violence and the bloodshed seem no longer necessary. The objects of jingoistic artifice – abstraction, idealism, imaginary pasts – are gone.

What is this new spirit of war and this new age of warriors – men and now combat-ready women? What is this unflinching recognition of mortal, imminent danger that no longer leans on the language of patriotism, religion or imaginary pasts? What is the new psychological stance of a poet who knows the arc of America's literary history well enough to suture Melville's undeceiving bullet to Eliot's impotent bang? It is new territory of thought that begs to be engaged in sophisticated dialogue. And there's a good chance that students have insights into these questions based on their own lives and their own perceptions of culture. But they require the language to talk with complexity about war and an understanding of the arc of history. And they need the opportunity to have that conversation. By studying war poetry we can help expand students' language and thinking about martial conflict. Observing how poets poignantly respond to the doubleness of war can help students think through difficult concepts and help them resist rigid or indoctrinated cultural thinking.

Bibliography

Allen, Hervey. *Wampum and Old Gold.* New Haven: Yale University Press, 1921.
Barlow, Joel. *The Columbiad: A Poem.* London: Richard Phillips, 1809.
Borden, Mary. *The Forbidden Zone.* London: Heinemann, 1929.
Eliot, T.S. *The Complete Poems and Plays, 1909-1950.* New York: Harcourt Brace, 1980.
Fuller, Randall. *From Battlefields Rising: How The Civil War Transformed American Literature.* New York: Oxford University Press, 2010.
Keats, John. *Selected Letters.* Ed. Robert Gittings. New York: Oxford University Press, 2002.

Key, Francis Scott. "Defence of Fort McHenry." *The Oxford Book of American Poetry*. Ed. David Lehman. New York: Oxford University Press, 2006. 18-19.

Lowell, Amy. *Pictures of the Floating World*. New York: Macmillan, 1919.

Melville, Herman. *Battle-Pieces and Aspects of the War*. New York: Harper, 1866.

Scott, Walter. *Marmion: A Tale of Flodden Field*. Edinburgh: Ballantyne, 1808.

---. *Lady of the Lake*. London: John Sharpe, 1810.

Turner, Brian. *Here Bullet*. Farmington, Maine: Alice James, 2005.

Twain, Mark [Samuel Langhorne Clemens]. *Life on the Mississippi*. New York: New American Library, 1961.

Whitman, Walt. *Leaves of Grass*. Boston: Small, Maynard, and Company, 1897.

Winn, James Anderson. *The Poetry of War*. New York: Cambridge University Press, 2008.

Sabine Sielke (Bonn)

To "Dwell in Possibility": On the Challenges and Rewards of Teaching and Studying Emily Dickinson

There is no dispute that Emily Dickinson (1830-1886), along with her contemporary Walt Whitman, is the most significant nineteenth-century American poet and one of the greatest writers in American literary history. As a modernist "making it new" long before paradigmatic modernist poets such as Ezra Pound, William Carlos Williams, and Marianne Moore appeared on the scene, Dickinson saw only a few of her almost 1800 poems published during her lifetime and engaged in a bold and single-minded poetic practice that was considered an oddity by many a reader. Due to both the New Critical appreciation of complex poetic forms, paradoxes, and ambiguities and to the feminist revision of Dickinson's work in the 1970s and 1980s, literary criticism in the second half of the twentieth century has contributed much to a thorough understanding of the poet's enigmatic experimentalist aesthetics, her daring insights into various modes of human existence, and the playful postures and gender-related power positions enacted in many of her texts. This criticism has also paved the way for a rereading of Dickinson as a figure fundamentally engaged with the politics and popular culture of her time. Readers meanwhile claim her as a writer highly conscious and critical of class ideologies, and include Dickinson, next to Herman Melville and Whitman, among the prominent Civil War poets. After all, Dickinson wrote most prolifically, most productively, between 1860 and 1865. But her "letter[s] to the World" (J. 441, Fr519), as she labelled her poems, proved to be far ahead of her time.

Meanwhile Dickinson's poems have become an essential component of high school curricula in the United States and there is, as I will show, ample reason why that is so. Dickinson may enjoy that status first and foremost because her poetry strikes us as so 'modern.' Her poetry makes for particularly interesting teaching material because it is so up-to-date in its concern with debates on the relation of religion, philosophy, and science, with issues of gender and power, and with the potential and the limits of writing itself. In fact, the difficulties that her single-minded, complex texts pose to both young and more experienced and learned readers are a challenge that, once met, offers many rewards. Trying to make sense of Dickinson's compressed and oddly punctuated lyrics, students acquire a sense of how to handle 'difficult texts' not so much by seeking to paraphrase their supposed content or by pinpointing what they could possibly mean to tell us, but by paying close attention to *how* they go about the telling. And 'telling' is not even as misleading a term as it might seem when it comes to poetry's subtle ways of showing. After all, many of Dickinson's most famous poems – including "My Life had stood – a Loaded Gun –" (J. 754, Fr764) and "Death is the supple Suitor" (J. 1445, Fr1470) – employ narrative modes to complex effect.

In fact, the world of Emily Dickinson is not as remote and opaque as it may seem. My standard advice to the student who encounters Dickinson's poems for the first time and voices bafflement – the standard reaction – has always been: Read her lyrics in large doses, in multitudes, in series. Only then do we begin to understand what she may have been after! This recommendation implies that the many figures we encounter in Dickinson's poems – the "supposed person[s]" (L. 268) that her writing gives voice to – become familiar characters to us as we read on and on; that later poems are updates on earlier texts; that the dashes which leave most of her poems open-ended are a kind of cliff-hangers; that the "booklets" in which she compiled groups of about twenty texts, first drafted on ordinary writing paper or scraps and then copied onto folded sheets of unlined stationary, now called 'fascicles,' may be viewed as analogous to the successive seasons of contemporary TV series; and that, in sum, we may apprehend novel dimensions of her work if we think about Dickinson by examining the way both the legend of her eccentric personality and her many aphoristic lines echo throughout contemporary popular culture. Previously "embodied" in dance performances by choreographer Martha Graham and set to music by Aaron Copland, among many others, Dickinson's poetry now reappears in many modes of material and visual culture and gets "inter-activated" in computer games and YouTube videos. In other words, when we simultaneously read Dickinson historically – as a key to modernism as well as to nineteenth-century New England culture and its many contradictions – and contemporaneously, as she is being remediated and remembered in contemporary (U.S.-American) pop cultures, the challenge of reading her work turns into the reward of seeing how (Dickinson's) poetry still matters and creates meaning today. This means that teaching and studying Dickinson may facilitate a considerable degree of cultural literacy.

In the following, I delineate a few paths that may take us there. In part one, I introduce Dickinson as a self-reliant member of the Amherst community who single-mindedly resisted a whole series of codes and conventions of femininity. This resistance, coupled with a deep, rigorously determined interest in literature and writing, may startle, even inspire, students. And it may explain, at least in part, why Dickinson eventually transformed from the "myth of Amherst" into a star and heroine of American poetry and into its "poster poet" (cf. figure 1). In part two, I pave inroads into some of Dickinson's poems to show how poetic form – the generous use of dashes, elisions, and odd syntax, for instance – carries subtle meanings and how our close attention to these aesthetics can subsequently lead us to an "'Undiscovered Continent' – No Settler had the Mind" (J. 832, Fr814). Dickinson's insight into phenomena that resist language is mind-boggling, and her poetics still manages to send shivers down one's spine, affirming the monumental power of a language sensitive to minute nuances. In a third and final section, I turn to materials made available by newer media, which have added entirely novel dimensions and approaches to studying Dickinson, while also engaging some of her many reincarnations in current popular culture. Seeing her turn into an event – as in marathon Emily Dickinson poetry readings – or reappear as an avatar in a video game, for instance, throws a different light on both the poet and the significance of that culture.

1. "The Soul selects her own Society –": On Having It Your Way

Dickinson is bound to strike any student as a strange bird who, through her very dedication and determination, may become quite

Figure 1. Penelope Dullaghan, Emily Dickinson Museum 2007 season poster, 18 x 27 inches.
© Penelope Dullaghan. Courtesy of the artist

dear to us. Born as the first daughter of Emily Norcross Dickinson and Edward Dickinson, a lawyer, congressman, and the treasurer of Amherst College, Dickinson lived most of her life in Amherst, Massachusetts, except for the year she spent at Mount Holyoke Female Seminary (1847-1848) in nearby South Hadley. The poet cared little for travelling, transgressing many boundaries in her mind and in her writing instead. "Vermont or Asia," she wrote in a late letter to her friend Elizabeth Holland, "[m]any of us go farther" (L. 685), suggesting that geographical distances don't matter.

To the Dickinson household also belonged her younger sister, Lavinia, and a slightly older brother, Austin, who became a lawyer like his father and moved next door after having married Dickinson's close friend Susan Huntington Gilbert. Susan Gilbert became both Dickinson's first critic and so intimate a friend that feminist criticism has speculated much about a possible sexual dimension of the women's relationship. Both as a childhood friend and as kin living across the lawn, Susan Gilbert received more letters from Dickinson than any other of the poet's correspondents. These letters are as compassionate as they are playful, interweaving accounts of family life and private matters with exchanges about books, ideas, and philosophical questions. Especially in the early exchanges with Susan Gilbert the reader can see the evolution of the wit, sensitivity, craft, and deep irony of Dickinson's writing. Reading these letters alongside selected poems reveals a mode of communication that appears both entirely foreign and strangely familiar to a contemporary reader. For just as we now compose emails addressing friends or colleagues located even closer than Dickinson's next door neighbor, we project and test different kinds of personae in these digital encounters, just as the poet did in her correspondence.

While Dickinson learned, as one of her poems puts it, to "see New-Englandly" (J. 285, Fr256), she also kept a clear, oftentimes ironic distance from Victorian values, Calvinist traditions, and conventional thinking. "Much Madness is divinest Sense –" reads one of her poems (J. 435, Fr620). "The Bible is an antique Volume –" begins another, "Written by faded Men" (J. 1545, Fr1577). This kind of critique, coming from the heart of a mid-19th century New England village, strikes us as daring and corrects our streamlined views of nineteenth-century cultures. Moreover, Dickinson had an avid interest in women's literature. As an ardent reader, she knew the Bible and Shakespeare by heart, was well familiar with the poetry of Henry Wadsworth Longfellow, James Russell Lowell, and the English romantics, and admired Ralph Waldo Emerson's and David Thoreau's writing. Yet she was most deeply inspired by women writers of her age and made reference in her letters and poems to George Eliot, the Brontë sisters, and Elisabeth Barrett Browning, whose work she considered "witchcraft." Reading other (women's) texts, Dickinson must have felt part of a conspiracy of authorship.

Like her sister, Dickinson did not marry and refused to convert to Protestantism, in this way missing out on the central moments in the making of ideal womanhood that her culture offered to young females. For Dickinson, it seems, this loss was clearly outbalanced by the personal liberties it allowed: literally embodying the "angel-in-the-house" figure that Victorian culture idealized, Dickinson managed to claim a "room of her own." Dickinson selected her social contacts carefully, and during her last fifteen years hardly left her family's house and grounds, privileging correspondence over personal meetings. "A letter always feels to me like immortality," she claimed in one of her letters, "because it is the mind alone without corporeal friend" (L. 330). Indeed, the "mind alone" became the preoccupation of much of Dickinson's poetry and poetics. "Soto! Explore thyself!" reads one of Dickinson's poems, composed in 1864. "Therein thyself shalt find / The 'Undiscovered Continent' – No Settler had the Mind" (J. 832, Fr814). The self, this "undiscovered continent," is central to Dickinson's mind: bracketing reality, the poet does not aim to account for *what* appears, but *how* it appears and affects the mind. Dickinson's verse thus does not primarily concentrate on the world of objects, but on consciousness as such. After all, "The Brain – is wider than the Sky –," "deeper than sea –," "just the weight of God –" (J. 632, Fr598).

Due to the fact that she hid most of her work in the bottom drawer of her desk and engaged in a kind of "show biz" (Keller 75), pretending to lead a reclusive, seemingly inconsequential life, the full extent of Dickinson's writing practice became evident only after her death, when relatives found the manuscripts that the poet had compiled. Whether Dickinson wanted her work to be published cannot be known clearly one way or the other. But if she were to publish, it seems, it had to be on her own terms. In 1862, she responded to the "Letter to a Young Contributor" which the editor and writer Thomas Wentworth Higginson had published in *The Atlantic*

Monthly. She sent Higginson four poems, a letter, and, in place of a signature, a separate envelope which included a card with her name, thus insisting that she meant for her person be understood as separate from the personae inhabiting her lyrics. Higginson found her verse "spasmodic," "uncontrolled" (L. 265), and not polished enough for publication, yet by 1890 admitted that he had failed to recognize the poetic power and cultural significance of Dickinson's verse and agreed to co-edit, with Mabel Loomis Todd, a series of selected poems. For the 1890 edition, Dickinson's texts – cryptic, compressed, and with little concern for conventions of grammar and genre – were adjusted to popular taste. Practising what Todd labelled "creative editing" (Franklin, *Editing* 23), Dickinson's first editors accommodated her violations of poetic decorum and made various alterations to the text, correcting verb forms, displacing the characteristic dashes with traditional punctuation, and sorting her untitled poems into categories like "Nature," "Love," and "Life," thus making clear-cut thematic divisions into which Dickinson's poems do not easily fit.

In fact, the power of Dickinson's verse results to a considerable degree from the ways in which it dissolves the distance between seemingly separate spheres and phenomena and piles layers of meaning on top of each other. "Come slowly, Eden" (J. 211, Fr205) and "Wild Nights – Wild Nights!" (J. 249, Fr269), for instance, two poems which delineate the passage to eternity, burst with sexual energy and reclaim death as desire and ecstasy. Likewise, poetry, at its best, is a torment for Dickinson, a sexual exhilaration, a discharge of destructive, fatal energy comparable to love and close to paradise: "To pile like Thunder to it's close / Then crumble grand away / While Everything created hid / This – would be Poetry – // Or Love – the two coeval come – / We Both and neither prove – / Experience either and consume – / For none see God and live –" (J. 1247, Fr1353).

After a series of editions that censored the idiosyncrasies of Dickinson's poetics to different degrees, in 1955 Thomas H. Johnson published a three-volume variorum edition, which also attempted to approximate the dates of the poems' production. In 1958, Johnson and Theodora Ward published Dickinson's letters in three volumes. Ralph Franklin's 1981 edition of the manuscripts of Dickinson's poems allowed readers to assess the nature of the original texts and to acknowledge their actual line breaks and exact use of punctuation. The poet frequently used dashes of varying length instead of the conventional commas and colons, and avoided, in particular, the closure that periods tend to imply. Ending a line or a poem with a dash instead, Dickinson's texts suggest that their meanings remain open-ended and carry beyond the physical frame of the text.

In light of this editing history, it is an eye-opening exercise to search the internet for Dickinson's poems. Students will not only discover, during such a search, different versions of the same poem; they will also note that many, even prominent, readers – like the U.S.-American novelists Siri Hustvedt and Richard Powers, who use Dickinson poems as epigraphs for their own books – are still reprinting old, garbled versions of her work. Comparing the old, "corrected" version of one of Dickinson's poems with the shape the same poem takes in one or both of the newer editions – or even "creatively editing" and "correcting" one of Dickinson's texts themselves – students can discover what difference a dash makes. Laying the regular print version next to the manuscript edition of a poem, we easily understand how printed editions tend to misrepresent Dickinson's work as they reduce the physical size of Dickinson's poems and obliterate the bold strokes of her handwriting. In fact, Dickinson's lyrics serve perfectly to show that by just looking at a poem – without even beginning to interpret its potential content, just by observing that it lacks titles, that stanzas break all of a sudden, and that conventional punctuation is amiss – we may "distil," as Dickinson puts it, many a subtle meaning.

2. "I dwell in Possibility – a fairer House than Prose": The Power of Poetry

It is important to remember that the significance of Dickinson in contemporary American literary history is not based on the fact that her writing was representative of her time; in fact, it was not. Her poems would hardly have fit the voluminous anthologies of American women's poetry that were published in the 1850s and 1860s. Putting one of these fairly conventional poems next to one of Dickinson's lyric texts therefore amounts to yet another illuminating enterprise. For Dickinson's poetics is based on a series of single-minded choices, driven by the poet's desire to extend the semantic register of poetic discourse, to push beyond the limits of language in order to explore uncharted territories, be they "the Colossal substance / Of Immortality" (J. 306, Fr630) or "that White Sustenance – / Despair –" (J. 640, Fr706).

Whereas her contemporary Whitman extended the poetic line beyond conventional iambic pentameter and opted for free verse, Dickinson selected the shorter lines characteristic of hymn meter and its variations (common, short, and long meter) as the formal frame of her poetry. Even though Dickinson thus did not abolish formal patterns as radically as did Whitman, William Blake, or Gerald Manley Hopkins, her choice of the ballad stanza, known to her through English hymnody, made her, as critics have observed, the only canonical nineteenth-century female poet who resisted the authority of standard blank verse. This does not mean that Dickinson entirely dispensed with iambic pentameter lines. Rather, she uses them rarely and in a highly functional manner. In the first and final lines of her poem "After great pain, a formal feeling comes –" (J. 341, Fr372), for instance, the monotony of the iambic meter embodies the immobility effected by extreme pain. At the same time, Dickinson also takes great liberties in the way she employs the metric conventions of the ballad stanza. Displacing the traditionally end-stopped line with enjambments, splitting lines, mingling different hymn meters in one poem, and working with off and slant rhymes, Dickinson turns the ballad stanza into a formal frame to bend, extend, and experiment with and to voice her critique of social and cultural conventions with ingenuous subtlety. "Tell all the Truth but tell it slant – / Success in Circuit lies […] The Truth must dazzle gradually / Or every man be blind –," Dickinson advises her reader in one of her poems (J. 1129, Fr1263).

Frequently, Dickinson's poems create suggestive tensions between form and content. In her poem "I rose – because He sank –" (J. 616, Fr454), for instance, irregular metric forms embed grammatically correct structures which transport highly controversial gender matters, evolving a female voice that, against all conventions, claims male power and authority. In other cases Dickinson's poems ironically align orthodox fulfilment of the ballad measure with explorations of cultural conformity. Dickinson's poem "She rose to His Requirement" (J. 732, Fr857), for instance, exposes the limits marriage sets on a woman's life ("She rose to His Requirement – dropt / The Playthings of Her Life / To take the honorable Work / Of Woman, and of Wife") by making the conventional frames of meter and marriage clash with the irregular syntax that dominates the second and central stanza of the poem ("If ought She missed in Her new Day, / Of Amplitude, or Awe – / Or the Prospective – Or the Gold / In using, wear away // It lay unmentioned – as the Sea / Develop Pearl and Weed").

In this text the constraint of matrimony corresponds to the regularity of the common meter, which is significantly disrupted, however, in the first line by an additional syllable and an archaic past tense ("dropt"). Semantically, the act of dropping indicates a decline from the playful "amplitudes" of premarital existence. By positioning this matter outside an otherwise regular formal frame, the poem associates marriage – a rise in a woman's social status – with loss (of pleasure) and suggests that the notion of marriage as the apex of women's lives conceals the renunciations matrimony demands of women. The alliteration of the *w* sound in "Work," "Woman," "Wife," "wear away," and "Weed" underscores that women's "honorable work" and the growth of "Weed" are in fact two sides of the same coin.

At the same time, the denied pleasures reassociate in rhetorical figures. Projecting passion, unbounded power, and infinity in Dickinson's poetry, the "Sea" in this poem symbolizes an undercurrent to women's conformity. Precious and rare, pearls are status symbols, female accessories as well as tropes of female sexuality, that Dickinson frequently employs as metaphors for poetry and its "business ... Circumference" (L. 268), thus aligning writing and femininity. "Weed," by contrast, denotes an organism that tends to overgrow and choke out more desirable vegetation. Repression of pleasure, the poem thus suggests, produces both constructive and destructive energy, or to put it differently: pressures to conform not only repress but also dislocate the desires they mean to control.

While Whitman's lengthy catalogue poems aim for inclusion and comprehensiveness, Dickinson's employ a disjunctive and highly elliptical syntax which seem to make many of her poems burst out of their seams. This effect is due both to the ambiguity of Dickinson's oftentimes riddling rhetoric and grammar and to a desire, driving much of her poetry, to represent aspects of human existence that tend to resist representation, such as pain, death, and immortality, as well as love and desire. Trying to put into poetic discourse dimensions of being that conventionally foreclose language, Dickinson's poems constantly push the limits of language's register; as in, for example, "After great pain, a formal feeling comes –." Indifferent to causes, the poem recollects and "formalizes" the effect of extreme pain as a state of paralysis and depicts a body cut loose from nervous control and separated from its social contexts: "The Nerves sit ceremonious, like Tombs – / [...] // The Feet, mechanical, go round – / Of Ground, or Air, or Ought – / A Wooden way / Regardless grown, / A Quartz contentment, like a stone –." Syntactically, Dickinson's depiction of paralysis tends toward disjunction and dismemberment, effected by parataxis and indeterminate prepositions as well as by deletion of conjunctions and adverbial endings ("mechanical"). On the level of content this immobility corresponds to a confusion of disparate semantic categories and a propensity to abstract ("Of Ground, or Air, or Ought –"). "This," the final stanza concludes, "is the Hour of Lead – / Remembered if outlived, / As freezing persons, recollect the Snow –, First – Chill – then Stupor – then the letting go –." Along with the last line's paratactical structures, the multiple dashes allow the poem to orchestrate the gradual loss of consciousness as an open-ended process.

Both Whitman and Dickinson are as much romantic poets as they are early modernists. Like Whitman and the English romantics, Dickinson is preoccupied with the relation of self and nature, the power of the imagination, and the limits of poetry. Unlike Whitman, however, who meant to put Emerson's transcendentalist philosophy into poetic practice and, in his poems, aims to bridge the gap between self and other or nature, Dickinson is highly skeptical of idealist convictions. She strongly resists the notions that nature gains its significance primarily through the perceiving consciousness, that words are directly fastened to visible things, and that the business of the philosopher or poet is to leap over the chasm of the unknown. Instead Dickinson recognizes nature's defiance of human understanding, be it scientific or philosophical, and cherishes perception itself: "Perception of an object costs / Precise the Object's loss – / Perception in itself a Gain / Replying to its Price – / The Object absolute – is nought – / Perception sets it fair / And then upbraids a Perfectness / That situates so far –" (J. 1071, Fr1103).

"Nature and God," she writes elsewhere, "I neither knew;" both remain strangers (J. 835, Fr803), of different worlds whose secrets are not to be revealed. No matter how close the human mind deems itself to nature, "nature is a stranger yet; / The one that cite her most / Have never passed her haunted house, / Nor simplified her ghost" (J. 1400, Fr1433). Rejecting Emerson's idealism and teleology, Dickinson insists on the separation between self and nature as a fundamental condition of human subjectivity. For Dickinson, identity – of self in relation to other or speaking subject in relation to objective world – is not to be achieved on this side of existence, but only in the beyond, in a state conventionally labelled eternity, immortality, paradise, or Eden. In a letter of March 1853 to Susan Gilbert, Dickinson compares eternity to an infinite embrace. "Bye and bye," she writes, "[eternity] will open it's everlasting arms, and gather us all" (L. 103). "There is no first, or last, in Forever –," she puts it to Susan later. "It is Centre, there, all the time –" (L. 288). "To crumbling men," reads one of her poems, eternity looks "firm" and represents "The only Adamant Estate / In all Identity –" (J. 1499, Fr1397). Viewed from the poet's privileged vantage points in "The Dying" (J. 906, Fr830), eternity indeed presents itself in the form of glimpses of identity, as the unmediated, mirroring gaze into the countenance of a beloved other (J. 625, Fr691). Somewhat paradoxically, by the use of broken language, the poet projects the beyond as a limitless space in which the human subject and (gender) differences dissolve, a condition of fulfilled wholeness, without desire – a condition that is unattainable on this side of existence.

In order to reclaim eternity for this side of life, Dickinson chose "For Occupation – This – / The spreading wide my narrow Hands / To gather Paradise –" (J. 657, Fr466). The poet repeatedly situates her speakers at the threshold of existence and consciousness, at the edge of eternity, on the margins of subjectivity and representation. In such poems death is not projected as a final moment, but as a process of dying, as in "I heard a Fly buzz – when I died" (J. 465, Fr591). In Dickinson's poems "The Admirations – and Contempts – of time – / Show justest – through an Open Tomb –." Presenting "The Dying – as it were a Height," a kind of observation tower, her texts take a bird's eye view on death, which alters perception, evolves a "Compound Vision [...] Back – toward Time – / And forward – / Toward the God of Him –," and "Reorganizes Estimate" (J. 906, Fr830). Thus the edges that Dickinson's poems ponder are not points in time but processes of border crossings. And for Dickinson these boundaries are not limitations but possibilities that open vistas. Accordingly, many of her poems have "Odd secrets of the line to tell" (J. 160, Fr132). As these lines transform into wide-open views, her speakers peep into the unknown, into paradise.

Considering the cultural context in which Dickinson was immersed, her preoccupations with death and eternity come as no surprise. (The fact that they do surprise us as twenty-first-century readers of her poems in turn tells us how much we have pushed our mortality to the margins of our attention.) The author's treatment of such popular themes, however, is breathtakingly unique and insightful, motivated, as it was, by a "Love for the Absent" (L. 31). Dickinson's investment in death and eternity was not a religious, certainly a spiritual, but first of all a poetic and poetological enterprise. Hers was that "still – Volcano – Life," in which conventions were temporarily blown to pieces by "A quiet – Earthquake Style –" (J. 601, Fr517), to recall one of her many oxymoronic figures.

From the 1890s onward readers have tried to take Dickinson on her own terms, even if many a reader objected to the peculiarities of her poetics. By the late 1970s, literary critics no longer focused on Dickinson's self-denials and renunciations but, rather, on her self-determination. Feminist perspectives, in particular, turned Dickinson into the heroine of American women's poetry whose concerns seemed to reach all the way to contemporary women's texts. And this very popularity and star status ushered Dickinson into many spheres of – analogue and digital – contemporary popular cultures as well.

3. "Never Too Much Dickinson": Poetry as Pop

While during her lifetime the poet shunned publicity, her legacy has since then become subject to a thriving "Dickinson industry," driven in part by a continuous desire to refashion our sense of who Emily Dickinson was. Recent scholarship projects the poet as expert gardener and healer, as philosopher and scientist, adding to her preoccupation with writing and making her days appear increasingly busy. Along similar lines, Alice Quinn reports, under the heading "Never Too Much Dickinson" in the blog section of the website of the Poetry Society of America, that from April to June 2010 the New York Botanical Garden featured the exhibition *Emily Dickinson's Garden: The Poetry of Flowers*, whose centerpiece was a re-creation of Dickinson's quintessential nineteenth-century New England garden. During this event, no lesser a figure than New York City mayor Michael Bloomberg himself recited a poem he had composed, borrowing the Dickinson line "'Hope' is the thing with feathers –" (J. 254, Fr314).

A large portion of the "Dickinson industry" is dedicated to remediating and thus recycling Dickinson's writing in multiple manners, making her significance both more sustainable and a matter of flux and constant (re-)construction. (The very fact that, in this way, canonized authors are subjected to continuous face-lifts is in itself an issue worth discussing with students.) There are a number of (mystery) novels and plays revolving around the poet, the 'mysteries' of her secluded life, and the radiance of her poetry, including William Luce's one woman, two-act drama *The Belle of Amherst* (1976), and fiction such as Jerome Charyn's *The Secret Life of Emily Dickinson: a Novel* (2010), Brock Clarke's *An Arsonist's Guide to Writers' Homes in New England: a Novel* (2007), Joanne Dobson's *Quieter Than Sleep: a Modern Mystery of Emily Dickinson* (1998), and Jane Langton's *Emily Dickinson Is Dead* (1985). Dickinson also inspired parts of William Styron's *Sophie's Choice* (1979) and Joyce Carol Oates's story "EDickinsonRepliLuxe," featured in *Wild Nights: Stories About the Last Days of Poe, Dickinson, Twain, James, and Hemingway* (2008), whose title pays tribute to Dickinson's poem "Wild Nights – Wild Nights!" (J. 249, Fr269). Journalist Simon Worrall's *The Poet and the Murderer: a True Story of Literary Crime and the Art of Forgery* (2002), by contrast, relates as if it were a thriller the "true story" of Mark Hofmann – a daring late twentieth century literary forger turned murderer whose major coup was to sell a fake Dickinson poem to the Jones library in Amherst.

Teachers and students can also consult recent films and TV productions on Dickinson: in 2008, the Famous Authors Series put out the DVD *Emily Dickinson,* which, as one commentator puts it on Amazon.com, can be recommended "for teachers to show to students as a less painful way of learning about Dickinson," less painful, I guess, than beginning with the poems themselves ("Dickinson the Poet and Person"). In the DVD *Emily Dickinson: A Certain Slant of Light* (2006), the award-winning actress Julie Harris takes viewers on a tour of the Dickinson Homestead on Amherst's Main Street and of Mount Holyoke Seminary (now College), where

Dickinson studied in 1847-1948. (Harris also starred in the original Broadway production of Luce's above-mentioned play, for which she won the 1977 Tony Award for Actress in a Drama and which was adapted for the TV screen in a filmed production, directed by Charles S. Dubin and available on video.) Without making the trip to Amherst, we can also visit the Emily Dickinson Museum, housed in the Dickinson Homestead online (http://www.emilydickinson museum.org). If we are lucky we can even catch one of the theater productions inspired by the poet's life and work, some of which are explicitly dedicated to making Dickinson more accessible to younger audiences.

All of this material reflects the fact that a large part of the interest in Dickinson remains biographically inclined and aims at visualizing a poet of whom exists but one confirmed daguerreotype image, taken ca. 1847. Closer to home, so to speak, is the transposition of poetry into music, which acknowledges both the historical and aesthetic proximity of the two media and Dickinson's personal favor for the hymn stanza. Whereas the dominance of iambic pentameter in nineteenth-century American poetry reinforces the traditional function of the lyric poem to project a speaker's voice, Dickinson's idiosyncratic choice of meter echoes the performative mode of the medieval ballad and its emphasis on sound rather than sense and "subject constitution." Accordingly, Dickinson's unconventional texts, both poems and letters, have inspired many musicians and composers, including Elliott Carter, the aforementioned Copland, and Leon Kirchner, to mention just a few prominent names. "Quiet, introspective Emily Dickinson" has become, as Valentine Cunningham puts it, "the darling of modern composers" and "is reckoned to be the poet most set to music ever" (17) – and here music means classical composition as well as hip hop and rap. YouTube offers a wide variety of oftentimes amateur musical renditions of her poems, reflecting the poet's impact on young readers in particular. Seeing and hearing "Calvin and Kevin rapping their nerdy hearts away" on Dickinson's "Some keep the Sabbath going to church" is as hilarious as it is touching and instructive (http://www.youtube.com/watch?v=-luFew0-el0). And there is much more to discover, perhaps in interdisciplinary cooperation with colleagues who actually teach music.

Or art, for that matter. Dickinson frequently reappears in the visual media, including painting, sculpture, and digital art as well as

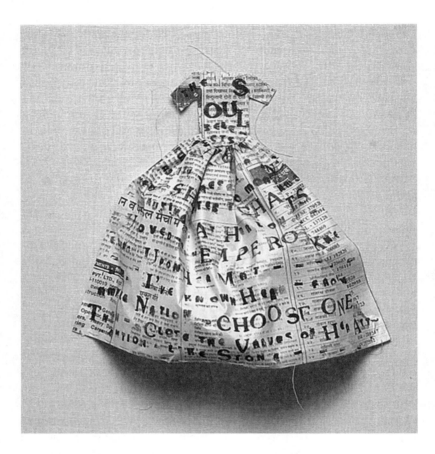

Figure 2. Lesley Dill, *Small Poem Dress (The Soul Selects ...)*, 1993 lithograph, newspaper; 10 x 8 x 2 inches; edition of 50; printed and published by Landfall Press, NM.
© Lesley Dill. Courtesy of the artist and George Adams Gallery, New York

cartoons and video games. We can trace the poet from Joseph Connell's 1950s box sculptures to Judy Chicago's famous *Dinner Party* (1974-79) and beyond: she is a constant reference, for instance, in the work of internationally acclaimed artists such as Lesley Dill (figure 2) and Barbara Penn (much of whose work is available to us on the internet).

Graphic artists who frame Dickinson in comics and cartoons obviously pick up on the "comic power" that critics like Suzanne Juhasz, Cristanne Miller, and Martha Nell Smith have ascribed to a poet hailed by other commentators (and cartoonists) as "Queen of the Neurotic Chicks" ("Emily Dickinson" blog post on *Toons Gone Feral*). A simple internet search unearths, for instance, a series of strips visualizing and mocking the narrative related in her poem "Because I could not stop for Death –" (see figure 3) – which has also inspired videos available on YouTube – as well as images that envision Dickinson having a soft spot for men with tattoos (see figure 4). Even Dickinson herself stars as cartoon artist. The website *Dickinson, Cartoonist* delineates some of the "cartoonist strategies" she used to "animate her words with visual designs," including cut-outs from a Dickens novel and drawings added around the Capitol building embossed on her father's Congressional stationery. Exploring these strategies, students easily see how modernist visual techniques, including the collage, have also evolved from literary practice. Moreover, even if, as Ed Park admits in an introduction to a *Poetryfoundation.org* series entitled "The Poem as Comic Strip,"

> [h]eightened language – one possible or partial definition of poetry – isn't the first thing one associates with comics [...] comic book artists take into account the way words appear on the page to a degree poets will find familiar. How many lines should accompany each image? How high should the dialogue balloon float? The ratio of printed words to blank space plays a role in whether a poem or strip succeeds.

And yet, if calculated from the printed versions of her poems, that ratio turns out to be highly misleading, since written by hand Dickinson's lyrics more often than not covered the page or scrap of paper in its entirety, leaving much less open space than it may appear.

Figure 3. Randall Munroe, *The Carriage* (http://xkcd.com/788/).

Figure 4. Emily Dickinson rendered by Nicole Hollander, creator of the cartoon strip "Sylvia" (see badgirlchats.com).

In 2005, the poet even became the center of the "Design Challenge: Emily Dickinson" posed to "master game design minds" during the Game Developers Convention in San Francisco. Will Wright, the overall winner of the competition, included his program as default software on a USB memory stick. "'USBEmily'," we can read in a review of the event on the "online gamesblog" of the *Guardian Unlimited*,

> would be an artificial personality, slightly unhinged, who would require the player, her psychiatrist, to manage her state of mind. [...] The various poles the character could veer towards would be romantically obsessed, utmost respect or suicidal, the last resulting in her self-deletion from the stick.
>
> Emily would contact you via email, Instant Message, while you were in the middle of an application or when you were online. She would be pervasive, asking if you want her to make a poem for you – a visual montage of first result images from a search using the two most relevant words from each line of one of her poems.
>
> The assumption was that the customer doesn't buy into Emily initially, but that he or she develops a relationship with her over time. ("Design Challenge")

Oh yes, Dickinson grows on us, and she may grow on us faster if we encounter her playfully. For as Dickinson's work and its echoes in contemporary popular cultures foreground, writing does not constitute a separate sphere, but closely interrelates with other arts and cultural practices. Exploring the intermedial connections between Dickinson's nineteenth-century verse and the material culture it is embedded in, on the one hand, and its current remediations, on the other, students may realize that what used to go by the label 'high art' and what many dismiss as merely pop can no longer be sorted out and set apart all that easily. In turn, we who consider cultural literacy a central objective of our enterprise as teachers may explore how it works to approach one of the greatest writers in American literary history from our end of the timeline and usher in digital Dickinson before turning to her nineteenth-century context. Web 2.0 has changed our lives and work and it changes how we view and interact with Emily Dickinson, both domesticating and othering the poet in the process. Some students may just purchase the "Emily Dickinson Lonely Heart Keychain" or crave the T-shirt, offered on www.littlebookwormz.com, displaying the caption "E is for Emily" under a cartoonish yet confident image of the poet's face. Wearing this "tee," they celebrate the poet and "rewrite" the "myth of Amherst." Others may prefer to liven up the "Contemporary Youth's Companion," a forum for poems and other writings by writers who are eighteen years old or younger featured on the *Dickinson Electronic Archives* (http://www.emilydickinson.org/titanic/cyc/cycdex.html). Yet others may simply want to read Dickinson's poems in series and experience the "joy in repetition" (Prince). No matter what one's personal preference may be in interacting with Emily Dickinson, there are innumerable ways in which the poet invites us to "dwell in possibilities" today.

Bibliography

Charyn, Jerome. *The Secret Life of Emily Dickinson: A Novel.* New York, NY: Norton, 2010.
Clarke, Brock. *An Arsonist's Guide to Writers' Homes in New England: A Novel.* Chapel Hill, NC: Algonquin Books, 2007.
Cunningham, Valentine. "The Sound of Startled Grass." *The Guardian* 19 October 2002: 17.
"Design Challenge : Emily Dickinson." *Guardian Unlimited Games Blog.* <http://blogs.guardian.co.uk/games/archives/game_culture/2005/03/design_challenge_emily_dickinson.html>.
"Dickinson, Cartoonist: Introduction." *EmilyDickinson.org* <http://www.emilydickinson.org/cartoon/carintro.html>.
"Dickinson the Poet and Person." Review of *Famous Authors: Emily Dickinson.* Amazon.com. http://www.amazon.com/Famous-Authors-Emily-Dickinson/product-reviews/B001GMH8QK>.
Dobson, Joanne. *Quieter Than Sleep: A Modern Mystery of Emily Dickinson.* New York, NY: Bantam, 1998.
"Emily Dickinson." *Toons Gone Feral.* 19 Jan. 2010. <http://toonstoonstoons.net/category/cartoon/poetry//>.
Franklin, Ralph W. *The Editing of Emily Dickinson: A Reconsideration.* Madison, WI: University of Wisconsin Press, 1967.
Franklin, Ralph W., ed. *The Manuscript Books of Emily Dickinson.* Cambridge, MA: Belknap Press, 1999.
Johnson, Thomas H., ed. *The Poems of Emily Dickinson.* 3 vols. Cambridge, MA: Belknap Press, 1979.
--- and Theodora Ward, eds. *The Letters of Emily Dickinson.* 3 vols. Cambridge, MA: Belknap Press, 1986.

Juhasz, Suzanne, Cristanne Miller and Martha Nell Smith. *Comic Power in Emily Dickinson*. Austin, TX: University of Texas Press, 1993.

Keller, Karl. "Notes on Sleeping with Emily Dickinson." *Feminist Critics Read Emily Dickinson*. Ed. Suzanne Juhasz. Bloomington, IN: Indiana University Press, 1983. 67-79.

Langton, Jane. *Emily Dickinson Is Dead: A Homer Kelly Mystery*. New York, NY: Penguin, 1985.

Luce, William. *The Belle of Amherst: A Play Based on the Life of Emily Dickinson*. Boston, MA: Houghton Mifflin, 1976.

Oates, Joyce Carol. *Wild Nights: Stories about the Last Days of Poe, Dickinson, Twain, James, and Hemingway*. New York, NY: Harper Collins, 2008.

Park, Ed. "The Poem as Comic Strip # 2, by Gabrielle Belle and Emily Dickinson." *Poetryfoundation.org*. Poetry Foundation. Web. 29 Aug. 2011. <http://www.poetryfoundation.org/article/179402>.

Prince. "Joy in Repetition." *Graffiti Bridge*. Paisley Park, Warner Bros. 1990.

Quinn, Alice. "Never Too Much Dickinson." *Blog of the Poetry Society of America*. Poetry Society of America. Web. 23 April 2010. <http://www.poetrysociety.org/psa/poetry/blog/never_too_much_emily_dickinson/>.

Smith, Martha Nell. "The Poet as Cartoonist: Pictures Sewed to Words." *Emily Dickinson: A Collection of Critical Essays*. Ed. Judith Farr. New Century Views. Upper Saddle River, NJ: Prentice Hall, 1996. 225-239.

Styron, William. *Sophie's Choice*. New York: Random House, 1979.

Worrall, Simon. *The Poet and the Murderer: A True Story of Literary Crime and the Art of Forgery*. New York, NY: Dutton, 2002.

Susanne Rohr (Hamburg)

On Being in Love with the World: Gertrude Stein's *Tender Buttons*

When asked whether they are familiar with the work of Gertrude Stein (1874-1946), most students will draw a blank. If they have heard of Stein, they might come up with the quotation "Rose is a rose is a rose," as this is probably Stein's most famous line of poetry, one that has even made it into colloquial speech. But when confronted with texts by this author for the first time, students, particularly undergraduates, tend either to make fun of them immediately or to dismiss them as incomprehensible. In any case, they will most likely be in despair at the prospect of dealing with Stein's work.

In short, when trying to familiarize students with Gertrude Stein's work teachers should be prepared to meet initial resistance. Yet there are other possible outcomes. The predictable reaction motivated one colleague, Dene Grigar, to use hypertext in her seminar on Stein's prose poem *Tender Buttons* (1914), and it seems to have been a successful experiment, as her conclusion reads: "What they [the students] had viewed originally as 'meaningless nonsense' [...] was instead revealed to them as an ingenious game in which they were invited to participate" (41). Nevertheless, and despite this particular happy ending, Gertrude Stein's reputation in the classroom leaves much to be desired, and it is one of the aims of this essay to remedy this rejection. Teaching the work of Gertrude Stein, even without the use of hypertext, is a most rewarding endeavor as she is if not "The Mother of Us All," in the words of the libretto she wrote for Virgil Thomson's opera, certainly one of the mothers of modernism.

Stein led a fascinating transatlantic existence. Born in Allegheny, Pennsylvania, she moved to Paris in 1903 with her brother Leo and became a passionate art collector. She also kept a famous salon where the avant-garde artists of her time met: Pablo Picasso, Henri Matisse, Georges Braque, Juan Gris, and many more. Stein was one of the first to appreciate the radical experiments of these artists and was as deeply influenced by their art as she in turn influenced them. After the end of the First World War, the first phase of extreme and iconoclastic modernist experiments – cubism, futurism, surrealism, and dada, as well as radical new forms of poetic expression – gave way to the second phase, which saw the production of literary masterworks such as John Dos Passos's *Manhattan Transfer* (1925), F. Scott Fitzgerald's *The Great Gatsby* (1925) and Ernest Hemingway's *The Sun Also Rises* (1926). Stein said of these gifted young visitors to her salon who had fought in the war and were struggling to cope with their traumatic experiences, "You are all a lost generation," coining an expression that came to describe an entire generation of writers. As Marianne DeKoven sums up, "She was at the center of three major modernist-avant-garde Parisian groups: the lesbian Left Bank [...], the bohemian Montmartre of Picasso [...], and the postwar scene of younger American expatriate modernists [...]" (479).

Yet Stein, the muse and "mother of them all," was herself the most daring author and experimenter, causing one contemporary critic, Robert E. Rogers, to wonder whether she was "mad" (32). Mad or a genius, Stein was "writing modernism out of the nineteenth century," as Georgia Johnston has aptly put it. Johnston here refers to Stein's first major work, *Three Lives* (1909), which she modelled on Gustave Flaubert's realist *Troi Contes* (1877), and which introduced Stein's famous technique of hypnotic repetition and the ensuing dynamization and aestheticization of the textual surface into a realist frame. Thus, teaching Stein and studying the developments characterizing her work allows for insights into the transitional phase from literary realism to modernism and provides a profound introduction to the project of modernism as a whole. What is more, her late work, particularly her novel *Ida* (1941), to a certain extent anticipates postmodernist literary techniques and concerns, so that Stein's work can be said to span three literary epochs.

Presenting Stein in this way requires, however, a thorough contextualization of her work in the dramatic cultural changes that took place around the turn of the century. I want to concentrate in this essay on exploring Stein's prose poem *Tender Buttons* (1914), so I cannot go into a detailed discussion of her other works and will only mention them in passing. I will, however, first sketch briefly those elements of the historical context of modernism and the history of ideas that might be instrumental in preparing students for analyses of Stein's work. As an amazing amount of secondary material on Stein comprises a discussion of her personal life – not a standard approach these days and one of the peculiarities of research on Stein – I will also give some key data from her rather unusual and exciting biography along the way.

1. The Upheavals of Modernism

Modernism roughly spans the period from the early twentieth century until the end of World War II, with its climax in the 1920s. It is an international, complex and heterogeneous phenomenon. In fact, it has become common usage to speak of various modernisms, in order to indicate the various strands and perspectives from which this epoch can be discussed and categorized. We might characterize modernism both as a form of cultural and artistic expression and as the expression of a certain uneasy awareness of or attitude toward the era's dominant currents. Sigmund Freud's 1930 seminal work *Das Unbehagen in der Kultur* (*Civilization and Its Discontents*) is an analysis of just this uneasiness, of an individual's warring tendencies to either obey or revolt against civilization's norms and regulations. Thus modernism is both a profound examination of received norms and traditions and a passionate attempt to break free from them and to explore radical new forms of expression.

Let us first have a closer look at the historical context. The turn of the century was first of all characterized by major technological developments and the ramifications of the daunting forces of industrialization. Dramatic societal changes ensued, most visible in the rapid growth of cities and the partitioning of urban areas into neighborhoods for the well to do, on the one hand, and slums on the other. Although this was a transatlantic and transnational development, American cities had to cope additionally with a massive influx of immigrants, bringing with it the challenge of integrating a multitude of cultural practices into American society. Furthermore, northern American metropolises, above all New York City, became prime destinations for African Americans who were migrating in great numbers from the southern states. In New York City, a flourishing of black American cultural expression emerged, the so-called "Harlem Renaissance," generally seen as the black counterpart to modernism. Important changes also occurred in the structure of gender relations as women began entering the work force now in great numbers. The traditional Victorian division into "separate spheres" for men and women, where the private sphere of the home was assigned to women and the public domain to men became increasingly difficult to maintain, if not actually obsolete. The "true woman," the woman obeying the rigid moral constraints of Victorianism, was slowly displaced by the concept of the more liberated "new woman," and the women's movement gained momentum, leading, in 1920, to women's suffrage in the U.S. Gertrude Stein, even in her European existence, was a lifelong keen observer of her original American culture and she continuously examined its changes in her works. One part of the already mentioned *Three Lives* (1909), "Melanctha," for example, concerns topics related to African American life in the U.S., whereas another part, "The Gentle Lena," investigates the sad existence of an immigrant woman. Stein's libretto for the opera *The Mother of Us All* (1947) in turn treats the life of Susan B. Anthony, one of the most prominent fighters for women's suffrage in the U.S.

Although these transformations were well under way during the second half of the nineteenth century, with the beginning of the twentieth century the situation culminated in a veritable shift of eras. The moral rigidity of the nineteenth century was displaced by a cultural climate in which men and women and members of all classes and races were beginning to probe the social stratification of nineteenth century society, which had largely been dominated by the norms of the now declining gentility. In other words, a whole cultural system, Victorianism, gave way to a new structure of cultural norms and values. Fundamental developments in the sciences shattered long held beliefs; for example, Albert Einstein's theory of relativity, formulated in 1905, overturned the definition of space and time as absolute quantities. Likewise, Sigmund Freud's new method of psychoanalysis, resting as it does on concepts of repression and the unconscious, deeply and frighteningly challenged the human self-images of control and rationality cherished in the nineteenth century. Furthermore, the speed of living increased considerably in the growing metropolises, where all of these changes became distinctly articulated and symbolically visible in the rise of the automobile, the rapid development of the motion picture and the shooting up of modern skyscrapers.

If all of these groundbreaking alterations were disquieting for many, they were celebrated emphatically by others. Avant-garde artists of the time revelled in the dramatic transformation and celebrated its speed and clamour. Artists felt that they were not only witnessing, but also actively participating in a breathtaking cataclysm, and they wanted to shape and represent it in completely new ways. Thus, Ezra Pound's imperative claim "Make It New!" became the battle cry for an entire generation of avant-garde artists who wanted to break free of the cultural traditions of the nineteenth century once and for all.

The epitome of this movement was probably the (in)famous "Armory Show" that took place in New York City in 1913 and exhibited the art of the European and American avant-garde. It introduced an amazed New York audience to cubist, fauvist and impressionist art, earned a great deal of ridicule and caused a veritable scandal. Countless articles satirized the disturbing art works that resisted any critical attempts to assess them along the realist lines to which the general audience had been accustomed. Of all the works of art, one in particular aggravated the critics: Marcel Duchamp's "Nude Descending a Staircase" (1912, Figure 1), now established as an outstanding modernist masterpiece. This painting displays the modernist project to perfection as it strikingly reflects the era's deep concern with the structures of human perception. Although explanations of cultural developments can certainly never be one-dimensional, one could argue that in dialogue with the dizzying speed and agitation of the age and the dazzling sense impressions to which city dwellers were exposed, the phenomena of human perception, consciousness and the exact nature of perceptual structures slowly shifted into the focus of cultural attention. In psychology, philosophy and the visual arts, the topic was taken up by many artists and scientists.

Thus in this vein Duchamp's painting tries to be truer than the eye, tries to show an existing reality that human perception cannot absorb. The painting wants to function like the newly developed stroboscope photography that slows or freezes an ongoing course of movement and makes visible to the human eye the sequence of singular elements of which it is composed. Much like the theory of

Figure 1. *Nude Descending a Staircase (No. 2)*, Marcel Duchamp. Oil on Canvas, 1912. 57 7/8 x 35 1/8 inches (147 x 89.2 cm). Philadelphia Museum of Art: The Louise and Walter Arensberg Collection, 1950.
© Succession Marcel Duchamp / VG Bild-Kunst, Bonn 2011

relativity or psychoanalysis, the artwork interrogates a dimension that eludes direct notice and even contradicts common sense as it dismantles the habit of the eye to combine discrete moments of movement into a unified flow of motion, thereby creating the illusion of unity or uniformity. To disclose illusions like this, to reveal the truth behind customary cognition and to show the fragments behind the impression of unity was one of the crucial concerns of modernism. It played itself out in cubism's abandoning of the central perspective and adoption of multiple vantage points in one painting as well as in dada's collages and assemblages and futurism's synesthetic experimental efforts to embody speed and sound visibly on the canvas.

The topic of human perception was not only explored widely in the visual arts; literature also took it up as a major subject. If the literary production of modernism's first phase was dominated mainly by dramatic poetic experimentation (major poets include T.S. Eliot, Ezra Pound and H.D.), the second phase belonged to prose, and a radical prose it was. As modernist writers in Europe and the U.S. embraced the topic of consciousness and the structures of perception in literature, they were looking for new forms of literary expression to represent the workings of the human mind. Derived from the work of the American psychologist and philosopher William James, the technique of "stream of consciousness" writing became the preferred method distinguishing major masterworks of the era, such as James Joyce's *Ulysses* (1922), William Faulkner's *The Sound and the Fury* (1929) and *Manhattan Transfer* (1925) by John Dos Passos.

Stream of consciousness, a particular point of view from which a story is told, is intended to represent thought processes and sense impressions. It aims to create the illusion that readers share a character's most intimate interaction with the world, the moment when a human being *creates* reality by directly interacting with his or her immediate perceptions. The point of view is located in a character's cognitive apparatus and seems to let the reader witness some kind of newborn reality as it emerges from the first, unordered sense impressions and their initial uncensored and provisional interpretations. As a consequence, the form of stream of consciousness is distinctly different from the orderly fashion of a coherent interior monologue or free indirect discourse, techniques used traditionally to represent thought processes, and is characterized instead by a radical fragmentation of syntactic coherence. Bits and pieces of sentences breathlessly scamper over the page, their vague connection indicated by dashes and series of periods.

Stream of consciousness is in a way the most subjective of all literary techniques of representation and points of view. As such it is a distinct challenge to the forms of the preceding literary realism that aimed to represent a kind of consensual and rational social reality. Very much like cubism's and dada's radical experiments with perspective in the visual arts, stream of consciousness in literature experiments with exploring dimensions of reality that had previously defied representation.

Interestingly enough, Gertrude Stein does not employ stream of consciousness as a method in her works, although her literary interests tie in closely with those of modernism. This is all the more surprising as she had been a student of philosophy and psychology under William James at Harvard and was thus intimately familiar with his work, particularly his research on the structures of cognition, knowledge, and experience and his philosophy of pragmatism. Stein was intensely interested in exploring the workings of consciousness and perception in her work, but she wanted to represent those processes through the stream of consciousness technique not as experienced by literary characters, but *by herself*. In "A Transatlantic Interview," given in 1946, she explains what she is after: "it was not solely the realism of the characters but the realism of the composition which was the important thing, the realism of the composition of my thoughts" (15-16). So at the core of all the disturbing aesthetic experiments that make reading Stein's texts such a challenge there is still an echo of the mimetic idea of truthful representation that had also governed the format of literary realism. In this case, however, it is a truthful representation not of *reality* but of the *process of constructing or composing reality* out of sense impressions. In other words, it is as if Stein turns herself into the object of critical examination and puts her own cognitive processes under scrutiny in order to understand how a coherent image of reality emerges out of a scattered series of sense impressions. The resulting representation is at once highly subjective – as it concerns an individual process of perception – and objective, as it displays epistemological structures that are not specific to an individual.

As this process is clearly an infinite one consisting of a series of distinct impressions that are smoothed into one coherent image, a truthful rendering, critical exploration and dismantling of this process calls for new techniques of representation (much like Duchamp's method in "Nude Descending a Staircase"). One of these is Stein's use of the continuous present as her favorite grammatical tense, as it allows her to create an endless stream of distinct moments, a "succession of nows." She composes certain sequences of sentences or parts of sentences that are repeated in slight variation over and over again, building up a kind of intense flow of hypnotic auditory effect when read aloud. These linguistic elements join together very much as do the single frames of a film sequence that, seen in succession, concatenate into a flow of a coherent optical impression, a somewhat cinematic effect of which Stein was quite conscious.

Consider for example the following quotation from Stein's portrait of Pablo Picasso (1909), where she tries to represent both the underlying rhythm of a particular personality and the different emphases of character traits in each new encounter with the same person: "One whom some were certainly following was one who was completely charming. One whom some were certainly following was one who was charming. One whom some were following was one who was completely charming. One whom some were following was one who was completely charming" (51).

Let us return to the interview mentioned above in which Stein makes important commentaries about her aesthetic intentions with unusual clarity. Here she herself establishes the relation between her style of writing and the compositional strategies of the visual arts, a topic that since then has been extensively treated in Stein criticism. Stein elucidates:

> Everything I have done has been influenced by Flaubert and Cézanne, and this gave me a new feeling about composition. Up to that time composition had consisted of a central idea, to which everything else was an accompaniment and separate but was not an end in itself, and Cézanne conceived of the idea that in composition one thing was as important as another thing. Each part is as important as the whole, and that impressed me enormously [...]. (15)

Stein here explains another one of her major compositional principles. If she exploited the technique of repetition with variation (which Stein herself incidentally did not call repetition but insistence) to the fullest extent in her early writing, the next phase of her work was characterized by a different aesthetic experiment. In trying to let each part of a particular composition be as important as the whole, she democratizes or de-hierarchizes language. That is, she does not construct sentences around dominating nouns (very often she replaces nouns by a deictic "this one" or "that one") but consciously grants elements like verbs, adjectives or adverbs equal value. Markus Poetzsch gives a hint as to the possible function of this verbal experiment: "Because Stein does not distinguish particular objects and their movements except through deixis, she invariably draws the reader beyond the text to the circumstances and moments of perception itself" (949). As Stein herself formulates it in the "Transatlantic Interview":

> I began to play with words then. I was a little obsessed by words of equal value. [...] I took individual words and thought about them until I got their weight and volume complete and put them next to another word, and at this same time I found out very soon that there is no such thing as putting them together without sense. [...] I made innumerable efforts to make words write without sense and found it impossible. (17-18)

Stein here explicitly refers to her major work of this period, *Tender Buttons* (1914), and refutes the claims of many later readers that the pieces of this poem make no sense at all. Let us now turn to a closer examination of this enigmatic masterpiece.

2. Expressing the Rhythm of the Visible World: Tender Buttons

In *The Autobiography of Alice B. Toklas* (1933), probably Stein's most famous book, in which she herself writes her autobiography by assuming the voice of her partner Alice B. Toklas, Stein describes her impulse to write *Tender Buttons* as "a desire to express the rhythm of the visible world" (145). What could she mean here?

This rhythm, it seems fair to say, is created in the cognitive processes of apprehending the world in sense impressions and subsequently interpreting these impressions in language. Stein in her attempt to trace this process aims to find a language suitable for this endeavor, a somehow fresh language that would not be obscured and worn by conventionality. Returning once more to the

"Transatlantic Interview," Stein here elucidates what she is after in *Tender Buttons*:

> I used to take objects on a table, like a tumbler or any kind of object and try to get the picture of it clear and separate in my mind and create a word relationship between the word and the things seen. […] I try to call to the eye the way it appears by suggestion the way a painter can do it. This is difficult and takes a lot of work and concentration to do it. I want to indicate it without calling in other things. (25)

Stein's comment provides a hint about the format of the text. *Tender Buttons* is a prose poem composed of three sections, titled "Objects," "Food" and "Rooms." The first two sections consist of over fifty poems (or stanzas) each that vary in length from one line to several pages. "Rooms" is one long poem. The poems in the first part describe everyday household objects that are used as titles, such as "A SELTZER BOTTLE," "A RED HAT" or "A HANDKERCHIEF." The second part continues with the description of various meals such as "BREAKFAST" and the food items that typically belong to them.

What generations of critics have found most troublesome about this text is the fact that the descriptions don't seem to match the titles. A familiar enough – even banal – domestic universe suddenly seems strange and out of control. Consider the famous first object:

A CARAFE, THAT IS A BLIND GLASS.

> A kind in glass and a cousin, a spectacle and nothing strange a single hurt color and an arrangement in a system to pointing. All this and not ordinary, not unordered in not resembling. The difference is spreading. (9)

As a first step in approaching this universe, a closer look at the genre form might be helpful. Prose poetry had its origin in France in the mid-19th century and from the beginning was credited with a somewhat subversive nature as it consciously goes against clear-cut genre definitions. It combines lyrical and prosaic characteristics in that it is not written in verse, yet it pays heightened attention to the rhythmic qualities of language and employs imagery typically found in poetry. Jonathan Monroe understands the ensuing aesthetic conflict between different literary genres politically, as a "symbolic reenactment of more broadly based social struggles" (18). In applying this reading to Stein's text, he concludes:

> [I]n *Tender Buttons* Stein rewrites the struggle between men and women as a struggle between prose and poetry. These struggles of gender and genre are themselves figured in Stein's text by objects of household labor that are the signs not only of the sexual subordination of women but of their economic subjugation as well [...]. (22)

If we follow this reading, we take the interconnection between gender and genre in Stein's text into account and read this prose poem in its hybrid form of "in-betweenness" as a critical examination of domestic female experience. And women's changing position in society is certainly a pertinent line of interpretation.

Stein, of course, does this examination of the domestic sphere in her very own way. Margueritte S. Murphy holds that "Stein exploits the vocabulary, syntax, rhythms, and cadences of conventional women's prose and talk, the ordinary discourse of domesticity, to create her own new 'language'" (383-84). Belinda Bruner in a recent publication supports this view: "Stein's insistence on the everyday, domestic content in *Tender Buttons* provides a context for her attempt to overthrow the metaphor and to dislodge readerly habits. Stein presents food and cooking as one way of getting to the *is* of things [...]" (426). Nicely put – yet *what* exactly does Stein describe, what kind of reality does she represent in her attempt to get "to the *is* of things"? Let us return to the very first of the described objects, the carafe.

There is a whole line of criticism, especially in vogue in the 1980s, that interprets this description in particular and Stein's work in general along the lines of poststructuralist or deconstructive thinking. This view is triggered by the enigmatic "spreading difference" here and elsewhere in Stein's work, difference being one of the favorite concepts of the postmodern critique of language. Her not making sense is celebrated as an attempt to subvert the law of the father, to transgress phallocentric norms in creating her own *écriture féminine*. Adhering to this line is Ellen Berry, who holds: "[...] Stein burns/bathes orgasmically in language, claiming language as her (our) own, in an eroticized linguistic space beyond paradox, beyond the sentences of the father. She ex-creates logical structures and 'excretes' a different language, one written with her body" (14).

Yet is the endless play of signifiers, spreading differences and the dissolving of meaning into a liquid flow of uncertainties the only way to interpret this description of a carafe? While I concede the usefulness of examining Stein's work from a postmodern perspective, I agree with Nicola Pitchford, who in her article "Unlikely Modernism, Unlikely Postmodernism" argues for interpreting *Tender Buttons* within the context of modernist concerns. She addresses the question of "how to draw useful distinctions *between* historical moments without repressing the diversity of writing *within* each period" (642, emphasis in original).

In this spirit I prefer to read the poem along the lines of Stein's interest in processes of perception. The poem starts with a paradoxical statement, an impasse really: "A carafe, that is a blind glass." Here, the object in question is clearly stated as "a carafe," and we would expect a further clarification of it after the insertion "that is." Yet the opposite happens, and our expectations are frustrated in that the carafe is surprisingly specified as "a blind glass." A carafe is made of glass, and as such its transparency is part of its essence – yet here the glass is opaque, or in another reading it is like a mirror that does not reflect what is put before it. What is put before it is the perceiving lyrical I/eye that cannot penetrate the nature of the object under observation as long as the perception is clouded by habitual patterns of cognition. Thus the attempt to conceptualize the object differently. First by seeing it generically as a "kind" of something and as something that is related to it, its "cousin," but not quite itself. Then the lyrical I/eye, as if turning a kaleidoscope, assumes the position of a painter and represents the carafe as broken down into its spectral colors.

Just as Duchamp tried to show another dimension of movement by splitting it up into its individual elements, the author here aims to find appropriate verbal expression for the physical qualities of glass. The image of the receptacle standing on the table in bright sunlight is conjured up, the light turning it into a blazing prism, thereby generating "a spectacle." The red spectrum creates the impression of a bleeding wound, a "hurt color" as part of a whole "arrangement" in a prismatic "system to pointing."

In this way, the carafe is finally seen in a fresh, maybe more truthful way, in a way that breaks with habits of conceptualization and is thus "not ordinary." Yet the account follows its own logic in that it is "not unordered in not resembling" established patterns of perception and description. As this is just the first object seen and delineated in an entirely unfamiliar way, the "difference" will certainly be "spreading" over the entire household and will evoke, in the whole of *Tender Buttons*, a new and bizarre domestic universe.

3. Shaking Tables and Caressed Nouns

In her contemplation of a table, Stein follows a different line of representation.

> A TABLE.
>
> A table means does it not my dear it means a whole steadiness. Is it likely that a change.
> A table means more than a glass even a looking glass is tall. A table means necessary places and a revision a revision of a little thing it means it does mean that there has been a stand, a stand where it did shake. (26)

Here, the lyrical I enters into a dialogue with the reader. The exchange starts with the assertion that the standard characterization of a table, its unchanging steadiness, is indeed true. Or is it? The lyrical I in a very polite yet somehow sly way seeks affirmation from the reader – "does it not my dear" – thereby giving the first hint that it does not and that our confidence will be shattered. To the contemplating I the table means more; it means something different; it even means the opposite of what it is habitually taken for. It means more than what you would see in a looking glass, the mirror just reflecting its steadiness. In a pragmatist move (after all, Stein was very much influenced by her teacher William James, one of the fathers of pragmatism), the lyrical I turns to contemplating what one would *do* with a table. In pragmatist thinking, what one *does* with or to a thing is what constitutes its *meaning*. In that way, it is not the table's steadiness that constitutes its meaning for the lyrical I but that one puts things on it in their "necessary places." Those necessities are, however, always subject to "revision;" they are constantly changing according to the needs of the user of the table. The aborted question of the beginning "Is it likely that a change" is now answered in the positive as it is precisely the continuous change that constitutes the meaning of a table for the lyrical I, not the steadiness that is conventionally ascribed to it. The table is thus in movement, it "shakes," and as this is a quite daring reinterpretation of what a table means, the lyrical I displays some persuasive power to assure itself that "it means it does mean [...] it did shake."

There are yet other strategies of representation to consider, as Stein investigates many forms of poetic experiment in *Tender Buttons*. In the "Food" section of the text, Stein contemplates chicken from various angles and ontological possibilities and presents us with four poems in a row, all titled "CHICKEN." While the first one tries to come to terms with the natural classification of the species by comparing it to pheasant, the second one ponders the linguistic dimension and rates chicken a "dirty word" because it is a fighting word and a way of calling someone a coward. The third poem finally understands chicken as food and part of a meal and pairs it with cress and potatoes. Consider the associations Stein invokes concerning the fourth possibility of how to understand chicken:

> CHICKEN.
>
> Stick stick call then, stick stick sticking, sticking with a chicken. Sticking in a extra succession, sticking in. (54)

Here Stein clearly plays with the possibilities of onomatopoetic description. She tries to capture the sound chickens make when they peck corn from the ground and the rhythm of this action. In this case, the birds are seen in their natural surroundings or the ambience of a farm, yet we are not presented with a description of the habitat or the way a chicken looks or the actual sounds it makes. Instead, the representation now shifts to the aesthetic level. When read aloud – which, by the way, is always imperative when dealing with Stein's work – "Stick stick call then" imitates the swift movements of the pecking bird's head and the following pause before the action restarts with "stick stick sticking." This representational strategy resembles the one Stein also employs in her much discussed poem "Susie Asado" (1913), a text from the same period in which she tries to poetically portray a Flamenco dancer:

SUSIE ASADO

> Sweet sweet sweet sweet sweet tea.
> Susie Asado […]. (57)

Again, when read aloud and fast, the repetition of "sweet" evokes the sound and movement of the swirling, whirling heels of a flamenco dancer that, as part of flamenco's characteristic choreography, come to a pronounced and abrupt stop, very much as "tea" abruptly ends the first line. Language is here, as in "CHICKEN," strictly employed for its aesthetic qualities of rhyme and rhythm, not for its function of transporting meaning. If, as Stein explains in the above quotation from the "Transatlantic Interview," she wanted in *Tender Buttons* to "create a word relationship between the word and the things seen," she designs this relationship in continually new ways. In cases like these the "word relationship" is a purely aesthetic one.

Yet there are more ways to read *Tender Buttons*. A whole field of feminist and gender-related research has concentrated on the erotic implications of the poem. This approach rests on the fact that a major change took place in Stein's personal life while she was writing *Tender Buttons*. She ended or altered her close and perhaps even suffocating relationship with her brother Leo and began her lifelong companionship with Alice B. Toklas. Leo moved out of the famous Parisian domicile Rue de Fleurus 27, Alice moved in, and the two settled into their domestic life. Many critics concentrate on isolating the repercussions of this move in Stein's work of that time. Shari Benstock, for instance, talks about breaking the "lesbian code" (161) and spelling out *Tender Buttons*'s "grammar of lesbian domesticity" (162) where "[s]exual expression is intimately linked to linguistic expression" (163). While I do not wish to challenge this approach, it seems to me that its results have by now become utterly predictable. Once the code is broken, the secret is out, so to speak. One of the favorite examples of this line of reading is the following poem in *Tender Buttons*:

RED ROSES.

> A cool red rose and a pink cut pink, a collapse and a sold hole, a little less hot. (24)

While the erotic and sexual allusions of this imagery are hard to miss, Rebecca Scherr, concentrating in her feminist reading on Stein's probing of the "tactile quality of language, its textures and the expression of 'touchability'" (193) adds convincing insights. She argues that *Tender Buttons* as a whole is a "meditation on the role of the senses in literary production" (195), and that while "RED ROSES" "draws simultaneously upon the visual, aural, and tactile sensory realms" (196), Stein's focus in the entire poem is on the tactile. In fact, Scherr concludes, "[s]everal passages seem to indicate the movement of the hand" (196). Stein herself makes a statement in *The Autobiography of Alice B. Toklas* that reinforces this view when she writes: "I always say that you cannot tell what a picture really is or what an object really is until you dust it every day [...]" (138).

According to this perspective, Stein creates a loving approach to the objects of her world. It is as if the author caresses her domestic universe, tries to take possession of it with all her senses and tries to find the appropriate verbal expression to match these sensuous experiences. In "Poetry and Grammar," an analytical text mainly dedicated to explaining her aesthetic strategies and poetics in *Tender Buttons*, Stein elaborates on the theme of being in love with the world:

> As I say a noun is a name of a thing, and therefore slowly if you feel what is inside that thing you do not call it by the name by which it is known. Everybody knows that by the way they do when they are in love and a writer should always have that intensity of emotion about whatever is the object about which he writes. (210)

In *Tender Buttons*, Stein in this way lovingly summons the objects of the world and sees how they answer. It is a play of poetic call and response in which Stein, as she explains, "called them [the things] by their names with passion and that made poetry" (235). Yet she doesn't want to idiosyncratically rename the world, but instead tries to find a way of "naming things [...] without naming them" (236). Hence she states the object under consideration in the title of the individual poem or stanza and follows it with descriptions that try to find a way of evoking the object "without naming it" again. In her reading of *Tender Buttons* Ulla Haselstein follows a related argument: "For the reader, the rule of the game is thus as follows: to recognize the text as the emergence of the thing and to thereby convert the appellation into a motivated name" (203, my translation).

As Stein puts it: "Anybody knows how anybody calls out the name of anybody one loves. And so that is poetry really loving the name of anything and that is not prose. Yes any of you can know that" (232). At this point we are led back to considerations of the genre form. If poetry is love and prose is reflection, then the prose poem, it seems to me, is a particularly apt form for Stein's project, as it allows for both the act of poetically "caressing nouns" (231) and the analytic and quasi-scientific interest in reflecting on processes of perception.

Let Gertrude Stein have the last word: "Well anyway [...] this is all that I do know [...] about prose and poetry. The rest will come considerably later" (246).

Bibliography

Benstock, Shari. *Women of the Left Bank: Paris, 1900-1940*. Austin, TX: University of Texas Press, 1986.
Berry, Ellen E. *Curved Thought and Textual Wandering: Gertrude Stein's Postmodernism*. Ann Arbor, MI: University of Michigan Press, 1992.
Bruner, Belinda. "A Recipe for Modernism and the Somatic Intellect in *The Alice B. Toklas Cook Book* and Gertrude Stein's *Tender Buttons*." *Papers on Language and Literature* 45.4 (2009): 411-433.
DeKoven, Marianne. "Gertrude Stein (1874-1946): Introduction." *The Gender of Modernism: A Critical Anthology*. Ed. Bonnie Kime Scott. Bloomington, IN: Indiana University Press, 1990. 479-488.
Grigar, Dene. "What Is Seen Depends on How Everybody Is Doing Everything: Using Hypertext to Teach Gertrude Stein's *Tender Buttons*." *The Dialogic Classroom: Teachers Integrating Computer Technology, Pedagogy, and Research*. Ed. Jeffrey R. Galin et al. Urbana; IL: NCTE, 1998. 27-42.
Haselstein, Ulla. "Gertrude Steins Porträts von Dingen." *Dinge – Medien der Aneignung: Grenzen der Verfügung*. Ed. Gisela Ecker et al. Königstein: Helmer, 2002. 197-217.
Johnston, Georgia. "Reading Anna Backwards: Gertrude Stein Writing Modernism out of the Nineteenth Century." *Studies in the Literary Imagination* 25.2 (1992): 31-37.
Monroe, Jonathan. *A Poverty of Objects: The Prose Poem and the Politics of Genre*. Ithaca, NY: Cornell University Press, 1987.

Murphy, Margueritte S. "'Familiar Strangers': The Household Words of Gertrude Stein's *Tender Buttons.*" *Contemporary Literature* 32.3 (1991): 383-402.

Pitchford, Nicola. "Unlikely Modernism, Unlikely Postmodernism: Stein's *Tender Buttons.*" *American Literary History* 11.4 (1999): 642-667.

Poetzsch, Markus. "Presence, Deixis, and the Making of Meaning in Gertrude Stein's *Tender Buttons.*" *University of Toronto Quarterly* 75.4 (2006): 946-956.

Rogers, Robert E. "*Tender Buttons*, Curious Experiment of Gertrude Stein in Literary Anarchy." *Critical Essays on Gertrude Stein.* Ed. Michael J. Hoffman. Boston, MA: G.K. Hall, 1986. 31-33 [1914].

Scherr, Rebecca. "Tactile Erotics: Gertrude Stein and the Aesthetics of Touch." *Literature Interpretation Theory* 18.3 (2007): 193-212.

Stein, Gertrude. *The Autobiography of Alice B. Toklas.* Illustrated. New York, NY: Harcourt, Brace, 1933.

---. "A Transatlantic Interview – 1946." *A Primer for the Gradual Understanding of Gertrude Stein.* Ed. Robert Bartlett Haas. Los Angeles: Black Sparrow Press, 1971. 15-35 [1962-1964].

---. "Picasso." *A Primer for the Gradual Understanding of Gertrude Stein.* Ed. Robert Bartlett Haas. Los Angeles, CA: Black Sparrow Press, 1971. 51-53 [1909].

---. "Poetry and Grammar." *Lectures in America.* Introduction by Wendy Steiner. Boston, MA: Beacon Press, 1985. 207-46 [1935].

---. "Susie Asado." *A Primer for the Gradual Understanding of Gertrude Stein.* Ed. Robert Bartlett Haas. Los Angeles, CA: Black Sparrow Press, 1971. 57 [1913].

---. *Tender Buttons: Objects – Food – Rooms.* New York, NY: Claire Marie, 1914.

Wolfgang Wicht (Potsdam)

"Language is made out of concrete things": The Imagist Movement and the Beginning of Anglo-American Modernism

Imagism is "a particular school" (Lowell 236) of innovative poetry and poetic conception that lasted from 1908 to 1917. It is one of the early varieties of multiple "modernisms" (Nicholls 1995) which sprang into life about the turn of the twentieth century, including Symbolism, Futurism, Dadaism and Surrealism, and which encompassed the genres of music and the pictorial arts as well as of poetry. As the compilers of the anthology *Some Imagist Poets 1916* noted, "with Debussy and Stravinsky in music, and Gauguin and Matisse in painting, it should have been evident to every one that art was entering upon an era of change" (Jones 137). In an exceptional and self-conscious manner, the Imagists reacted to the unequalled social transformations, crises and modernizations in economy, technology, the sciences, philosophy and culture, not to speak of the spirit of political revolt which expressed itself variously in industrial strikes, Fabianism, socialist movements and suffragette agitation. Their response, however, was strictly literary, never overtly social or political. In a typical manner, the Imagist poets represented the modernist condition, which Raymond Williams brilliantly summarizes as follows,

> Liberated or breaking from their national and provincial cultures, [...] encountering meanwhile a novel and dynamic common environment from which many of the older forms were obviously distant, the artists and writers and thinkers of this phase found the only community available to them: a community of the medium; of their own practices. (45)

To unearth Imagist poems today might help us to learn from "the grammar school of modern poetry" (Perkins 329) and gain a paradigmatic insight into the major shift in aesthetic form and conception at the beginning of the twentieth century.

Differing from the local circulation of modernist conceptual drafts and writing practices, which nonetheless claimed universal significance, Imagism established itself as a transatlantic London-based Anglo-American movement. Five of the "core group members" (Hamilton 468) were American (Ezra Pound, Hilda Doolittle, Amy Lowell, William Carlos Williams and John Gould Fletcher), and three were English (T.E. Hulme, F.S. Flint and Richard Aldington). Their ambition was to break with conventional versification (rhyme, metre, rhythm, the stanza) and the emotional, sentimental verbiage of both the American genteel poets and the late-Victorian and Edwardian versifiers. As the philosopher and critic T.E. Hulme emphasized in his "Lecture on Modern Poetry," probably presented to the Poets' Club in November 1908, "the new forms are deliberately introduced by people who detest the old ones" (*The Collected Writings* 51).

The "general distaste for the slushiness and swishiness of the post-Swinburnian British line" (Pound, *The Selected Letters* 181), however, was not a stimulus to the Imagist movement alone. It also guided those poets who did improve the quality – in meaning and form – of poems by modifying conventional patterns, poets such as Rupert Brooke, James Flecker, Harold Monro, Ralph Hodgson, William Davies, W.E. Henley and others, whose poems were published in the influential volumes of *Georgian Poetry*, edited by Edward Marsh, private secretary to Winston Churchill between 1912 and 1920. These poets accomplished what Ross (1965) appropriately calls "the Georgian Revolt." *The New Freewoman* (1913, from 1914 *The Egoist: An Individualist Review*), founded by the young philosopher and feminist Dora Marsden and edited by Harriet Shaw Weaver, became a mouthpiece of anti-hegemonic thinking, and Pound, who was invited to edit its literary pages, also made it the major forum for Imagist writing. It also published the first critical insider-accounts of the new movement, "Modern Poetry and the Imagists" by Richard Aldington (1 June 1914) and "The History of Imagism" by F. S. Flint (1 May 1915). Conrad Aiken's "The Place of Imagism" in the New York *New Republic* (22 May 1915) and further American articles, published in *The Little Review* and *Atlantic Monthly* in 1914, 1915 and 1916, for a large part kept their distance, and even censured the new movement. Typical titles were, for instance, "Poetry Versus Imagism" and "The New Naiveté" (cf. Jones 33-34). Harold Monro aspired to make *Poetry Review* (1911, from 1912 *Poetry and Drama*), the journal of the English Poetry Society, "the representative organ of the younger generation" (qtd. in Ross 62), which was open to both experimental and conventional verse. Apart from the literary coteries, however, single, exceptional, writers paved the way to, and lastingly shaped, the poetic revolution of the twentieth-century: W.B. Yeats and T.S. Eliot, Carl Sandburg, post-Imagist Ezra Pound and William Carlos Williams.

In hindsight, for critics, and even for the poets themselves, the significance of Imagism has been a matter of dispute. For some scholars, Imagism was a revolution in the literature of the English language and, as Pratt has it, "the most original movement in English literature in this century" (*Homage to Imagism* 75). Stephen Spender affirms that "the aims of the imagist movement in poetry provide the archetype of a modern procedure" (110). Others describe it as "a movement whose history was brief, broken and querulous, whose poetic results were minuscule" – in short, "a small affair" (Hough 9); or blame its "barren aestheticism which was, and is, empty of content," as John Gould Fletcher (213), who had once been an Imagist himself, once insinuated. With the barbarity of World War I and the impact of "usury age-old and age-thick / and liars in public places" in mind, Ezra Pound (*Selected Poems* 100) distanced himself from his transitional Imagist involvement in his poem of 1920, *Hugh Selwyn Mauberley*,

> For three years, out of key with his time
> He strove to resuscitate the dead art
> Of poetry; to maintain "the sublime"
> In the old sense. Wrong from the start – (*Selected Poems* 98)

From the perspective of the literary historian, "the advent of the imagists," as Helen Carr notes in her comprehensive "group biography" of the movement, "marked the beginning of Anglo-American modernism" (1). For a short period, it was representative of those poets who nourished their antipathy to representational art and all things Victorian. Since then, its outstanding poems and its conceptual thinking have not fallen into oblivion, but rather have been included in anthologies and academic discussion. Imagism was, as the subtitle of Stanley Coffman's influential study indicates, "a chapter for the history of modern poetry."

The man who became the first "ringleader" (Flint, qtd. in Jones 15) of the Imagist movement was, by common critical consent, T.E. Hulme, born in 1883 and killed in action in 1917, a student of Bergsonian philosophy, essayist and author of six poems, five of them published in *The New Age* in February 1912 and republished as an appendix to Pound's small volume of poems, *Ripostes* (1912). In 1908, Hulme gathered around himself a literary discussion group called the Poets' Club. The Club's anthology *For Christmas MDCCCCVIII* included his first poems, "A City Sunset" and "Autumn." Before long, he met the poet F. S. Flint (1885-1960), who, as poetry critic of *The New Age* from 1908, advocated a radical departure from traditional techniques in his reviews (see Martin 12). Hulme and Flint formed another circle, which met at the Eiffel Tower restaurant in Soho every Thursday from 25 March 1909 onwards. Hulme dominated both clubs, tirelessly explicating his ideas. Influenced by Rimbaud and Laforgue, and in close alliance with Flint, he first appropriated, and then distanced himself from, French Symbolist poetry.

Hulme developed his theoretical notions in their most condensed form in an essay entitled "Romanticism and Classicism," written in either 1909 or 1914, and in a "Lecture on Modern Poetry," which he read in 1908. As he suggests in the essay, poetry, for him, is "a visual concrete" language, which

> always endeavours to arrest you and to make you continuously see a physical thing, to prevent you gliding through an abstract process. It chooses fresh epithets and fresh metaphors [...] Visual meanings can only be transferred by the new bowl of metaphor. Images in verse are not mere decoration, but the very essence of an intuitive language. (1994 70)

The call for "fresh" and "unexpected" (70) images goes along (in the "Lecture") with the massive rejection of "the old metric system," reserved for an "older Art," which originated in "a religious incantation" (54). He emphasizes that regular metre

> is cramping, jangling, meaningless, and out of place. Into the delicate pattern of images and colour it introduces the heavy, crude pattern of rhetorical verse [...]. It is a delicate and difficult art, that of evoking an

image, or fitting the rhythm to the idea . [... There are] two methods of communication, a direct, and a conventional language. The direct language is poetry, it is direct because it deals in images. The indirect language is prose, because it uses images that have died and become figures of speech. [...]

This new verse resembles sculpture rather than music; it appeals to the eye rather than to the ear. It has to mould images, a kind of spiritual clay, into definite shapes. This material, the ὕλη [matter] of Aristotle, is image and not sound. It builds up a plastic image which it hands over to the reader, whereas the old art endeavoured to influence him physically by the hypnotic effect of rhythm. (54-56)

Conspicuously, Hulme's ideas herald the high-Imagist and Vorticist conceptions and considerations submitted by Flint, Pound, Wyndham Lewis and others. Their essence is the "shift from the thing seen to a tangible objectification of the sign; the image is re-conceived as a physical force, a 'real solid'" (Comentale and Gasiorek 12). All in all, the *image* and non-conventional rhythmic structure are the primary means of shaping the new poetry. According to Flint, Hulme also coined the word *imagism* at the meetings of the group. But it was Pound who introduced the term as the proper emblem of the poetic movement in 1912.

The correlation between Hulme's thinking and verse writing takes obvious shape in what is considered his outstanding poem:

Autumn

A touch of cold in the Autumn night –
I walked abroad,
And saw the ruddy moon lean over a hedge
Like a red-faced farmer.
I did not stop to speak, but nodded,
And round about were the wistful stars
With white faces like town children. (Jones 48)

The poem in fact presents a single "plastic image" (see above, Hulme 56) of a particular moment, made up of concrete objects, or material images appealing to the eye, discerned by the auctorial speaker, who himself becomes part of the objective scene. The two similes (lines 4 and 7) are particularly powerful, pairing markedly distinct levels of signification, thus establishing "fresh metaphors" (see above, Hulme 70). The rhythm of the end-stopped lines of irregular length oscillates between iambic, dactylic and spondaic feet. The words are marked out by distinctly different vowels, but sound patterns are created as well by assonance and alliteration. The poem might be considered a model of how language can become sculptural, visual, direct and firmly shaped.

Ezra Pound (1885-1945) attended the Eiffel Tower evenings for the first time on 22 April 1909. He had arrived in London in September 1908 and soon found his way into literary circles. In succeeding years, his reputation as a scholar and innovative poet expanded rapidly. His preference for the Provençal troubadours, Dante and the Japanese *haiku* (also *hokku*; Pound, *Selected Letters* 17) merged with his personal musings over a lyrical expression that would no longer revel in topics such as Spring, young man's fancy, love, provident nature, weather and men fighting battles or going on voyages, but that would rather be beautiful, free from didacticism, and true to the object, or thing, seen (Letter to William Carlos Williams of 21 October 1908; 1982 4-6). His ideas struck a chord with the views of Hulme, Flint and Ford Hermann Hueffer (from 1919 on known as Ford Madox Ford; 1873-1939), the editor of the literary periodical *The English Review*, whose innovative conceptions he began to translate into his own terms.

In October 1912, in a note placed in *Ripostes*, Pound explicitly referred to a new poetic school which he named "Les Imagistes" (qtd. in Jones 18), the French denotation being a typical Poundian mannerism, as well as a means of distinguishing the group from *les Symbolistes*. The Imagists, then, started as a group of three, consisting of Pound himself, Hilda Doolittle (H.D.; 1886-1961) and Richard Aldington (1892-1962). H.D., who had been engaged to Pound in America, arrived in London in October 1911. She married Aldington in 1913. Both of them acted as assistant editors of *The Egoist* during the following years. Pound began to hold readings at his rooms and to collaborate with the Chicago poet Harriet Monroe (1860-1936), who founded *Poetry: A Magazine of Verse* in 1912 in order to champion new verse. Pound did not hesitate to submit six poems written by the "Imagistes" H.D. and Aldington to the journal. In a letter to Monroe (October 1912), speaking of H.D., he emphasized that

> [t]his is the sort of American stuff that I can show here and in Paris without its being ridiculed. Objective – no slither; direct – no excessive use of adjectives, no metaphors that won't permit examination. It's straight talk, straight as Greek! (*Selected Letters* 11)

An anthology of Imagist verse, *Des Imagistes*, was edited by Pound and published in New York and London in March and April 1914. It presented 34 poems by eleven contributors, nine by Aldington, seven by H.D., six by Pound, five by Flint, and one each by Hueffer, William Carlos Williams, Skipwith Cannell, Amy Lowell, Allan Upward, John Cournos and James Joyce. At about the same time, however, Pound felt that the contours of Imagist principles were becoming indistinct. He changed the title of an article he was writing from "Imagisme" to "Vorticism," thus expressing his sympathy with this more radical movement, which was initiated by Wyndham Lewis (1882-1957), and also represented by the painter Edward Wadsworth and the sculptor Henri Gaudier-Brzezka. Its magazine *Blast: A Review of the Great English Vortex* appeared in June 1914 and published poems by Pound and manifestos by Lewis, who argued, for instance, that "Our Vortex rushes out like an angry dog at your Impressionist fuss. Our Vortex is white and abstract with its red-hot swiftness" (qtd. in Stock 202). Vorticism, emerging from Imagism, deftly and ironically articulated its hostility toward Futurism, Symbolism and Sentimentalism, albeit for a very short time. The second edition of *Blast* was published in July 1915; and that was it.

Attracted by the innovations of Imagist verse, the American poet Amy Lowell (1874-1925) headed for London in 1913 in order to meet Pound. An "Imagist Dinner" she gave in London in July 1914 was attended by all members of the movement. Lowell's purpose was to bring out a second anthology of Imagist verse with the help of Aldington and H.D. Pound was nervous about the fact that "Miss Lowell would set up a new and wider movement with lower standards" (Stock 206), and refused to participate. In a letter of 1 August 1914, he told her that

> I should like the name 'Imagisme' to retain some sort of a meaning. It stands, or I should like it to stand for hard light, clear edges. I can not trust any democratized committee to maintain that standard. Some will be splay-footed and some sentimental.

On 12 August, he added that "I should, as I have said, like to keep the term associated with a certain clarity and intensity" (*Selected Letters* 38-39). As a consequence, Pound dissociated himself from Lowell's "democratic beer-garden" (letter to Harriet Monroe, January 1915 in *Selected Letters* 48), though he continued to reassert his own Imagist principles for some time. For her part, Lowell stuck to her purpose and arranged, with the support of "a sort of informal committee" (Jones 134) and her substantial financial resources, the anthologies *Some Imagist Poets*, published in April 1915 (37 poems), May 1916 (32 poems) and April 1917 (26 poems). The poets represented were Aldington, H.D., Flint, Lowell, Fletcher and Lawrence. *Post festum*, another *Imagist Anthology*, edited by Glenn Hughes, followed in 1930. Lowell publicized Imagism in America after her return in 1915, delivering dozens of lectures. However, the 1917 edition of *Some Imagist Poems* marked in fact the end of the Imagist movement. The poets embarked on their individual literary careers.

The preface to the 1915 anthology states "certain common principles" that "united" the authors of the poems. These essentials were

> 1. To use the language of common speech, but to employ always the *exact* word, not the nearly-exact, nor the merely decorative word.
> 2. To create new rhythms – as the expression of new moods – and not to copy old rhythms [...]
> 3. To allow absolute freedom in the choice of subject. It is not good art to write badly about aeroplanes and automobiles [...]
> 4. To present an image (hence the name: "Imagist"). We are not a school of painters, but we believe that poetry should render particulars exactly and not deal in vague generalities, however magnificent and sonorous [...]
> 5. To produce poetry that is hard and clear, never blurred nor indefinite.
> 6. Finally, most of us believe that concentration is of the very essence of poetry. (Jones 135)

For his part, Pound simultaneously suggested in a letter to Monroe of January 1915 that in poetry

> [t]here must be no book words, no periphrases, no inversions [...] There must be no interjections. No words flying off to nothing [...]

> Rhythm must have a meaning. It can't be merely a careless dash off, with no grip and no real hold to the words and sense, a tumty tum tumty tum tum ta.
>
> There must be no cliches, set phrases, stereotyped journalese [...].
>
> Objectivity and again objectivity, and expression: no hindside-beforeness, no straddled adjectives [...].
>
> Language is made out of concrete things. General expressions in non-concrete terms are laziness; they are talk, not art, not creation. They are the reaction of things on the writer, not the creative act *by* the writer. (*Selected Letters* 49)

Notwithstanding their disagreement about the purity of the Imagist idea and the arrangement of the Imagist anthology, both the editors and Pound still nurtured closely related maxims. These maxims also contained the fundamental assumptions which characterized Imagist thinking from the start.

The three initial essentials of Imagism were focussing the poetic text on concrete signifiers, economy of language, and the use of non-regular rhythm. F.S. Flint specified the "few rules" in a contribution to the March 1913 issue of *Poetry*, prefacing them with a general characterization of the school:

> The *imagistes* admitted that they were contemporaries of the Post Impressionists and the Futurists; but they had nothing in common with these schools. They had not published a manifesto. They were not a revolutionary school; their only endeavor was to write in accordance with the best tradition, as they found it in the best writers of all time, –in Sappho, Catullus, Villon. They seemed to be absolutely intolerant of all poetry that was not written in such endeavor, ignorance of the best tradition forming no excuse. They had a few rules, drawn up for their own satisfaction only, and they had not published them. They were:
> 1. Direct treatment of the "thing," whether subjective or objective.
> 2. To use absolutely no word that did not contribute to the presentation.
> 3. As regarding rhythm: to compose in sequence of the musical phrase, not the sequence of a metronome.
>
> By these standards they judged all poetry; and found most of it wanting. They held also a certain "Doctrine of the Image," which they had not committed to writing; they said that it did not concern the public, and would provoke useless discussion. (Jones 129)

Flint's argument obviously summarizes what the Imagist discussion groups had been deliberating during their meetings. The attention given to Sappho, Catullus, Villon and the best writers of all time as a point of reference suggests in fact the preferences of Pound, as well as his dominant impact upon the course of debate. Flint also marks off Impressionism and Futurism as different from Imagism, since the *Imagistes* "were not a revolutionary school" (129). The three 'rules' proper are supplemented by a fourth one, somewhat ominously circumscribed as evocation of the image, the explication of which Flint postpones at this point.

Though poetry and poetical conceptions are two different things, the fact cannot be ignored that theory and practice were closely interrelated in early Modernist literature. The conscious desire for artistic innovation must needs develop into explicit reflections on what a poetic text stands for, and simultaneously into poetic texts that represent in practice what is considered new in appropriate linguistic forms. The complementary shape of poem and conception becomes transparent when Flint's 'rules' are brought face to face with one of his poems:

> The Swan
>
> Under the lily shadow
> and the gold
> and the blue and mauve
> that the whin and the lilac
> pour down on the water,
> the fishes quiver.
>
> Over the green cold leaves
> and the rippled silver
> and the tarnished copper
> of its neck and beak,
> toward the deep black water
> beneath the arches
> the swan floats slowly.
>
> Into the dark of the arch the swan floats
> and into the black depth of my sorrow
> It bears a white rose of flame. (Jones 80)

Though "black/white" is full of possibilities, not excluding classical ones, Flint's swan is *not* a classical or mythological symbol of beauty and purity, not to speak of Mary, the mother of Christ. It is, along with the quivering fishes, a *thing* in a particular natural surroundings, which is treated directly in linguistic signifiers. The sequence of words is structurally ordered: simple sentences are arranged by bracketing the first with the last lines of the stanzas. Thus, a whole is constituted of what one might call an image. This image also comprises, in the end, the subjective emotion of the author, or observer, which turns the objective phenomenon of "the deep black water" into a metaphor of emphatic subjective feelings: "the black depth of my sorrow." Ambiguously, object and subject are at one and the same time both related and not related with each other. Rhythmically, a subtle stress pattern is established, which is not identical with *verse libre* as such. Tribrachs mark the beginnings of the first lines of the three stanzas; anapaests the beginnings of lines two to four in the first two stanzas; anapaests and iambs are variably combined; spondees put emphasis on strategic words (black water, swan floats, black depth, white rose). This repetition and variation of rhythmic units indeed creates a musical effect, which gives impact to the image and affects the feelings of the reader.

In the preface to the 1916 anthology of *Some Imagist Poets*, the editors even assert that "rhythm is the most important quality in [Imagist] technique." They cautiously dissociate themselves from the French Symbolists' understanding of *vers libre*, demanding a perfect balance of flow, arguing that

> [t]he definition of *verse libre* is – a verse-form based upon cadence. Now cadence in music is one thing, cadence in poetry quite another, since we are not dealing with tone but with rhythm. It is the sense of perfect balance of flow and rhythm. Not only must the syllables so fall as to increase and continue the movement, but the whole poem must be as rounded and recurring as the circular swing of a balanced pendulum. It can be fast or slow, it may even jerk, but this perfect swing it must have, even its jerks must follow the central movement. (Jones 138)

Less cautiously, William Carlos Williams declared his breach with *vers libre*, confessing that "I do not believe in *verse libre*, this contradiction in terms. Either the motion continues or it does not continue, either there is rhythm or no rhythm. *Vers libre* is prose" (qtd. in Perloff 114). The practice of the Imagist conception of rhythm, however, could find no better explication than in Flint's poem.

In the *Poetry* issue of March 1913, Flint's 'rules' were supplemented with further exemplifications by Pound in an essay entitled "A Few Don'ts by an Imagiste." Pound added an explanation of the "certain doctrine of the image," which basically echoed what Hulme had suggested five years earlier. For Pound,

> [a]n "image" is that which presents an intellectual and emotional complex in an instant of time [...].
>
> It is the presentation of such a "complex" instantaneously which gives that sense of sudden liberation; that sense of freedom from time limits and space limits; that sense of sudden growth, which we experience in the presence of the greatest work of art.
> [...]
>
> Use no superfluous word, no adjective, which does not reveal something.
>
> Don't use such an expression as "dim land *of peace*." It dulls the image. It mixes an abstraction with the concrete. It comes from the writer's not realizing that the natural object is always the *adequate* symbol.
> [...]
>
> Use either no ornament or good ornament.
> [...]
>
> Don't be "viewy" – leave that to the writers of pretty little philosophic essays. Don't be descriptive; remember that the painter can describe a landscape much better than you can, and that he has to know a deal more about it [...]. (Jones 130-132)

The negative advice contained in the "few dont's" obscures rather then illuminates a clear-cut exposition of the literary project. But the first sentence, to which item four of the principles in the preface to the 1915 anthology might be added, helps us to understand what the somewhat mysterious term "image," and hence "imagism," denotes. *Image* is distinguished from particular instances such as metaphors, similes, particular signifiers and other formal means that constitute the poetic text in detail. It does not designate the imagery that appears at particular points in the text, as some reference works imply. The *image* is meant to present wholeness; it is epiphanic, a moment of sudden revelation; it is complex, combining the intellectual with the emotional; it has a visual quality, resembling sculpture; it has a musical quality as well, "fitting the rhythm to the idea" (Hulme); its characteristics are concentration, "objectivity and again objectivity," and concreteness – in a language "made out of concrete things" (Pound, *Selected Letters* 49). In the following year Pound added the proposition that

> [the] image is not an idea. It is a radiant node or cluster; it is what I can, and must perforce, call a VORTEX, from which, and through which, and into which ideas are constantly rushing. (qtd. in Zach 237)

The proposition is not free of a certain vagueness. It does not properly define the image but rather describes it in a metaphoric, though highly illustrative, manner. In his article "As for Imagisme," written for *The New Age* of 28 January 1915, Pound augments this vorticist "pattern-unit" by explicitly pointing to the dimension of its subjective creation, of "that emotional force [that] gives the image." He accentuates the fact that "intense emotion causes pattern to arise in the mind," suggesting that

> [n]ot only does emotion create the "pattern-unit" and the "arrangement of forms," it creates also the Image. The Image can be of two sorts. It can arise within the mind. It is then "subjective". External causes play upon the mind, perhaps; if so, they are drawn into the mind, fused, transmitted, and emerge in an Image unlike themselves. Secondly, the Image can be objective. Emotion seizing up some external scene of action carries it intact to the mind; and the vortex purges it of all save the essential or dominant or dramatic qualities, and it emerges like the external original.
> In either case the Image is more than an idea. It is a vortex or cluster of fused ideas and is endowed with energy. If it does not fulfil these specifications, it is not what I mean by an Image. (*Selected Prose* 344-345)

Maintaining "that the 'organising' or creative-inventive faculty is the thing that matters" (347), Pound in fact undermines the thesis of the direct treatment of the "thing." At the same time, however, he sustains the Imagist emphasis on form. According to his "vorticist position," personal creativity and depersonalized form constitute integral parts of a whole. He asserts that "energy, or emotion, expresses itself in form," and that "when an energy or emotion 'presents an image,' this may find adequate expression in words" (346).

A major example of how an Imagist intellectual and emotional complex in an instant of time is constituted is Pound's celebrated *haiku*

IN A STATION OF THE METRO

The apparition   of these   faces   in the crowd   :
Petals   on a wet, black   bough   . (*Selected Poems* 53)

As Pound himself clarified in his "Vorticism" article of 1914, the poem was inspired by a host of beautiful women and a child that struck his imaginative eye when alighting from a metro train in Paris. It speaks for the strength of Imagist poetry that the author was in possession of a poetical conception and a formal pattern that allowed him to sculpt a concise, hard and utterly concrete linguistic artefact out of his subjective impression. In their materialized objectivity, reinforced through the typographical layout, the two lines correspondingly strike "upon the imaginative *eye* of the reader" (Pound, qtd. in Jones 133) in a powerful way.

Kenner suggests that the poem is "a simile with 'like' suppressed" (185). But obviously the poem does not present a figure of speech which explicitly compares two seemingly disparate things, which would be recognizable by the use of 'like' or 'as.' The omission of the conjunction, beyond its rhythmical effect, modifies the explicitness of the comparison. As a result, the two units, whilst still interconnected, face each other. Two moments of linguistic intensity join together. An "imaginative fusion" (Pratt and Richardson 82) is generated which juxtaposes a present visual impression with an absent imagined picture, without superimposing one reference on top of the other. Both sentences stay close to the concrete. A parallel construction is created, affirmed by the conspicuous correspondences of part and whole, "face–crowd," "petals–bough," in lines one and two. On the representative plane, a fundamental contradiction between the modern city and the phenomena of nature is highlighted. To this extent, the poem might be read as an "image" which denotes the immanent Imagist tension between an explicitly urban, innovative, literary movement and its poetic emphasis on the concrete objectivity of natural things.

In a letter to Harriet Monroe of 30 March 1913, Pound notes that "in the 'Metro' hokku, I was careful, I think, to indicate spaces between the rhythmic units, and I want them observed" (*Selected Letters* 17). Emphasizing the special typographical arrangement (which is unfortunately ignored in anthologies and later editions of Pound's poetry), the poet draws the reader's particular attention to the fact that the "spatial unity" created by the text "is identical with the aural suggestion produced by a musical score" (Rabaté 66). Undeniably, what the preface to the anthology *Some Imagist Poets 1916* calls "the sense of perfect balance of flow and rhythm" (Jones 138) takes supreme shape in "Metro." Pound superimposes a different rhythmic structure over the basic rhythms of six iambs in the first and four trochees in the second line. The iambs are resolved in three fourth paeons; the trochees in a first paeon and a dispondee:

Thĕ ăppărītĭon   ŏf thĕse   fācĕs   ĭn thĕ crōwd   :
Pētăls   ŏn ă wēt, blāck   bōw   .

The twelve feet of the first line are marked by only three stresses, whereas the seven feet of the second line have four stresses. The prosodic differences additionally underline the disparate nature of the 'simile.' The dance-like vivacity changes *rallentando* into a strong final accent. It is not the beat of the metronome that gives the *image* its rhythmical structure but rather the sequence of a musical phrase, or "the rhythm wave" ("A Few Dont's," Jones 133). But basically, metronomic regularity and free cadence still overlap. As in music, the notes on Pound's 'sheet of music' allow, and even demand, interpretation and performance.

In other words, the Imagist *image*, in both its musicality and its poetic direct treatment of an object, is of necessity reader-oriented. Hulme was conscious of the problem of appropriation, referring to "the new art of the Reader: Sympathy with the reader as brother, as unexpected Author" (*Further Speculations* 93). It is the reader himself who must experience and decode the aesthetic and cognitive possibilities contained in the linguistic artefact. As Hamilton has it, "by merely priming source domains in the minds of their readers, Imagists could count on readers to complete the task and carry out the meaning-making procedures of mapping, inference, and interpretation" (473). Take, for example, H.D.'s much-cited poem pertaining to a Greek mythological mountain nymph:

Oread
(S.I.P. 1915)

Whirl up, sea –
Whirl your pointed pines,
Splash your great pines
On our rocks,
Hurl your green over us,
Cover us with your pools of fir. (Jones 62)

Like Pound's "Metro," the poem is exceptional as regards its exciting musical rhythm. All the lines, varying in length between three and eight feet, are marked by three stresses; the basic trochaic metre changes into spondees (lines 2, 3, 5), dispondees (lines 1, 4) and a first paeon (line 6). The musical character is intensified by an impressive complexity of sound figuration, which employs anaphora, initial rhyme (whirl/hurl), identical rhyme (whirl; pines), alliteration (pointed pines), assonance (sea/green), pararhyme (over/cover, hurl/fir) and repetition (your). But under the surface of the form, marked by the compactness of sound patterns, lurks the problem of interpretation. It can only be solved by the reader who has to find the key to this presentation of an intellectual and emotional complex in an instant of time. Does the desire of the mountain nymph, who seems to be a non-authorial speaker (but is she?), imply destruction, or renewal? Or is there no message at all, just the mere evocation of an image, i.e. an aesthetic artefact as such? A vortex through and from which ideas are rushing?

Wacior neatly summarizes that the Imagists "capture the unique nature of a singular experience in an objective, precise, condensed and fresh way" (41). However, the relationship between the subject of the perceiver and the object of perception needs further commentary. To strive towards objectivity means to put the stress on semiotic construction, which 'performs' the linguistic notation of particular pre-linguistic objects and at the same time creates independent, self-representational objectivity through language. The signified is assumed to be a pre-linguistic *thing*, which, however, experienced by the author of the poem, is converted into "a tangible objectification of the sign" (Comentale and Gasiorek 12). In philosophical terms, the Imagist conception might be compared to phenomenological theory. Husserl, for instance, noted that "phenomenological experience as reflection must avoid interpretive constructions. Its descriptions must reflect accurately the concrete contents of experience, precisely as these are experienced" (13). It is exactly this avoidance of interpretive poetic constructions that the Imagists desired. The semiotic interrelationship between the word and the thing was meant to deconstruct the moralistic and metaphysical contents of poetic texts. In Pound's "The Encounter," the authorial I experiences an objectively given constellation which by means of the creative act of the writer changes into a surprising tangential simile:

> The Encounter
>
> All the while they were talking the new morality
> Her eyes explored me.
> And when I arose to go
> Her fingers were like the tissue
> Of a Japanese paper napkin. (*Selected Poems* 53)

The image created by the text indicates that the author is not at all concerned with the discussion of morality, but rather with a peculiar personal experience which in turn is objectified in the form of a purely linguistic correlative. The Imagist poem no longer serves as the transcendent means of representing subjective feelings, ethics, ideology and philosophy. The poetic ordering of lyrical reflection is replaced by the order of semiotic construction. On this premise, it is not the poem that transmits experiences and ideas; as suggested above, it is the reader who experiences the poetical image. Poetry is not meant to inspire sympathy, benign emotions and moral thinking but rather to arouse the reader's aesthetic pleasure, remote from all ulterior aims.

To strive towards objectivity, or the complex image, produces its immanent negativity. A fundamental thesis of Imagism is that the image stands for itself, presenting an intellectual and emotional complex; it does not represent, or symbolize, anything else. Focussed on 'thingness,' the image provides an antitype to the Romantic idea that poetry is the most philosophical form of writing:

> its object is truth, not individual and local, but general, and operative; not standing upon external testimony, but carried alive into the heart by passion [... P]oetry is the spontaneous overflow of powerful feelings; it

takes its origin from emotion recollected in tranquillity. (Wordsworth 35-39)

In a tacit way, however, the Imagist desire to merge the object and the sign is in fact intentional, perhaps even more intensely than the Wordsworthian spontaneous 'philosophy' was meant to be. The Imagist poet speaks to himself, as lyrical poets generally do, but his subjective voice speaking in a poem is suppressed, in contrast to the distinct voice of the Romantic poet. It was only Pound who knew by 1915 that the poet's energy and emotion "create" the self-referential work of art, based on procedures in the nervous system and the mind, and it was Pound who discerned the two types of the Image, that which arises within the mind and that which refers to an external phenomenon reflected in the mind. But in general the true Imagist desire was to create an *image* in precise poetic form. The emphasis on the object of presentation suppresses the significance of the human subject *as* the purpose and performer of representation. In this way, the Imagist programme is one of narrowing; it refuses to accept the entire tradition of lyrical poetry since the Renaissance. On the other hand, it is also broadening; it is oriented towards the reader who is summoned to "work" with, and make personal, social and even political sense of, the emotional and intellectual complexity of the poetic text.

Bibliography

Carr, Helen. *The Verse Revolutionaries: Ezra Pound, H.D. and the Imagists.* London: Jonathan Cape, 2009.
Coffman, Stanley K. *Imagism: A Chapter for the History of Modern Poetry.* Norman, OK: University of Oklahoma Press, 1951.
Comentale, Edward P., and Andrzej Gasiorek, eds. *T.E. Hulme and the Question of Modernism.* London and Surrey: Ashgate, 2006.
Fletcher, John Gould. *Life is My Song.* New York: Farrar and Rinehart, 1937.
Flint, F. S. "History of Imagism." *The Egoist.* 1 May 1915.
Hamilton, Craig A. "Toward a Cognitive Rhetoric of Imagism." *Style* 38.4 (2004): 468-490.
Hough, Graham. *Image and Experience: Studies in a Literary Revolution.* Westport, CT: Greenwood Press, 1978.
Hughes, Glenn. *Imagism and the Imagists.* Stanford: Stanford UP, 1931.

Hulme, T. E. *Further Speculations*. Ed. Sam Hynes. Minneapolis: University of Minnesota Press, 1955.

---. *The Paris Lectures*. Trans. Peter Koestenbaum. The Hague: Martinus Nijhoff, 1964.

---. *The Collected Writings of T. E. Hulme*. Ed. Karen Csengari. Oxford: Clarendon Press, 1994.

Jones, Peter, ed. *Imagist Poetry*. Harmondsworth: Penguin, 1985 [1972].

Kenner, Hugh. *The Pound Era*. Berkeley, CA: University of California Press, 1971.

Korg, Jacob."Imagism." *A Companion to Twentieth-Century Poetry*. Ed. Neil Roberts. Oxford: Blackwell, 2001. 127-137.

Lowell, Amy. *Tendencies in Modern American Poetry*. New York: Macmillan, 1917.

Martin, Wallace. "'The Forgotten School of 1909' and the Origins of Imagism." *A Catalogue of the Imagist Poets*. Ed. J. Howard Woolmer. New York: J. Howard Woolmer, 1966. 7-38.

Nicholls, Peter. *Modernisms: A Literary Guide*. London: Macmillan, 1995.

Perkins, David. *A History of Modern Poetry: From the 1890s to the High Modernist Mode*. Cambridge, MA: The Belknap Press of Harvard University Press, 1976.

Perloff, Marjorie. *The Dance of the Intellect: Studies in the Poetry of the Pound Tradition*. Cambridge, MA: Cambridge UP, 1985.

Pound, Ezra. "Vorticism." *Fortnightly Review* 46.1 (September 1914): 465-467.

---. *Selected Poems 1908-1959*. London: Faber & Faber, 1981 [1975].

---. *Selected Prose 1909-1965*. Ed. William Cookson. London: Faber & Faber, 1978.

---. *The Selected Letters of Ezra Pound, 1907-1941*. Ed. D.D. Paige. London: Faber & Faber, 1982 [1950].

Pratt, William, and Robert Richardson, eds. *Homage to Imagism*. New York: AMS, 1992.

---. *Ezra Pound and the Making of Modernism*, New York: AMS, 2007.

Rabaté, Jean-Michel. *1913: The Cradle of Modernism*. Malden, MA: Blackwell, 2007.

Ross, Robert H. *The Georgian Revolt 1910–1922: Rise and Fall of a Poetic Ideal*. Carbondale, IL: Southern Illinois UP, 1965.

Spender, Stephen. *The Struggle of the Modern*. London: H. Hamilton, 1965.

Stock, Noel. *The Life of Ezra Pound*. Harmondsworth: Penguin, 1985 [1970].

Wacior, Slawomir. *Explaining Imagism: The Imagist Movement in Poetry and Art*. Lewiston, NY: Edwin Mellen, 2007.

Williams, Raymond. *The Politics of Modernism: Against the New Conformists*. Ed. Tony Pinkney. London: Verso, 1989.

Woolmer, J. Howard, ed. *A Catalogue of the Imagist Poets*. With Essays by Wallace Martin & Ian Fletcher. New York: AMS, 1966.

Wordsworth, William. "Preface to 'Lyrical Ballads.'" *Englische literaturtheoretische Essays 2: 19. und 20. Jahrhundert.* Ed. Rüdiger Ahrens. Heidelberg: Quelle und Meyer, 1975. 26-44.

Zach, Natan. "Imagism and Vorticism." *Modernism.* Ed. Malcolm Bradbury and James McFarlane. Harmondsworth: Penguin, 1976. 228-242.

Brian M. Reed (Seattle)

Confessional Poetry: Staging the Self

Confessional poetry is one of the most common yet confusing terms within the study of post-World War II American verse. Its origins can be traced back to a famous review of Robert Lowell's collection *Life Studies* (1959) by the literary critic M. L. Rosenthal. He complained that "[t]he use of poetry for the most naked kind of confession grows apace in our day." Although, he conceded, Lowell's previous publications had demonstrated his familiarity with T.S. Eliot and Ezra Pound – authors whose "indirection masks [their] actual face and psyche from greedy eyes" – now even he has fallen prey to the *Zeitgeist*. Perversely, he "removes the mask. His speaker is unequivocally himself, and it is hard not to think of *Life Studies* as a series of personal confidences, rather shameful, that one is honor-bound not to reveal" (154).

Over the last half century, Rosenthal's label "confessional" has become convenient short-hand for a cohort of post-World War II American poets, including Lowell, John Berryman, Sylvia Plath, Anne Sexton, and W.D. Snodgrass. This group of writers is typically seen as less a school or a movement than a cohort of talented individuals whose poetry, especially from the late 1950s and the 1960s, shares important formal and thematic traits. They are known for writing a "highly personal poetry" that exhibits little "aesthetic distance separating the poetic 'I' from the author." Rightly or wrongly, one expects their verse to contain a parade of "minutely accurate or only slightly distorted autobiographical details," regularly featuring "direct treatment of shameful and taboo subjects – mental illnesses, violence, divorce, masturbation, operations, alcoholism, [and] incest" (Horváth 9).

The confessional poets occupy a curious place in the history of twentieth-century American poetry. While their verse might not fit perfectly the definitions of postmodernism offered by theorists such as David Harvey, Fredric Jameson, and François Lyotard, it nonetheless clearly positions itself as coming after, and even superseding, literary modernism. More specifically, in their best-known and most representative lyrics the confessional poets tend to reject the impersonal elevated style characteristic of Anglo-American modernism. "In contrast to the obscurity and erudition of High Modernist poetry," Rita Horváth explains, "Confessional poems seek immediate apprehension [...]. The syntax of Confessional poems is rarely convoluted; their patterns of allusion are not excessively cryptic; the poems tend to be less condensed and more repetitive than High Modernist poems" (13).

The confessional poets are also understood as introducing a mode of composition that has had widespread impact on subsequent generations of American writers. Literary critics in fact frequently use the word *confessional* somewhat loosely to refer to any contemporary verse that stylistically or thematically recalls such volumes as Lowell's *Life Studies*, Berryman's *Dream Songs* (1969), Plath's *Ariel* (1965), Sexton's *Live or Die* (1966), and W.D. Snodgrass's *Heart's Needle* (1959). In this expanded sense, *confessional* often possesses negative connotations that echo Rosenthal's review. That is, the term can imply the desire to make self-indulgent, lurid revelations instead of attending to matters of craft. Marjorie Perloff's *Differentials* (2004), for example, takes great pains to show that poets can write well about autobiographical subjects without making talk-show-like histrionic "confessions" to prove their "authenticity" (133).

Why should one teach confessional poetry if it is held in such low esteem nowadays? First, poets such as Berryman, Lowell, Plath, and Sexton are among the few post-World War II American poets with a high level of name recognition both inside and outside of the academy. Plath in particular has become part of the American pop cultural imagination. Promoted by feminist scholars and the women's movement more generally in the later 1960s and '70s, today she is a celebrity. She has shown up in everything from Hollywood biopics such as *Sylvia* (2003) – where she was played by Gwyneth Paltrow – to science fiction television programs such as *Warehouse 13*. (In the 2009 episode "Breakdown" her typewriter proves to be a dangerous magical relic with the power to deprive people of their will to live.) Students, in my experience, are eager to study confessionalism. They have heard of it, they find it exciting, and it informs their preconceived notions of what constitutes poetry and the poetic vocation.

Preconceptions can also be prejudices, of course; hence the second reason to study confessional poetry. One of its legacies is to reinforce the commonplace notion that poetry is a *cri de coeur*, a bold expression of deeply-held beliefs and emotions. Unless they are unusually well read, when arriving in my classroom students have a propensity to ignore the distinction between a poem's speaker and its author. They want to read the "I" on the page as voicing an author's personal experiences rawly and immediately. They dislike poems that disavow sincerity, elude intelligibility, or otherwise eschew a stereotypically 'confessional' scenario in which authors are imagined to give audiences special access to the ebb and flow of powerful emotions.

Most literary critics, of course, deem this author-focused mode of reading and the texts that reward it to be naïve and narrow. Yes, many poems seek to stir strong passions. Not all do. Some emphasize wit, sound play, philosophical argument, etc. Moreover, rare indeed is the poet whose confessions are one-hundred-percent unedited and spontaneous. Writers make an array of choices as they compose, and many of these go into the creation and maintenance of personae (Latin, significantly, for *masks*) through which to speak. Much poetry by the confessionals purports to be from-the-heart, but on closer inspection this quality almost always turns out to be an effect produced through self-conscious artistry. This aperçus relates to a third, more theoretical reason to study confessional poetry. The confessional poets writing in the 1950s and 60s did not in fact advocate a poetics of sincere self-expression (unlike many of their imitators and epigones, who badly misread them on this point). They began writing autobiographical verse in full awareness that their poetic personae were artificial, or better yet, *theatrical* creations. Far from subscribing to the popular belief that poems provide unmediated access to a writer's heart and soul, they delighted in what Judith Butler has called the *performativity* of the self. The "I" in Berryman, Lowell, Plath, Sexton, and Snodgrass is through-and-through a fiction – but so too, they implicitly acknowledge, is identity itself. All poems, autobiographical or not, are performances. They might vary in order, kind, and result, but one cannot differentiate cleanly between sincere and insincere utterance, or artful and artless self-expression. These are not easy lessons, but they are a necessary prelude to advanced literary study. If students can let go of the real/fake binary when reading verse, they are ready to grapple with more difficult fare by such postmodern poets as John Ashbery, Lyn Hejinian, and K. Silem Mohammad, all of whom experiment aggressively with the relationship between author, text, reader, and world.

How could one ever reach such an endpoint in an actual classroom? A teacher can only do so patiently and inductively. Lowell's "Waking in the Blue" (1959) is a good starting point, partly because of the subject matter. It describes an extended stay in a psychiatric institution in 1957-1958 by a poet who "suffered all his life from manic depression, and was hospitalized almost annually for decades" (Kirsch 28). Moreover, Lowell was teaching at the time at Harvard University, and there are many vivid stories about his public breakdowns: "Lowell showing up at William Alfred's house and declaring that he was the Virgin Mary; Lowell talking for two hours straight in class, revising a student's poem in the style of Milton, Tennyson, or Frost; Lowell wandering around Harvard Square without a coat in the middle of January, shivering, wild-eyed, incoherent" (Atlas 328). "Waking in the Blue" allows a teacher to tackle head-on popular but mistaken assumptions about confessionalism.

On first reading or listening to the poem, students are frequently mystified because so much remains un- or understated. Lowell relies on his audience having a thorough familiarity with the history of the Boston area, especially the small details that indicate differences in class. For example, McLean Hospital, the lyric's setting, was founded in the early nineteenth century, and it has served a long line of wealthy and famous patients, including the novelist David Foster Wallace. This storied institution serves as a backdrop for a drama of social division. On the one hand there are the patients. On the other are the attendants who care for them.

The poem opens with a vignette about one of the latter, a "night attendant" who is "a B.U. sophomore," that is, a second-year undergraduate at Boston University. Having earlier fallen asleep reading a philosophy textbook titled *The Meaning of Meaning* (1923), he now wakes up and "catwalks down our corridor." In these lines, the speaker lets readers know that the "night attendant" is working to put himself through college; that he is having trouble balancing the demands of work and study (hence his falling asleep); and that he attends a respectable university but not an Ivy League one. These facts prepare one for a passage later in the poem that describes the attendants more generally: they have "crew cuts," are Roman Catholic, and do their work cheerfully (they "twinkle"). Crew cuts here signify healthy robust masculinity: in the 1950s they would have been associated with the military and with team sports such as rowing and football. "Roman Catholic" would have implied "from an immigrant background," perhaps Irish, Italian, or Polish. The attendants are "bachelors" because jobs in a mental hospital, while okay as a way to make money while single, are not for respectable married men, let alone ones with children. These young men, in short, are squarely part of the American mainstream, untroubled by the conformity and labor that bourgeois normality demands.

In contrast, the patients at McLean's belong to a higher social stratum. Lowell calls them "thoroughbred," as if they were expensive Arabian race horses. He also links them to the *Mayflower* that brought the Pilgrims to the New World in 1620. They are, one infers, part of the Protestant elite that had dominated the region for more than three hundred years. And two of them, it seems, attended Harvard University, which had been educating that elite since 1636. The first, "Stanley," was an "all-American fullback," a celebrated football player in the distant era when Harvard dominated American athletics as well as academics. The second man, "Bobbie," is "Porcellian '29," in other words, a Harvard graduate from thirty years previous who belonged to the Porcellian Club, an exclusive undergraduate secret society. Although technically there is no such thing as a hereditary aristocracy in the United States, these men come close. Accordingly, Lowell talks about Stanley's "kingly [...] profile" and compares Bobbie to Louis XVI. This last comparison is barbed, of course, since Louis XVI was beheaded in 1792. But these quasi-aristocrats do exemplify a kind of decadence or endgame. They "ossified young," that is, exhibit arrested development, acting decades younger than they ought. They are "mental cases" and "screwballs." The class raised to lead is now kept confined under surveillance. They are so powerless that even their razors are "locked" so that they cannot commit suicide. They no longer even have the power to decide to live or die.

The class division between attendants and patients is starkly binaristic, even exaggeratedly so. Were all the workers at McLean's in 1957-1958 truly youthful unmarried coreligionists with identical haircuts? Was everyone receiving treatment in fact an eccentric aging Harvard alum? The speaker fancifully presents with Manichaean clarity what was surely a real but messier opposition. Why? It makes the poem more *dramatic*. After one clarifies the poem's social subtext, different aspects of "Waking in the Blue" begin to draw one's attention, especially the pronounced artifice that Lowell employs throughout the poem. His language is controlled, ironic, and self-consciously literary:

> Azure day
> makes my agonized blue window bleaker.
> Crows maunder on the petrified fairway.
> Absence! My heart grows tense
> as though a harpoon were sparring for the kill.
> (This is the house for the "mentally ill.") (81)

The length of the lines varies from three to eleven syllables, and the number of stressed syllables per line ranges from two to five. This variability would seem to suggest free verse, but if one scans the lyric, the meter turns out to be predominately iambic. There is prominent rhyme, too – "day" / "fairway" and "kill" / "ill" – but it is awkwardly interspersed with end words that do not rhyme ("bleaker," "tense"). Finally, there is intense local sound play, including assonance ("azure," "agonized," "absence"); consonance ("bleaker," "maunder," "hearts," "harpoon," "sparring"); and internal rhyme ("crows," "grows"). Lowell makes use of the resources of traditional poetic form, but he is also deliberately off-kilter, oscillating between overly obvious sound patterning and its equally conspicuous absence. There are other oddities, too, such as the sarcastic echo of the cliché "absence makes the heart grow fonder" and the misapplication of the adjective "agonized" to a "window" (only living beings – like the poem's speaker – can endure "agony"). The verse in "Waking in the Blue" resembles Joan Sutherland singing the mad scene in Donizetti's *Lucia di Lammermoor* (1835): a master of conventional technique simulates insanity by showcasing and exaggerating her talents in the midst of a ragged, inconsistent, improvised delivery.

This operatic analogy might be a tad strained, but it is useful nonetheless. Arias can be powerfully stirring, yet no one would deny that they are also through-and-through artificial. Opera plots are nonsensical, emotions are often excessive given the situation, and nobody naturally breaks into coloratura. If one thinks of a confessional poem as akin to an aria, it can suggest rewarding paths for inquiry. Instead of the truth or falsity of what is said, a reader focuses on the *performance* itself. How is it staged? Who are the characters? What does the piece reveal about the soloist? Approached from this standpoint, "Waking in the Blue" is striking because of the amount of space it devotes to other people. Why not reveal more about the speaker's past, symptoms, and sufferings? Why not talk about blame or revenge? The word "I" appears only three times in the poem, and this "I" does not do very much: "I grin," have breakfast, "weigh two hundred pounds," and "strut." If this is a mad scene like Lucia's, are readers supposed to feel sympathy – or what precisely?

Like many of Lowell's ostensibly autobiographical lyrics, "Waking in the Blue" engages in *metonymic portraiture*, the indirect characterization of a speaker via a detailed presentation of the people, places, and things that surround him. Although the speaker might spend most of the lyric talking about Stanley and Bobbie, he is in a roundabout way introducing himself to the reader, too, by way of the company that he keeps. Like them, he is a "screwball," an ersatz aristocrat, and someone who "ossified young." In the above passage, the poem mentions a "harpoon"; later Stanley will be called a "seal," Bobbie compared to a "spermwhale," and then finally "I" reveals that he wears a "sailor's jersey." All of these men are on the same sea voyage, so to speak, and "I" fit right in, indeed, am "cock of the walk" (an American idiom originally referring to the toughest of the flat boatmen and keel boatmen working on a river). The poem ends with a moment of clarity: "We are all old-timers." The speaker now *explicitly* groups himself with the ludicrous decrepit patients at McLean's. He could have distanced himself – claimed to be a brilliant poet or otherwise special and superior – but instead he recognizes that he, too, is privileged but ridiculous. "I," and the class to which "I" belong, is an anachronism. The others, the solicitous attendants with crew-cuts, are likely "our" successors and heirs.

If "Waking in the Blue" is a confessional poem, what exactly does it confess? As Adam Kirsch puts it, the poet with "candor [...] reveals himself at one of his most frightening and shameful moments" (29). Such a confession, though, is hardly shocking or newsworthy in the age of Oprah Winfrey and Lindsey Lohan. Now that psychiatric treatment has lost much of its stigma, one can return to "Waking in the Blue" and see that it does not say anything especially lurid about its speaker, or by extension Lowell himself. The speaker does not traipse about naked, engage in abject behaviors, or endure humiliation *à la* Olivia de Havilland in *The Snake Pit* (1948). In addition, one neither learns – nor needs to learn – much about Lowell's own life. It might deepen a reader's appreciation, for example, to know that one of his ancestors served as president of Harvard, but the poem neither offers that fact nor requires it to be effective.

Half a century later, two things stand out about "Waking in the Blue." First is its achieved artistry. Lowell revisits the genre of the *aubade*, the awakening-at-dawn poem, but instead of love, the speaker is disturbed by mania, a less celebrated variety of madness. The lyric features lines of different lengths with an irregular rhyme scheme, a tried-and-true means of miming an overwhelmed ecstatic state that dates back to Pindar. Its metonymic portraiture is systematic, and it climaxes elegantly in a cards-on-the-table moment ("We're all old-timers"), which insures that readers will go back and interpret Stanley and Bobby as the speaker's alter egos. The whole poem, in other words, is written so carefully and rationally that, whether the *speaker* comes across as ill, the *poet* seems to have full command of his faculties. The poem might have an autobiographical basis, but Lowell has thoroughly reworked that material to create the equivalent of a dramatic monologue for a character named 'Robert Lowell.'

The second aspect of "Waking in the Blue" that stands out is its insistence on connecting private tragedy to public issues. Confessional poets have a longstanding reputation for ignoring Cold War politics and creating a literature of personal complaint. "Waking in the Blue," though, expresses a deep uneasiness about dramatic changes underway in the United States in the 1950s. The unprecedented expansion of higher education in the country after World War II coincided with the explosive growth of large corporations and an accompanying increase in jobs in middle management. In 1957 Edward Young coined the word *meritocracy* to describe the shifting distribution of authority underway in the period. Scores on tests and evaluations were increasingly replacing family ties and inherited wealth as the qualifications for high-paying, high-status positions. This business-world revolution had literary parallels. Institutions such as Harvard were opening their doors to talented individuals from utterly undistinguished families (for example, Lowell's future rivals John Ashbery, Robert Creeley, and Frank O'Hara). Lowell might trace his family name back to the *Mayflower*, and he might be related to the canonical poets James Russell Lowell and Amy Lowell, but there was no guarantee that his inherited advantages would translate into long term literary success. Looking at the attendants at McLean's, Lowell could have been thinking about Jack Kerouac, whose *On the Road* was published in 1957. A descendent of working-class Catholic Quebecois immigrants, Kerouac grew up in the mill town of Lowell, Massachusetts – named after the poet's ancestor Francis Cabot Lowell (1775-1817). "Waking in the Blue" takes a *donnée* – time spent in a mental hospital – and uses it to comment on a period of transition in American society and culture.

Once students become comfortable with "Waking in the Blue," they are ready to move on to other confessional poems such as Lowell's "Skunk Hour" (1959), Sexton's "Wanting to Die" (1966) and Snodgrass's "April Inventory" (1959). A lyric such as Plath's "Cut" is a particularly good choice. The event that serves as its *donnée* took place in October 1962 in a kitchen while the poet was preparing food. The setting, like Lowell's, is removed from public view, but this time it is an everyday domestic space as well as "that space of the home most identified with the feminine" (Hammer 154). Similarly, instead of a breakdown leading to a hospital stay – a break from routine – the proximate cause of Plath's poem is a wholly mundane accident:

> What a thrill –
> My thumb instead of an onion.
> The top quite gone
> Except for a sort of hinge
>
> Of skin,
> A flap like a hat,
> Dead white.
> Then that red plush. (*Collected* 235)

What makes this moment extraordinary is the speaker's tone. One would normally expect a person to respond to such an ordeal with fear, anger, or numbness, not excitement ("what a thrill"). Stranger still is the reaction to seeing her own blood. The word *plush* refers to textiles with a cut nap or pile that feels like velvet; such cloth is often used in upholstery or in dresses. It connotes luxury and sensuality. It is as if by nearly slicing off the "top" of her thumb the speaker suddenly becomes alive and aware and aroused, "red plush" replacing "dead white." While not perhaps mentally ill in a clinical sense, there does seem to be something wrong or odd about a speaker who so delights in accidental self-mutilation. (She later will say "I am ill.")

Just as in "Waking in the Blue," the poem's form reinforces the impression that this is like an operatic mad scene. Plath's lines might be shorter than Lowell's, but they vary in length from one stress to three, and although the meter remains iambic throughout, there are numerous substitutions, both anapestic ("of a sort," "like a hat") and spondaic ("dead white"). The opening two lines add further metrical complications. The first line is catalectic, that is, missing an opening unstressed syllable ("WHAT a THRILL"), and the second line has a feminine ending (the *-ion* in "onion"), a hypermetrical unstressed syllable. These variations, before the poem's meter has been firmly established, render it unclear for several lines whether Plath is writing free verse in an Imagist vein or, like Lowell, engaging in the exaggerations and syncopations within regular meter that conventionally convey intense passion. She also pushes further in inventive ways the irregular rhyme scheme of "Waking in the Blue." Strictly speaking, the first eight lines contain no end rhymes, but that does not prevent them from sounding like they make excessive use of the device. Four lines in a row have slant rhymes ("onion," "gone," "hinge," "skin"), and she makes free use of internal rhyme ("instead," "dead," "red"; "quite," "white"). There are also insistent chains of assonance, both schwas ("thumb," "of," "onion," "of," "plush") and garish short *a*'s ("hat," "flat," "that"). The intensity and frequency of the sound play approaches the level of nursery rhymes or incantations. If the romantic ode is still distantly audible as precedent for the prosody of "Waking in the Blue," Plath presses traditional form so far it teeters on the boundary between doggerel and irrational word-magic.

Characteristically, Plath goes further than Lowell, too, in her imbrication of the private and the public. "Waking in the Blue" allegorizes a single moment in American history. "Cut" tackles a more ambitious topic. It suggests that victims of violence almost compulsively seek the meaning behind and the reasons for the trauma that they have endured. Even as blood wells from the sliced thumb, so too does a cascade of metaphors spill from the poem's speaker. First, she evokes the early settlement of New England by comparing her injured digit to a "pilgrim" whose "scalp" is "axed" by an "Indian." Next comes the Revolutionary War. She renames the blood cells pouring from her thumb a "million soldiers [...] Redcoats every one." Last is World War II: the thumb is a "Kamikaze man." While early biologists were wrong about the principle *ontogeny recapitulates phylogeny* – the idea that as organisms grow they repeat previous stages of evolutionary development – Plath's poem implicitly proposes a cultural analogue. Any time one maims flesh the act extends the long history of hurting others, from the primordial past to the present. Bloodletting is only intelligible as something that *has happened before*. Those previous incidents provide the words, reference points, and topoi that make something as disruptive and painful as a wound both thinkable and communicable.

Plath's speaker goes on to offer further disturbing propositions. When she places a bandage on the thumb – which she has just labeled a "Homunculus," a "little human" – its pristine white "[d]arkens and tarnishes" from the blood, and she calls it a "Gauze Ku Klux Klan / Babushka." While still unblemished, the gauze makes her think of the distinctive white hood of the notorious racist cross-burning organization the Ku Klux Klan. Then, after the bandage becomes bloody, it reminds her of the red head scarf stereotypically worn by a *babushka*, a Russian grandmother. To appreciate this latter image, one has to recall when the poem was written. The poet cut her finger during the same month that the Cuban Missile Crisis dominated the news and the USA and the USSR almost went to war. Given this Cold War context, the speaker's use of a Russian word would have been disconcerting, especially when applied to her own body. Her injured thumb suddenly becomes strangely foreign, as if part of another woman altogether, an alien from the other side of the Iron Curtain. The poem suggests that, after there has been a "cut," everything, even its alleviation, is interpretable in relation to violence and its history. Notice that the "cut" here *precedes* the beginning of the poem. It is a kind of secular Fall, an act that inaugurates a spreading "stain" that, like the blood soaking through the gauze, taints whatever it touches. Blood and death become pervasive, geographically as well as historically. Such a vision can be paralyzing, insofar as it levels distinctions between different kinds of trauma and lumps all victims and perpetrators into fixed, opposed categories. Nonetheless, it also asserts ties between private incidents and public events. Personal tragedies come to occupy the same stage as world-historical ones.

Plath's catalogue of metaphors culminates at the poem's end, when she juxtaposes two images of bleeding flesh. First is a "[d]irty girl," a young woman who is menstruating ("The balled / Pulp of your heart / Confronts its small / Mill"). Second is a "[t]repanned veteran," a soldier who has had a hole drilled or scraped into his skull. Why introduce a natural nonviolent process such as menstruation into a poem full of images of warfare? Plath shows that even the menstrual cycle is implicated in the long history of (interpreting) spectacles of bleeding bodies. The speaker *herself* associates the shedding of the uterine lining with images of hurt and harm. Intentionally or not, she restates patriarchal assumptions about the female body as an inferior, 'wounded,' or 'castrated' variant on the proudly phallic 'whole' male body. In effect, "Cut" shows that in mid-twentieth century American society a woman's body is never fully hers to command. It is inevitably caught up in narratives, discourses, and histories that freight it with externally imposed meanings.

Significantly, in presenting this message, Plath is complicit in the very dynamic that she opposes. That is, she focuses her audience's gaze on a woman's body, nominally her own, and she demonstrates for those onlookers how one might interpret the flesh on display. The speaker's tone, careening from ecstasy ("thrill," "fizz," "celebration") to self-disgust, reflects, first, her heady discovery that the female body is not outside language, somehow *unspeakable*. She relishes putting herself into the spotlight because it initiates an outpouring of tropes and free association. By becoming poet-like, she comes close to taking control of her own self, and her destiny. That breakthrough, though, also leads to the discomfiting discovery that, while she can take charge of how she performs in front of an audience, the language given to her, and the stage on which she soliloquizes (and the body she ventriloquizes), are not of her choosing. The freedom she experiences is at first intoxicating. But it also proves largely illusory. In terms of the larger cycle of *Ariel* poems, she reaffirms that, whatever her considerable erudition and verbal talents, she remains a mother and housewife, coerced into a role she never asked for or wanted.

Once students better understand confessional poetry from the 1950s and 60s they are prepared to read later verse that also receives that label. It becomes possible to look at a poem such as Sharon Olds's "The Bra" (2008), for example, and say why, however often she is called 'confessional,' she only superficially deserves to be grouped with a writer like Plath:

> It happened, with me, on the left side, first,
> I would look down and the soft skin of the
> nipple had become like a blister, as if it had been
> lifted by slow puffs of breath
> from underneath. It took weeks, months,
> a year. And those white harnesses,
> like contagion masks for conjoined twins
> – if you saw a strap showing, on someone
> you knew well enough, you could whisper, in her ear,
> It's Snowing Up North. (37)

Olds invites a prurient eye to witness her speaker's passage through puberty. Thematically, one could relate it to "The Cut" and other Plath poems in which she draws attention to the female body. Olds, though, writes in slack free verse which sometimes breaks its lines phrasally and other times features brutal enjambment ("the / nipple," "had been / lifted"). The above passage could be rewritten in prose without doing it much violence. Metaphors, too, accumulate haphazardly. The speaker's breasts are injured flesh ("blister"); slowly inflating balloons ("lifted by slow puffs of breath"); and then the faces of "conjoined twins." The bra is a "harness," "contagion masks," and snow. Collectively, these tropes suggest the uncanniness of a changing body, the way in the throes of puberty a person seems invaded by, controlled by, external forces over which she has no control. But the selection is arbitrary; one could add more or take a few away without ruining or undermining the impact. In comparison to Plath's brilliant consistent use of historical imagery, Olds seems to have engaged in a brainstorming exercise and produced an artless jumble. One could argue that the poem thereby becomes less like an off-putting soliloquy and more like an actual person talking – except that "like contagion masks for conjoined twins," for instance, is too strange and strained a simile for ordinary conversation. Just as she uses the cusp between childish innocence and adult experience to provoke an eroticized gaze, so too Olds seems to encourage admiration for her ability to generate unusual tropes higgledy-piggledy. Her artistry, though, is rudimentary by Plath's standards, her exhibitionism insufficiently ironized, and she evinces no awareness that she is rewarding, not criticizing, the objectification of a woman's body. "The Bra" is a sample of what critics have in mind when they speak dismissively of contemporary confessionalism.

It would be a mistake, however, to assume that confessionalism as a vein within American literature is entirely tapped out. There are poets such as Laura Kasischke who have studied mid-twentieth century verse attentively and who self-consciously and skillfully build on its accomplishments. "Miss Congeniality" (2007) is a monologue from the point of view of a gifted young woman who has chosen to conform to gender expectations as a route to success:

> Like flowers, my friends. Nodding, nodding. My
> enemies like space, drifting
> away. They
>
> praised my face, my enunciation, the power
> I freely relinquished (6)

This passage opens with a surreal moment of distorted perception reminiscent of Plath's "Tulips" (1965) before the "I" admits that she has "freely" traded true power, self-determination, for conventional beauty, praiseworthy feminine behavior, and the simulacrum of power that popularity among her peers provides. Kasischke might not employ regular meter, but she is as close a student of Plath's form as her content. The poem's variable line lengths, irregular stanza breaks, and rampant enjambment suggest a distraught speaker, even as a concentrated use of assonance and consonance weave Plath-like sinews of sound between the words (the long a's in "space," "away," "they," "praised," "face," "enunciation" and the r's in "flowers," "friends," "drifting," "praised," "power," "freely," "relinquished"). The poem as a whole compares the effort for a woman to succeed on American society's terms to a kind of zombie beauty pageant in which she continues play-acting long after she might as well be dead. In addition, the speaker comments that she gave a "speech [...] about peace, in praise of the war" (7). Published during the second George W. Bush administration, "Miss Congeniality" suggests that normative femininity, and the popular culture that supports it, is complicit in the United States' wars in Iraq and Afghanistan. After all, it is most uncongenial to take a public stand against a president during a time of conflict. How much better, if put on the spot, to repeat patriotic platitudes about bringing peace to the rest of the world.

A number of Kasischke's poems are explicitly based on her life. They express the confusion of a member of Generation X, raised on grunge, rap, and postfeminism, who grows up to become a suburban soccer mom. In contrast, "Miss Congeniality" is only indirectly autobiographical. Nevertheless, it is a worthy present-day representative of the confessional tradition, as practiced by Lowell and Plath. Like them, Kasischke writes theatrically and vividly, aware that characters (and people) fashion themselves performatively through their speech and behavior. Moreover, again like them, she teaches that supposedly private traits – one's appearance, hygiene, and health – are bound up in larger networks of power, pressure, and pleasure. Kasischke is not unique in these respects. One could also cite poems by such prominent contemporary American poets as Henri Cole, Terrance Hayes, Timothy Liu, and D.A. Powell. At its best, confessional poetry of all eras elucidates the intertwining of the individual and the social while also demonstrating an impressive level of craft and polish. Identity is an artificial construct. By accentuating their artistry confessional poets drive that point home.

Bibliography

Atlas, James. "Robert Lowell in Cambridge: Lord Weary." *Robert Lowell: Interviews and Memoirs*. Ed. Jeffrey Meyers. Ann Arbor: University of Michigan, 1988. 318-334.
Hammer, Langdon. "Plath at War." *Eye Rhymes: Sylvia Plath's Art of the Visual*. Eds. Kathleen Connors and Sally Balley. New York: Oxford University Press, 2007. 145-157.
Horváth, Rita. *Never Asking Why Build – Only Asking Which Tools: Confessional Poetry and the Construction of the Self*. Budapest: Akadémiai Kiadó, 2005.

Kasischke, Laura. *Lilies Without*. Saint Paul, MN: Ausuble, 2007.
Kirsch, Adam. *The Wounded Surgeon: Confession and Transformation in Six American Poets*. New York: Norton, 2005.
Lowell, Robert. *Life Studies*. New York: Farrar, 1959.
Olds, Sharon. *One Secret Thing*. New York: Knopf, 2008.
Perloff, Marjorie. *Differentials: Poetry Poetics Pedagogy*. Tuscaloosa, AL: University of Alabama Press, 2004.
Plath, Sylvia. *Collected Poems*. New York: Harper, 1981.
Rosenthal, M. L. "Poetry as Confession." *The Nation* 189 (19 Sept. 1959): 154-155.

Heinz Ickstadt (Berlin)

Frank O'Hara and the "New York School": Poetry and Painting in the 1950s

1.

In times of artistic upheaval, when conventions are questioned, traditions re-examined, and literary or artistic institutions perceived as bastions of the Old, the forces of rebellion tend to cooperate and interact. Boundaries are crossed: those of established forms and between genres, but also those between the different artistic media. The agents of the New, then, also become the ferment of a small yet growing audience of the New, ignored or critically rejected by a general public still dominated in its aesthetic preferences by the various institutions of Literature and Art (by criticism, academia, publishing, or the museum).

This was true of the modernist rebellion in the 1910s and 1920s in Europe as well as in the United States. William Carlos Williams's cooperation with the painter Charles Demuth and his exchanges with the artists of the Alfred Stieglitz circle in New York would be one example, Gertrude Stein's fascination with the Cubists in Paris and her creative dialogue with Picasso another.

Dialogue between the arts also characterizes a second wave of avant-garde experimentation during the early fifties. By then, modernism itself had become an institution via the critical opinions of T.S. Eliot (the period's literary "Pope") and the aesthetics of the New Criticism, which had become academic doctrine. A new generation of artistic rebels thus found itself in a situation comparable to that of its modernist forebears: "When we all arrived in New York or emerged as poets in the mid 50s or late 50s," Frank O'Hara remembers, "painters were the only ones who were interested in any kind of experimental poetry and the general literary scene was not. Oh, we were published in certain magazines and so on, but nobody was really very enthusiastic except the painters" (Allen 3).

This may have been characteristic especially of the New York scene with its tightly interwoven network of clubs, cafés, galleries, performance venues and intense party life where essentially the same crowd met, talked, discussed and regrouped itself endlessly. Yet the united attack on the center by artists and poets from the margins occurred in other places as well. In San Francisco, poets like Lawrence Ferlinghetti, Michael McClure and Gary Snyder initiated the San Francisco Poetry Renaissance and were in close contact with the New York Beats who wandered between the East and West coasts. At Black Mountain, a private alternative college in the mountains of North Carolina, the poet Charles Olson established an interdisciplinary curriculum in which poets, painters, dancers and composers participated who would later become famous. (Among them were the poet Robert Creeley, who edited the *Black Mountain Review,* and the painters Franz Kline and Robert Rauschenberg. Dancers, like Merce Cunningham, and composers, like John Cage, joined the staff periodically.)

These groups, although in contact with each other and united in their rejection of established concepts and practices of Art, were nevertheless quite different in the stylistic modes of their rebellion. The academization of poetry and poets during the forties and throughout the fifties had transformed modernism into a new classicism (or what was also called "High Modernism" to distinguish it from an earlier, more radical phase). It emphasized objectivity of form over subjective ("romantic") self-expression and made rhetorical figures like paradox, irony, ambiguity or metaphor the very basis of good poetry. The doctrine was explained and made eminently teachable through a series of precise formal analyses in the New Criticism's handbook of interpretation, Cleanth Brooks and Robert Penn Warren's *Understanding Poetry* (1938). Eliot's poems and essays provided the model and conceptual basis for a generation of academic modernists (poets like Allen Tate, John Crowe Ransom and Robert Penn Warren) whose most accomplished representative was Robert Lowell, at the time thought by many to have the linguistic subtlety and intellectual stature to succeed Eliot.

Resistance against this new formalism took predictable paths: it rediscovered everything that had been banned by the self-restrictive conservatism of Eliot and his followers – most importantly the emotionally engaged and performative subjective voice, as cultivated in the self-projecting rhetoric of the Beat poets. It also meant a turning away from the concept of a traditional form in rhyme or meter (even from the subtle rhythmic variations of Eliot's "blank verse") and to individual breath as the basic principle that determined the length of the line. (Charles Olson expounded this concept of organic form based on breath in his seminal essay "Projective Verse.") This went hand in hand with a rejection of the "Metaphysical Poets" (John Donne and Andrew Marvell, the great religious poets of the early seventeenth century, whose linguistic density Eliot set up as poetic model for modern poetry) and with the rediscovery of Walt Whitman, whose rhetoric and 'formlessness' the New Critics had despised. The latter also had little appreciation for what they considered the empty iconoclasm of Dada and the French Surrealists. Precisely these iconoclastic ruptures with tradition, however, were embraced by both the poets and the painters of the New York scene in their attack on "depth" and "meaning" and their creation of dissonant and broken-up surfaces. As a result of this sudden inversion of established hierarchies, a poet finally came into his own who had long been neglected by academic critics because his conception and practice of poetry had been so consciously directed against everything that T.S. Eliot stood for: William Carlos Williams. Williams, who had once declared that "the whole house [of poetry] had to come down" before it could be rebuilt (*Selected Essays*, 163) and whose poems emphasized the simplicity of "speech" and the dignity of everyday objects, now became the father figure of a new generation of poets whose existence was effectively propagated by Donald Allen's path-breaking anthology, *The New American Poetry 1945-1960* (which came out in 1960).

How great the distance between the representatives of an established modernism and the young rebels on the margins had become may be illustrated by two episodes, one concerning Allen Ginsberg, the other Frank O'Hara. In a gesture meant to introduce the young into the circles of the intellectual establishment, Ginsberg and some of his friends were invited to Columbia University, from which Ginsberg – formerly a student of the eminent critic Lionel Trilling – had been expelled a few months earlier. (The previous speaker in this series of lectures and readings had been T. S. Eliot himself.) The report of the event by Trilling's wife Diana (in *The Partisan Review* of 1959) wavers between acknowledging the fear of cultivated intellectuals like herself *vis-à-vis* the irrationality of the new cultural barbarians, the disgust she felt for their tasteless self-staging, and her amazement that Ginsberg was nevertheless able to move her. (Pictures of the event, as well as of the "Beat Scene" in general, show how modestly – at least in terms of attire – these rebels staged their protest. The cultural shock of the counter-culture of the late sixties that was to shake American universities to their foundations was still to come.)

The second episode occurred three years later, when Robert Lowell and Frank O'Hara were both invited to give a reading of their poems at Wagner College on Staten Island. O'Hara started off with the remark that the poem he was about to read had just been written on the Staten Island Ferry. To which Lowell, for whom such irreverence toward the work of art was inconceivable, replied that he never wrote his poems on either ferryboats or subways, thus sternly underlining the modernist credo of craftsmanship and professional seriousness (Perloff 13). The poem O'Hara read on this occasion was simply called "Poem" (one of many with that title):

> Lana Turner has collapsed!
> I was trotting along and suddenly
> it started raining and snowing
> and you said it was hailing
> but hailing hits you on the head
> hard so it was really snowing and
> raining and I was in such a hurry
> to meet you but the traffic
> was acting exactly like the sky
> and suddenly I see a headline
> LANA TURNER HAS COLLAPSED!
> there is no snow in Hollywood
> there is no rain in California
> I have been to lots of parties
> and acted perfectly disgraceful
> but I never actually collapsed
> oh Lana Turner we love you get up
> (*CP* 449)

The poem unmistakably shows O'Hara's signature: its conversational casualness, its self-deprecating irony, its penchant for the absurd, its courting of the light and superficial, its charming and life-affirming acceptance of the moment and the everyday, its declaration of love toward a "you" that includes a nameless lover as well as Lana Turner and the collective "you" of the audience – all these are easily recognizable aspects of his style. Its playfulness is as far removed from Olson's ponderous myth-conscious poetry as it is from Ginsberg's prophetic and declamatory style. And yet, although "Poem" is characteristic of O'Hara's tone, it is only one of his modes in a wide spectrum of stylistic versatility which drew on many different sources:

> His best poems fuse what he called the "charming artifice" of Apollinaire (and of a host of other French poets from Rimbaud to the Surrealists) with the bardic voice of Mayakovsky, the colloquial speech of Williams or the late Auden, the documentary precision of Pound's *Cantos*, and the Rilkean notion of being "needed by things." (Perloff xxxiii)

But his poems also draw on paintings by his various New York painter friends, among them Larry Rivers, Jasper Johns, Philip Guston, Jane Freilicher, or Grace Hartigan. In what follows I shall trace this creative interaction between the arts in several of O'Hara's poems, placing them in the context of the New York art scene and analyzing the exchange they document in form and subject matter.

2.

Even though he called himself and his group "non-Academic and indeed non-literary poets" (*CP* 512), O'Hara was a highly style-conscious and educated writer who knew, like few other contemporary American poets did, the poetry and art works of European modernism. He had, like John Ashbery and Kenneth Koch (as well as, several decades earlier, T.S. Eliot), studied at Harvard before he came to New York in 1951, at the age of 25. However, he was "non-literary" inasmuch as his poems attempt, in their often skillful artlessness, to undermine a modernist aesthetic that insisted on the finished product.

As assistant curator at New York's Museum of Modern Art and organizer of several exhibitions of contemporary painting, O'Hara had expert knowledge of the American (especially of the New York) art scene. He witnessed the arrival of Abstract Expressionism in the early fifties (and its different manifestations in the works of Jackson Pollock, Franz Kline, Willem de Kooning, or Barnett Newman). He also experienced the rise of Pop Art in the mid-fifties and after, and was aware of the different paths it took in the works of Andy Warhol, Robert Rauschenberg, and Claes Oldenburg. He knew them all personally and wrote about them in his art reviews (collected in *Art Chronicles*) and in the catalogs to the exhibitions he organized.

In this second modernist rebellion against established forms and concepts of art, the painters (not the poets) were the path-breakers, for the simple reason that none of the artists prominent in the 1930s and 1940s (Ben Shahn, Grant Wood, Thomas Hart Benton) had the status of a T.S. Eliot or the theoretical underpinning that Eliot received from the New Critics. The then dominant mode of realistic representation (modified by stylistic echoes of the modernist innovations of a decade earlier) had exhausted itself by the end of WWII. Therefore the rise of the Abstract Expressionists was not only greeted with relief but acclaimed as proof that the U.S., as the leading modernizing nation, had also surpassed Europe culturally and become the new homeland of modernism in the arts. It gave Jackson Pollock (who had been a disciple of the regionalist painter Thomas Hart Benton) and Philip Guston (who had painted murals for Roosevelt's Federal Arts Project during the 1930s) an opportunity to re-invent themselves as path-breaking American modernists. So fast, in fact, had the Abstract Expressionists moved from the margins to the center that within a decade they provoked a counter-movement directed against abstraction and back toward representation – away from what was criticized as "modernist elitism" to a more Pop(ular) Art dedicated to ordinary objects, or signs of objects – the semiotic material of urban culture.

For O'Hara, the conflicts between these different schools were largely irrelevant. What counted for him was the quality of the individual imagination – no matter how it expressed itself. He saw originality in Andy Warhol and Claes Oldenburg as much as in Jackson Pollock and Willem de Kooning. Recalling the stylistic range of O'Hara's favorite texts (the material and referential concreteness of William Carlos Williams's and Ezra Pound's poetry, the dissonant brilliance of surrealism's linguistic surfaces), these painters defined a wide spectrum of expressive possibilities, between intense visual perception (particular moments in a continuous flow of sensuous experience, or the pure joy in the materiality of things) and sudden imaginative leaps into the dreamlike, subconscious and fantastic. They mark the poles of abstraction and concreteness between which O'Hara's own style fluctuates. From this spectrum, O'Hara took what he needed in response to a certain situation, or to a certain mood – be it depression or, as in the following example, joyous affirmation which he expressed in exuberant, sometimes extravagant, word-play.

HAVING A COKE WITH YOU

is even more fun than going to San Sebastian, Irún, Hendaye, Biaritz, Bayonne
or being sick to my stomach on the Traversa de Gracia in Barcelona
partly because in your orange shirt you look like a better happier St. Sebastian
partly because of my love for you, partly because of your love for yoghurt
partly because of the fluorescent orange tulips around the birches
partly because of the secrecy our smiles take on before people and statuary
it is hard to believe when I'm with you that there can be anything as still
as solemn as unpleasantly definitive as statuary when right in front of it
in the warm New York 4 o'clock light we are drifting back and forth
between each other like a tree breathing through its spectacles

and the portrait show seems to have no faces in it at all, just paint
you suddenly wonder why in the world anyone ever did them
                                                                       I look
at you and I would rather look at you than all the portraits in the world
except possibly the *Polish Rider* occasionally and anyway it's in the Frick
which thank heavens you haven't gone to yet so we can go together the first time
and the fact that you move so beautifully more or less takes care of Futurism
just as at home I never think of the *Nude Descending a Staircase* or
at a rehearsal a single drawing of Leonardo or Michelangelo that used to wow me
and what good does all the research of the Impressionists do them
when they never got the right person to stand near the tree when the sun sank
or for that matter Marino Marini when he didn't pick the rider as carefully
as the horse
               it seems they were all cheated of some marvellous experience
which is not going to go wasted on me which is why I am telling you about it
(CP 360-361)

This love poem, addressed to an anonymous "you" (who, we know, was O'Hara's lover, the dancer Vincent Warren), combines casual coolness with emotional intensity – just as its trivial title comes to stand for an ecstatic acceptance of life ("fun") through the experience of love. The poem is full of allusions to visits to New

York museums (in the past or the near future) as well as to specific works of art (to Marino Marini's equestrian sculptures and to the "Polish Rider," once thought to be the work of Rembrandt). And yet it values life above art and treasures the concretely experienced moment (at 4 o'clock on a New York afternoon) more than remembered or imagined episodes in exotic Spain. The poem is literally centered in "I look" – line 13 in a poem of 25 lines – which is a "marvellous experience" because it is a looking "at you" whose "orange shirt" is echoed in the "fluorescent orange tulips" – just as the organic flow of energy, transmitted in the act of loving looking, is set against "statuary" art works. The poet counters these works' "stationary" solemnity with the intense experience of the moment whose energizing fluidity and lightness is caught and embodied in his poem.

The moment's exuberant playfulness is apparent in the speaker's associative drifting between places (Spain and New York), between outside and inside (park and museum), between natural and artistic objects – the beauty of art in each case surpassed by the grace and actual presence of the "you" in motion – a "you" who looks "happier and better" than, let's say, the suffering St. Sebastian in Mantegna's painting and moves more elegantly than Duchamp's famous "Nude Descending a Staircase." The poem's breathless flow is neither interrupted nor brought to a close by punctuation. There is no final period, nor does a period mark the break between the two sentences of which the poem is composed (the first beginning with the title, the second with "I look"). The only element of syntactic structure that meets the reader's eye – the anaphora "partly" at the beginning of lines 3-7 – seems to be offering a logic for love when in fact it lists non-sequiturs: a logic of emotion beyond reason which culminates in the playfully absurd image of "a tree breathing through its spectacles."

It is the perfection and aliveness of the lived moment (in comparison to which all art works suffer from the fact that they are *only* art and not Life) that is eventually revealed as the poem's *raison d'être*, since the very flow of the experience it celebrates also implies its own evanescence. So that "telling you about it" – to "you," the lover, as well as to "you," the reader – is the only way of making the ecstatically felt Now permanent despite its fluidity and transience.

The desire to bring art as close to life as possible, and to make the energy of life present in his own art, marks all of O'Hara's poetry and accounts for the life-sustaining function art had for him. Like William Carlos Williams, who as a practicing physician wrote many of his poems during office hours between patients, O'Hara wrote prolifically, regardless of place and occasion, apparently caring more about the process than the product of his creativity, his casual production having its equivalent in the careless treatment of his drafts. After his premature and grotesquely accidental death at forty in 1966 (he was run over by a jeep on Fire Island), his editor literally found hundreds of poems jotted down on all kinds of paper and thrown into the drawers of his desk. Just as in Williams's case, this raised questions about his seriousness as an artist and the merits of his art. But as one of his friends wrote about him, "I didn't realize right away – the critics, for a long time, didn't either – that if you took poetry so much for granted as you did breathing, it might mean you felt it was essential to your life" (Berkson and LeSueur, 43). For O'Hara, writing poetry was an everyday activity, as necessary as eating or having sex, and the poems he wrote were, in that sense, "non-art" everyday objects in a world of everyday phenomena, despite their linguistic extraordinariness. They were artistically conscious attempts at creating, against modernism's insistence on the finished product, an open, a processual form – an unfinished aesthetic object that was not only "in" the world but also taking part in it, thus revealing the fundamental continuity between art and life.

It was this concept – in addition to a shared feeling of place and cultural moment – that connected O'Hara with the world in which he moved. By the late fifties, his charismatic personality, his "radiant magnetism" (Ashbery, in Berkson and LeSueur, 21) and the "explosive effect" it had on people (Koch, in Berkson and LeSueur, 26) had made him the center of that world – attracting fellow poets like John Ashbery, Kenneth Koch, LeRoi Jones (later Amiri Baraka), James Schuyler and Barbara Guest, as well as his other artistic friends: the painters, dancers and composers. It was an erotically charged and predominantly gay scene providing occasion for passionate relationships along with constant intellectual stimulation. O'Hara's unceasing curiosity eagerly responded to the metropolitan excitement of New York as well as to the dynamically shifting art scene of the period, in which experimentalism in the arts seemed fundamentally connected with a willingness to also experiment with ways of living: "living every moment," according to Marjorie Perloff, "as if it were his last" (117).

Gertrude Stein's work – especially her portraits – has been frequently understood as applying the structural principles of Cubism to the literary text. However, such comparisons across the boundaries of artistic media may offer analogies at best, since each medium is distinctly different in its inherent possibilities as well as its limits of expression. It would therefore be problematic to call some of O'Hara's surrealist poems "abstract expressionist," or some of the *Lunch Poems* literary versions of Pop Art. On the other hand, it is clear that the mutual awareness of what the painters and poets were doing, the "extraordinary rapport" (Perloff 76) between them, left its mark on poems as well as paintings of the New York circle. Evidence of such extensive dialogue between the arts are several projects of collaboration O'Hara undertook with Larry Rivers and Jasper Johns (among others). Although these works are not particularly memorable, they underline the appropriateness of Marjorie Perloff's calling O'Hara "a poet among painters," which I take to mean not only that he lived and moved among painters but that he also was a "painterly poet" who yet kept the difference between both artistic media very much in mind – as he explored and explained, tongue-in-cheek, in his witty poem

Why I am Not a Painter

I am not a painter, I am a poet.
Why? I think I would rather be
a painter, but I am not. Well,

for instance, Mike Goldberg
is starting a painting. I drop in.
"Sit down and have a drink" he
says. I drink; we drink. I look
up. "You have SARDINES in it."
"Yes, it needed something there."
"Oh." I go and the days go by
and I drop in again. The painting
is going on, and I go, and the days
go by: I drop in. The painting is
finished. "Where's SARDINES?"
All that's left is just
Letters, "It was too much," Mike says.

> But me? One day I am thinking of
> a color: orange. I write a line
> about orange. Pretty soon it is a
> whole page of words, not lines.
> Then another page. There should be
> so much more, not of orange, of
> words, of how terrible orange is
> and life. Days go by. It is even in
> prose, I am a real poet. My poem
> is finished and I haven't mentioned
> orange yet. It's twelve poems, I call
> it ORANGES. And one day in a gallery
> I see Mike's painting called SARDINES.
> (*CP* 261-262)

In contrast to the poem discussed previously, the tone of this one is again in O'Hara's casual, cool, and self-ironic mode. There is much coming and going, little talk and some drinking, while time goes by and the works of both painter and poet progress – seemingly in different directions. And yet, in explaining why he is not a painter, O'Hara demonstrates more than anything else the affinity between the poet's and the painter's practice. In this poem, the painter (one of his close friends, Michael Goldberg) turns the visually concrete object, sardines, into something literary: letters; and the poet, "I," who has a painter's idea of color in mind when he starts writing (orange, a color his friends Grace Hartigan and Willem de Kooning, but also O'Hara himself, treasured as a color of vitality), loses the idea in the flow of words released or generated by it. Both poet and painter evidently prefer process to subject matter and emphasize surface over meaning. In the end, what was originally meant to be represented is lost, or, rather, abstracted, in the process of composition, a last trace of reference remaining only in the titles: "Sardines," which is indeed a painting by Michael Goldberg, and "Oranges," which is indeed the title of a series of poems ("Oranges: 12 Pastorals") by Frank O'Hara, which made Grace Hartigan paint twelve paintings called "Oranges" exhibited together with O'Hara's poems of that title in 1953.

Although Hartigan was by no means the only painter of the New York circle who responded to O'Hara's poetry, the reverse was more frequent. Thus, O'Hara composed poems about two specific paintings by Jackson Pollock and Larry Rivers. While Rivers's painting, especially, confirms O'Hara's skepticism of labels – Rivers being by no means a clear-cut "Abstract Expressionist" – it seems useful to recall the definition of Harold Rosenberg, a critic who was eminently responsible for the movement's success and impact.

> At a certain moment the canvas began to appear to one painter after another as an arena in which to act – rather than as a space in which to reproduce, re-design, analyze, or 'express' an object, actual or imagined. What was to go on the canvas was not a picture but an event. [...] The painter no longer approached his easel with an image in his mind; he went up to it with material in his hand to do something to that other piece of material in front of him. The image would be the result of this encounter. (qtd. in Baigell, 3)

This famous characterization of the painting process as "action painting" echoes Pollock's statement of not being *opposite* a canvas but "*in* [the] painting":

> When I am *in* painting, I am not aware of what I am doing. It is only after a sort of 'get acquainted' period that I see what I have been about. I have no fears about making changes, destroying the image, etc. because the painting has a life of its own. I try to let it come through. It is only when I lose contact with the painting that the result is a mess. Otherwise there is pure harmony, an easy give and take, and the painting comes out well. (*Art Chronicles*, 39)

Pollock's *Number 1, 1948* is evidently conceived as a field of forces, or, as O'Hara says, it projects space as a "field of incident": although there seems to be some center, it appears to have exploded, its fragments hurled toward a periphery where lines form whirls of energy that catch the eye and pass it on from one whirl to another. And yet the lines are potentially moving in all directions, are in any case not contained by any spatial limit or frame but "continue out into all four areas of space surrounding its boundaries" (*Art Chronicles,* 14 and 32). O'Hara's poem "on" Pollock's painting reads:

> Digression On Number 1, 1948
>
> I am ill today but I am not
> too ill. I am not ill at all.
> It is a perfect day, warm
> for winter, cold for fall.

> A fine day for seeing. I see
> ceramics, during lunch hour, by
> Miró, and I see the sea by Léger;
> Light, complicated Metzingers
> and a rude awakening by Brauner,
> a little table by Picasso, pink.
>
> I am tired today but I am not
> too tired. I am not tired at all.
> There is the Pollock, white, harm
> will not fall, his perfect hand
>
> and the many short voyages. They'll
> never fence the silver range.
> Stars are out and there is sea
> enough beneath the glistening earth
> to bear me toward the future
> which is not so dark. I see.
> (*CP* 260)

In his essay on Pollock, O'Hara describes *Number 1, 1948* as having "ecstatic, irritable, demanding force, incredible speed and nervous legibility in its draftsmanship" (*Art Chronicles*, 31). In his poem on the painting, however, he seems to deal with hardly any of this. As a matter of fact, its lightness of touch, its balancing of seemingly contradictory statements which posit the ill and tired body against the heightened awareness of the mind's eye, appear to counteract and offset Pollock's emphasis on force and energy. It thus seems to respond rather to what Pollock called the "pure harmony, the easy give and take" of the act of painting. On the one hand, the poem stresses the processual aspects of the picture, its adventurous, boundary-crossing push beyond the frame of space and time toward a boundless field of revelation/liberation, but, on the other, it emphasizes balance, harmony and perfection: "harm will not fall" since we (the readers/viewers) are led by the master's "perfect hand." This finds an echo in the poem's balanced regularity: four lines in the first and third stanza, six lines in the second and fourth, the rhyme of the first stanza completed in the only other, the final rhyme: "sea" and "see." O'Hara's poem should thus be understood not (or not only) as a translation from the visual into the verbal medium but as representing the painting in its emotional impact on the viewer: its healing, balance-restoring, liberating and life-giving energy enables the speaker to see beyond the limits of his precarious physical state. It thus re-enforces his initial effort at self-persuasion that things are better than they are ("I am not ill at all;" "I am not tired at all"). "Seeing," then ("A fine day for seeing. I see" and again, at the end, in emphatic repetition: "I see"), does not only connote the perception of an object (i.e. the painting), nor even the process of perceiving it, but rather sight as achieved insight or enlightenment: a way of seeing as a way of being, which makes it possible for the speaker to accept and reaffirm life.

The second poem of O'Hara's I shall discuss in this context is on Larry Rivers's "Washington Crossing the Delaware." Like the one on Pollock's painting it stands in a curiously inverse relationship to its object of reference. Rivers's picture is, of course, a parody of the nineteenth-century historical painting by Emanuel Leutze (decorating a wall of the American Congress in Washington), which had become part of the national iconography. "What could be dopier," Rivers comments in an interview with O'Hara, "than a painting dedicated to a national cliché [...] What I saw in the crossing was quite different. I saw the moment as nerve-wrecking and uncomfortable. I couldn't picture anyone getting into a chilly river around Christmas time with anything resembling hand-on-chest heroics" (*Art Chronicles*, 112). Leutze's picture clearly tries to tell national history by condensing heroic legend in the general's determined gaze toward the other shore. Washington is the leader and representative of a people who literally (and metaphorically) sit with him in the same boat. Rivers's painting, in contrast, conveys an air of the roughly sketched and the unfinished – a deliberate gesture of profanation. He also de-dramatizes and parodies the privileged and historically sacred moment by taking the temporal element out of the picture, replacing the Now of directed will and determination in Washington's body language with spatial dispersion: the people's collective purpose gathered in the gesture of their leader toward the other shore is dissolved and groups of people are loosely placed around the slightly de-centered (and somewhat damaged) figure of Washington. (His right boot seems to have been replaced by what appears to be a plaster cast, his head looks bandaged, etc.) The outlines of all figures and objects are blurred, except for the General's face which, in Leutze's picture, is seen in profile, while Rivers lets him stare at the spectator open-eyed and open-mouthed.

This is how O'Hara responds to the painting:

> ON SEEING LARRY RIVERS'
> WASHINGTON CROSSING THE DELAWARE
> AT THE MUSEUM OF MODERN ART
>
> Now that our hero has come back to us
> in his white pants and we know his nose
> trembling like a flag under fire,
> we see the calm cold river is supporting
> our forces, the beautiful history.
>
> To be more revolutionary than a nun
> is our desire, to be secular and intimate
> as, when sighting a redcoat, you smile
> and pull the trigger. Anxieties
> and animosities, flaming and feeding
>
> on theoretical considerations and
> the jealous spiritualities of the abstract,
> the robot? they're smoke, billows above
> the physical event. They have burned up.
> See how free we are! As a nation of persons.
>
> Dear father of our country, so alive
> you must have lied incessantly to be
> immediate, here are your bones crossed
> on my breast like a rusty flintlock,
> a pirate's flag, bravely specific
>
> and ever so light in the misty glare
> of a crossing by water in winter to a shore
> other than that the bridge reaches for.
> Don't shoot until, the white of freedom glinting
> on your gun barrel, you see the general fear.
> (*CP* 233)

O'Hara's version continues the parodistic intention of Rivers's painting ("his nose / trembling like a flag under fire," "to be more revolutionary than a nun is our desire"), yet he reintroduces the temporal and dramatic by starting with an emphatic "Now." And yet, although O'Hara makes lighthearted fun of the national icon, "the beautiful history," from beginning to end, there is also an unmistakable gesture of loving appropriation. Although one critic maintains that "O'Hara's Washington is cold, afraid, an incessant liar and a killer" (Breslin in Stich, 213), it seems to me that O'Hara transforms the father of the nation rather into a representative figure of a different kind: as a lover of the immediate, he is alive in his awareness of the possibility of death. For the reality of the "physical event" reduces all revolutionary rhetoric to mere "smoke." Through Rivers's eyes and beyond them, O'Hara recognizes beneath the heroic Washington of the legend a risk-conscious existential spirit who belies the pious stories of popular mythology (that he was unable to tell a lie, for instance). His venture towards "a shore / other than the bridge reaches for" is thus the object not only of the general's but also of (our) general fear.

If O'Hara was, according to Perloff, a "Poet among Painters," he was also a "City Poet," the title Brad Gooch gave to his voluminous biography (published in 1993). In a sense, all poems and paintings of O'Hara's New York circle could be called "city art" since they, directly or indirectly, respond to the energy and excitement of New York's metropolitan ambience. Yet some of his *Lunch Poems* (1964), especially, enact a process of perception centered in the casual and roaming eye of the flâneur, recording, apparently at random, whatever image it collects while strolling along Broadway. "Now when I walk around at lunchtime" ("Personal Poem"). There is, in these poems, no attempt to reflect on or to connect these random perceptions. The attention of the speaker appears to be directed to everything which comes to the eye (or, often self-ironically, to the mind's eye) with equal intensity: "if / I ever get to be a construction worker / I'd like to have a silver hat please / and get to Moriarty's where I wait for / LeRoi and hear [...]" ("Personal Poem"). The movement of the eye duplicates the movement of the street – the speaker's eye is that of the leisurely walker in the city who moves along with the movement that surrounds him. Motion, fluidity, change and chance are structural principles. "How I hate subject matter," O'Hara writes elsewhere, "and all things that don't change;" and again: "The surface and the meaning – the one is the other" (*CP* 275 and 497). There is a measure of affirmation and well-being which puts advertisements, billposters, purchasable goods, the glistening torsos of laborers, names of restaurants, the memory of friends (together with their names) and the poems of Pierre Reverdy on the same level of appreciation.

This blurring of urban space and art space is also of importance to Claes Oldenburg, another of O'Hara's favorites. Oldenburg's environment, "The Street," consisted of the discarded objects visitors had found in the street and brought into his studio. In a similar fashion Robert Rauschenberg chose the objects for his assemblages from the material he had collected within a certain amount of time and within a certain segment of city space (a neighborhood block, for instance). In addition, it is important to remember, as Lawrence Alloway reminds us in his various books on Pop Art, that this is essentially an art of and about urban signs and sign systems: it absorbs city material as well as material already processed through the media, discovering creative possibilities in the aesthetic reproduction of material we recognize from contexts of daily sight or use. By thus making familiar objects suddenly unfamiliar, Pop Art certainly opens a new space for aesthetic contemplation. Yet it also signals an essential affirmation of contemporary culture as the very basis and condition of its own creativity.

In one of his best known lunch poems, "A Step Away from Them," O'Hara seems to follow the aesthetic strategies of Rauschenberg's "flâneur who becomes bricoleur" (Conrad 303), his idly strolling observer-speaker collecting not objects, however, but visual impressions, isolated moments of perception, casually registered by the roaming eye. Many of O'Hara's poems may remind one of William Carlos Williams's random glimpses and revelations (I am thinking, for instance, of Williams's "The Right of Way," *Collected Earlier Poems* 258), but in contrast to Williams they seem to be mere assemblages of random moments: they are neither revelations, nor do they move toward a revelatory climax. At one point, "everything suddenly honks" – but why? It just happens. The poem appears to have no logical frame of argument or sequence except that it begins with the beginning of the lunch hour and ends with its end. There is no attempt made to interpret perception, to create meaning, nor any attempt to differentiate between the important and the irrelevant – everything that comes to eye or mind exists on the same level of significance. We are not told who Bunny is [the poet Violet Lang, a long-time friend from Harvard], nor John Latouche [a well-known New York librettist]; O'Hara indiscriminately merges private with public knowledge. One should also notice that, to fend off sentimentality (which he loathed), the potentially loaded memories of their deaths (like Pollock they died in 1956) are immediately trivialized: "But is the /

earth as full as life was full, of them?" The poem creates surface just as the speaker's eye glides along surfaces.

A Step Away from Them

It's my lunch hour, so I go
for a walk among the hum-colored
cabs. First, down the sidewalk
where laborers feed their dirty
glistening torsos sandwiches
and Coca-Cola, with yellow helmets
on. They protect them from falling
bricks, I guess. Then onto the
avenue where skirts are flipping
above heels and blow up over
grates. The sun is hot, but the
cabs stir up air. I look
at bargains in wristwatches. There
are cats playing in sawdust.
       On
to Times Square, where the sign
blows smoke over my head, and higher
the waterfall pours lightly. A
Negro stands in a doorway with a
toothpick, languorously agitating.
A blond chorus girl clicks: he
smiles and rubs his chin. Everything
suddenly honks: it is 12:40 of
a Thursday.
    Neon in daylight is a
great pleasure, as Edwin Denby would
write, as are light bulbs in daylight.
I stop for a cheeseburger at JULIET'S
CORNER. Giulietta Masina, wife of
Federico Fellini, *è bell' attrice*.
And chocolate malted. A lady in
foxes on such a day puts her poodle
in a cab.
    There are several Puerto
Ricans on the avenue today, which
makes it beautiful and warm. First
Bunny died, then John Latouche,
then Jackson Pollock. But is the
earth as full as life was full, of them?
And one has eaten and one walks,
past the magazines with nudes

>   and posters for BULLFIGHT and
>   the Manhattan Storage Warehouse,
>   which they'll soon tear down. I
>   used to think they had the Armory
>   Show there.
>   A glass of papaya juice
>   and back to work. My heart is in my
>   pocket, it is Poems by Pierre Reverdy.
>   (CP 257-58)

In her book on O'Hara, Marjorie Perloff has worked out in detail the characteristics of this style of surface and immediacy. She sees the movement of his poems as centered in the wandering (and wondering) I/eye, the casual glance of the flâneur drifting along in the experiential flow of urban life, caught in the movement of the city street. And yet, if we look again at "A Step Away From Them," couldn't what seems like a series of visual impressions also be taken as a collage of pre-coded images? The image of the workers, for instance, eating sandwiches and drinking coke with bare torsos and "yellow helmets on" resembles an advertisement for Coca Cola; and the following image of the avenue "where skirts are flipping / above heels and blow up / over grates" we know from many posters and photographs – most famously as a photograph of Marilyn Monroe. The urban space of O'Hara's poems is iconized space: partly because the observer registers advertisements and posters (the well-known Times Square advertisements for brands of cigarettes and whiskey, now gone: "the sign blows smoke, the waterfall pours lightly"), but partly also because his impressions themselves resemble photographs or advertising images. O'Hara thus playfully blurs the borderline between the culturally known image and what is individually seen or felt: "the lady in foxes on such a day," the avenue made warm and beautiful by the presence of several Puerto Ricans. Naturalizing and personalizing a pre-coded language, he creates a witty style of mere surface which unmistakably bears his signature, but is also part of an everyday culture that has become the 'natural' context of our own everyday experience – a context of images which we, through his poems, recognize in its familiarity, yet also learn to see with fresh eyes.

But placing so much emphasis on O'Hara's creation of linguistic surface may itself be too easy and too superficial a response to the complexities of his poetry. It does not appear to apply, for instance, to what is perhaps his most accomplished poem, "The Day Lady Died." On the one hand, this may not even seem to be a characteristic poem since it does have a climax and is centered in a privileged moment of epiphany. On the other, it brings out what I would call the secret subtext of all of Frank O'Hara's poetry: there is the casual surface, composed of random collections of the aimless walker, the visual bricolage of the roaming I/eye, and at the same time a pull toward closure, toward a climactic moment at once final and unavoidable that his poetry – in its determined, often frantic affirmation of life – is meant to resist or counter.

> The Day Lady Died
>
> It is 12:20 in New York a Friday
> three days after Bastille day, yes
> it is 1959 and I go get a shoeshine
> because I will get off the 4:19 in Easthampton
> at 7:15 and then go straight to dinner
> and I don't know the people who will feed me
>
> I walk up the muggy street beginning to sun
> and have a hamburger and a malted and buy
> an ugly NEW WORLD WRITING to see what the poets
> in Ghana are doing these days
>   I go on to the bank
> and Miss Stillwagon (first name Linda I once heard)
> doesn't even look up my balance for once in her life
> and in the GOLDEN GRIFFIN I get a little Verlaine
> for Patsy with drawings by Bonnard although I do
> think of Hesiod, trans. Richmond Lattimore or
> Brendan Behan's new play or *Le Balcon* or *Les Nègres*
> of Genet, but I don't I stick with Verlaine
> after practically going to sleep with quandariness
>
> and for Mike I just stroll into the PARK LANE
> Liquor Store and ask for a bottle of Strega and
> then I go back where I came from to 6th Avenue
> and the tobacconist in the Ziegfeld Theatre and
> casually ask for a carton of Gauloises and a carton
> of Picayunes, and a NEW YORK POST with her face on it
>
> and I am sweating a lot by now and thinking of
> leaning on the john door in the 5 SPOT
> while she whispered a song along the keyboard
> to Mal Waldron and everyone and I stopped breathing
> (*CP* 325)

Note the discrepancy between text and title. The title announces awareness of a special day and date, the day Billie Holiday died (and playfully, even lovingly puns on the singer's name in Jazz circles: Lady Day). She dies three days after Bastille Day. This historic day the speaker does remember – before July 17, 1959, becomes engraved in his memory as the Day Lady Died. However, the text refers to the event of Lady's death only in the last four lines when her photo, accidentally and casually perceived on the title page of the *New York Post*, brings back the memory of her performance. In one of the many ironies of the last line the shock of her death merges with the remembered moment of aesthetic revelation when "everyone and I stopped breathing," The remembered moment is thus at once a shocked *memento mori* and a consolation: art evoking death and yet transcending it. But, although the text suggests such uncharacteristic depth of meaning, it cannot rest in it. If the poem seems to culminate in a moment of cognition, one could also argue that this privileged moment is constantly delayed: "I walk up the muggy street," "I go on to the bank;" "And I am sweating a lot by now" – is this the result of the heat of the New York summer? Or of the speaker's rising inner tension of trying *not* to think of Billie Holiday? He appears to be absorbed by the trivialities of the everyday world in which he moves, his attention fully directed toward the objects that surround him. Although the speaker seems to learn about Billie Holiday's death only when his eye casually falls on her photograph, it would also seem possible that he, like the reader, knows from the very beginning that this is indeed the day Lady died – the distracted attention he pays to the ordinary, the casual awareness of the everyday constituting more than anything else an elaborate strategy to hold the overwhelming knowledge of (her) death at bay.

If so, the poem could be regarded as evidence of a strategy that failed. Yet it also gives testimony to the elegant heroism of O'Hara's whole poetic enterprise since, for him, the need for writing was most of all a need to resist the powerful pull toward death – that cause and agent of creative urgency in life as well as art. In his tribute to O'Hara, the composer Morton Feldman expressed this tension in O'Hara's poetry perceptively: "Who but the dead know what it is to be alive? Death seems the only metaphor distant enough to truly measure our existence. Frank understood this. That is why these poems, so colloquial, so conversational, nevertheless

135

seem to be reaching us from some other, infinitely distant place" (Berkson and LeSueur 14). By risking the life-affirming openness of the roaming eye, the fluid form as a way of writing and a way of living, he, like his Washington of the trembling nose, negotiated the "general fear" of that final random moment when "everyone and I" will stop breathing.

In his eulogy for O'Hara, Feldman also recalls the reaction of an eminent painter on hearing the news of Pollock's death in a car accident: "'That son of a bitch – he did it.' I understood," Feldman continues, "Pollock had wrapped up an era and walked away with it," adding, with O'Hara's early death in mind: "To die early – before one's time was to make the biggest coup of all, for in such a case the work perpetuated not only itself, but also the pain of everyone's loss. In a certain sense the artist makes the pain immortal when he dies young" (Berkson and LeSueur 12). The outpouring of poems and tributes in memory of O'Hara seemed to confirm Feldman's assessment, as did the impact his poetry had on a younger generation of poets: Ted Berrigan, Ron Padgett, Frank Lima, Lewis MacAdams and Anne Waldman, among others. And yet, he is most remembered as the poet of a period and of a place: the resurgence of the avant-garde in the New York art scene of the fifties and early sixties and the extraordinary dialogue between the arts that he so energetically promoted and that shaped his work. Whether he will be remembered as more than the most exciting poet of the New York circle (his friend John Ashbery having been away in Paris during much of that time and only reaching fame and academic elevation long after O'Hara's death), remains an open question. After all, wrapping up an era and walking away with it can also imply one's being defined by it. Marjorie Perloff sensed this when she, in a new preface to her book on O'Hara (originally published in 1977 and republished in 1998), tries to free him from a confinement that, in a sense, she herself had created for him:

> Indeed, just as it is no longer enough to read O'Hara's poetry as the verbal counterpart of New York abstract expressionist painting, so it no longer seems satisfactory to view him primarily as a founding father of New York Poetry, a school allied [...] primarily with Black Mountain, the Beats, and the so-called San Francisco Renaissance. (xxvii)

Instead she suggests a path that would lead out of the synchronicity of "school" or period to the "poetics of our moment," to an awareness that O'Hara's linguistic experiments found continuity and echo in the experimentalism of the language poets: of Charles Bernstein, Ron Silliman and several others. This may well be – although the ancestral line leading to contemporary poetics can be drawn much more solidly in the case of John Ashbery, whose work developed and matured during many decades and has now reached a level of achievement that death denied to his friend. And yet O'Hara's poems are so rich in their diversity of tone and linguistic inventiveness that, like the poems of Hart Crane (a poet he greatly admired), they will always be rediscovered and returned to, if only for the sheer joy in life and language they so brilliantly embody.

Bibliography

Allen, Donald, ed. *Frank O'Hara: Standing Still and Walking in New York*. Bolinas, CA: Grey Fox Press, 1975.
Alloway, Lawrence. *American Pop Art*. New York, NY: Macmillan, 1974.
Baigell, Matthew. "Abstract Expressionism." *Dictionary of American Art*. New York, NY: Harper & Row, 1982. 1-4.
Berkson, Bill, and Joe LeSueur, eds. *Homage to Frank O'Hara*. Berkeley, CA: Big Sky, 1978.
Breslin, James. "Frank O'Hara, Popular Culture, and American Poetry in the 1950s." *Made in U.S.A*. Ed. Sidra Stich. Berkeley, CA: University of California Press, 1987. 212-219.
Ferguson, Russell. *In Memory of My Feelings: Frank O'Hara and American Art*. Los Angeles, CA: The Museum of Contemporary Art, 1999.
Gooch, Brad. *City Poet: The Life and Times of Frank O'Hara*. New York, NY: Alfred Knopf, 1993.
O'Hara, Frank. *The Collected Poems*. Ed. Donald Allen. Berkeley, CA: University of California Press, 1985.
---. "Jackson Pollock." *Art Chronicles, 1954-1966*. New York, NY: George Braziller, 1975. 12-39.
---. "Larry Rivers: Why I Paint As I Do." *Art Chronicles, 1954-1966*. New York, NY: George Braziller, 1975. 106-20.
Perloff, Marjorie. *Frank O'Hara: Poet Among Painters*. Chicago, IL: University of Chicago Press, 1998 [1977].
Rosenberg, Harold. *The Anxious Object*. Chicago, IL: Chicago University Press, 1966. 39-48.
Wilentz, Elias, ed. *The Beat Scene*. New York, NY: Corinth Books, 1960.

Williams, William Carlos. *The Collected Earlier Poems.* New York, NY: New Directions, 1951.

---. *Selected Essays.* New York, NY: New Directions, 1954.

David Huntsperger (Southfield, Michigan)

Postmodern Poetic Form in the Classroom

Teaching the various experimental and seemingly arbitrary forms of postmodern American poetry can be challenging, and the difficulty begins before one even approaches a poem. For in discussing postmodern poetry, we are immediately confronted by a definitional problem: What is postmodern? To a certain extent, this problem applies to periodization itself, and one might similarly inquire into the definition of romanticism or modernism. But in the case of postmodern poetry, the question is more pressing, in that we are dealing with a period that – arguably – continues into the present moment. Indeed, some critics seem to use the term 'postmodern' as though it were more or less interchangeable with 'contemporary.' In terms of simple chronology, such usage is not especially problematic. Postmodernism in American poetry may be said to begin in the mid-twentieth century, and if it has ended, there is no clear umbrella term for the many poetic praxes that have characterized the poetry of this new millennium.

Yet when applied to American poetry, the term "postmodern" suggests more than the cultural epoch between modernism and the present. The term suggests a continuation and extension of the radical experimentation of modernists such as T.S. Eliot, H.D., Ezra Pound, Gertrude Stein, Jean Toomer, William Carlos Williams, Louis Zukofsky and the many other avant-garde poets whose work flourished in the first half of the last century. Because of the enormous influence that avant-garde modernists have had on postmodernists such as David Antin, Amiri Baraka, Charles Bernstein, Robert Creeley, Robert Duncan, Allen Ginsberg, Lyn Hejinian, Susan Howe, Denise Levertov, Charles Olson and Ron Silliman (to name only a few), the 'post' in the latter term often seems less important than the 'modernist.' Thus, reading difficult postmodern works such as Howe's *The Europe of Trusts* or Olson's

The Maximus Poems will provide formal challenges similar to those issued by modernist works like Eliot's *The Waste Land* or Pound's *Cantos*.

Nevertheless, important differences do distinguish postmodernists from their predecessors. For example, there is a certain impromptu, provisional, performative quality to some postmodern poetry that is absent from most high modernism (Williams might be taken as an exception here). Charles Altieri identifies in postmodernism a "sense of poetic openness to worldly contingencies," and he finds this openness exemplified in the work of Ginsberg, Robert Lowell and Olson (794). In my experience, this "openness to worldly contingencies" – the seemingly casual and off-handed spontaneity of certain postmodern works – has a particular appeal to students, who find it liberating to imagine poetry as a kind of quotidian communication instead of a collection of timeless cultural artefacts. The postmodern practice of writing poems that emulate informal notes or spontaneous jottings may be contrasted to (or combined with) the postmodern practice of arranging verse into stanzas or concrete visual patterns, and both of these formal praxes may in turn be contrasted to a more rigidly structured formal principle in postmodern American poetry: proceduralism. A number of postmodern poets have used predetermined rules, constraints, or procedures to generate the content of their poetry. While it is relatively simple to enumerate these and other postmodern formal praxes, it is not so easy to offer a single definition of postmodernism that will be both succinct and accurate. Thus, it may be more helpful to fall back on Paul Hoover's broad definition of postmodern American poetry. According to Hoover,

> '[P]ostmodern' means the historical period following World War II. It also suggests an experimental approach to composition, as well as a worldview that sets itself apart from mainstream culture and the narcissism, sentimentality, and self-expressiveness of its life in writing. Postmodernist poetry is the avant-garde of our time. (xxv)

The definition primarily focuses on what postmodernism is not, but it does capture both the time period and the experimental quality that help to define postmodern poetry. By way of expanding upon and qualifying Hoover's definition, we might also consider Altieri's distinction between modern and postmodern aesthetics. According to Altieri, modernism "based its heroic sense of constructivist genius on the capacity of the art work to gather diverse properties within an intensely unified field of balanced forces" (794). Postmodernism, on the other hand, privileges

> those features of textuality that distribute the compositional forces into processes of weaving and unweaving meanings as a divided judgment tries to understand the competing desires imposed upon it by the various cultural codes shaping its imaginary investments. (794)

In Altieri's assessment, modernism aspires to balance and completion; postmodernism does not. Postmodernism allows meaning to remain provisional (woven and then unwoven). This is a significant distinction, for it points to the fundamentally exploratory nature of much postmodern poetry. While the poetry of the high modernists often seems monumental and final, the poetry of postmodern experimenters can sometimes seem casual, occasional, incomplete, improvisatory, asymmetrical, or formulaic.

Defining postmodern poetry is an important consideration for educators, but even more important is the problem of how to present these texts to students, and how to guide students through the reading process. (It's worth noting that some postmodern texts experiment so radically with language that 'reading' may not be the correct term for what we do with them.) Starting with form can be particularly effective because thinking about form requires students to think like poets. To understand why a given form might be effective in presenting (or fragmenting or obfuscating) a given subject matter, students have to consider the formal decisions that the poet has made. Of course, separating form from content creates an artificial distinction that will not hold up very well under scrutiny, but it is a useful pedagogical tool. By asking our students to think provisionally about form in its own right, we encourage them to appreciate poetry as a unique genre and to start reading more attentively and more receptively. In doing so, students gain the opportunity to appreciate poetic language in general, and experimental poetry in particular. Following Hejinian's lead, we might even think of our students' reading as a fundamentally exploratory activity. If this is so, then it is perhaps less important that our students produce a 'correct' reading than that they investigate the semantic possibilities that a given form provides. Hejinian "posits descriptive language and, in a broader sense, poetic language as a language of inquiry, with analogies to the scientific methods of the explorers" (*Language* 148). As our students begin to explore postmodern form, we might encourage them to adopt a reading practice appropriate to this "language of inquiry." Applying Hejinian's writing methodology to reading, we might think of reading itself as a kind of "inquiry." Her observation that "an initial, essential recognition of difference – of strangeness – develops only with attention to single objects, while others are temporarily held in abeyance" (157) might inform a reading strategy. The "strangeness," the weird unfamiliarity of many postmodern forms, can actually become an enjoyable challenge for students, provided that they are not convinced that their teachers have some ultimately authoritative reading in reserve. After all, there is nothing especially enjoyable about exploring a new textual frontier only to be told later that your explorations were a waste of time because a map already existed.

If thinking about form encourages our students to think like writers, then it may also be the case that thinking like writers helps our students to understand form. This has been true in my experience. Students can learn a great deal from emulating or creatively engaging with forms in conjunction with more traditionally critical activities. For example, students might be given an opportunity to substitute a creative writing assignment for an essay. But such an opportunity will not be particularly useful in helping students understand form unless the assignment requires a conscious and reflective engagement with the formal choices underlying the poem. The procedural constraints invented between 1971 and 1975 by postmodern poet Bernadette Mayer and other members of the poetry workshop at St. Mark's Church in New York provide suggestive prompts to the production of formally reflexive poetry. The following procedures strike me as particularly useful:

> Rewrite someone else's writing. Maybe someone formidable. (Mayer 531)

> Get a group of words (make a list or select at random); then form these words (only) into a piece of writing – whatever the words allow. Let them demand their own form, and/or: Use certain words in a set way, like, the same word in every line, or in a certain place in every paragraph, etc. Design words. (531)

Cut-ups, paste-ups, etc. (Intersperse different material in horizontal cut-up strips, paste it together, infinite variations on this). (532)

Use (take, write in) a strict form and/or try to destroy it, e.g., the sestina. (532)

Make a pattern of repetitions. (533)

The first suggestion (rewriting the work of another poet) immediately foregrounds the issue of form by calling attention to the difficulty of separating form and content. In trying to rewrite poetry, we are confronted with a number of questions to which there are no clear answers. What exactly does it mean to rewrite the work of another poet? Is it to emulate a particular tone or style? Is it to replace subject matter with similar subject matter using a different form? Is it to replace subject matter with different subject matter using the same form? And what is the subject matter of a poem? Vocabulary? Setting? Narrative? Imagery? Even if a student focuses primarily on emulating a certain style or voice, the student will probably take into account the way that the original poem looks on the page, and this is a fine beginning to any consideration of form. The second suggestion (using a predetermined vocabulary) puts the emphasis almost completely on form in the broadest sense. The words are already there. It is in the formation of these words into sentences, lines, stanzas (or perhaps some agrammatical, asymmetrical arrangement) that the artistry lies. The third suggestion (constructing cut-ups) recalls the dadaistic roots of Mayer's poem recipes. Moreover, it recalls the importance for avant-garde poetry of collage and other artistic techniques borrowed from the visual arts. After all, form in modern and postmodern poetry comprises much more than rhyme and meter arranged into stanzaic patterns, though such traditional patterning remains important within the poetry of the second half of the twentieth century. Mayer suggests this with her fourth suggestion, to "[u]se [...] a strict form." The fifth suggestion might almost be said to contain a summary of poetic form at its most fundamental level: "Make a pattern of repetitions." Certain examples of free verse and of concrete poetry would be difficult to describe as patterns of repetitions, but this is nevertheless a useful definition of many postmodern forms, particularly if we assume that the notion of variation is implicit in the notion of repetition. In any case, students can learn much about poetic form by beginning to construct forms themselves, and experiments such as those suggested by Mayer and her workshop can facilitate this process. Whether reading or writing postmodern poetry, students benefit from thinking of this genre as both experimental and exploratory. There is something exciting – perhaps even liberating – in learning that form is not an inherited tradition to be understood, internalized, and slavishly followed but a set of directions that *you* (the poet, the student) can construct yourself.

For the remainder of this essay, I will present individual postmodern poems as pedagogical artefacts, and in doing so I will attempt to keep form always in view. Free verse is a useful starting place, because one almost inevitably teaches this form in any survey of modern or postmodern poetry. In my own teaching, I have found it useful to emphasize the fact that interesting postmodern free verse poems are far from formless, even when they feel improvisatory or offhanded. Let's take Robert Creeley's oft-anthologized "I Know a Man" as an example. The poem is arranged into four unrhymed tercets – a simple form that students should be able to recognize without difficulty. But the poem is of formal interest not because of the stanzaic arrangement but because of the tension between this arrangement and the poem's grammar. Because the poem is composed of a single sentence (or a sentence according to Creeley's idiosyncratic punctuation), enjambment is pervasive. The question for students, then, concerns the relationship between this enjambment and the subject matter of the poem. One might ask students to consider how this enjambment compliments Creeley's narrative of existential crisis and bad driving. Here is the poem in its entirety:

> As I sd to my
> friend, because I am
> always talking, – John, I
>
> sd, which was not his
> name, the darkness sur-
> rounds us, what

> can we do against
> it, or else, shall we &
> why not, buy a goddamn big car,
>
> drive, he sd, for
> christ's sake, look
> out where yr going. (40)

The use of the shorthand "sd" and "yr" is a typical Black Mountain School homage to Pound, but students do not need to know this in order to grasp the fact that the poem, with its lack of capitalization and its use of an ampersand, seems to emulate a note-book style, as though it were a mere momentary jotting down of a thought. This style combines with Creeley's use of comma splices and his omission of quotation and question marks to produce a breathless, hurried feel. That the speaker seems too pressed to wait for a response from his friend only enhances this effect. (One is perhaps reminded of Jack Kerouac's fictionalized adventures in *On the Road*.) In light of the final (funny) stanza, we might start to think of the line breaks as reinforcing the theme of driving. More specifically, we might see some of these line breaks as a formal representation of erratic driving. Line breaks tend to emphasize the final word in a line; among poets working in free verse it is sometimes taken as a matter of common sense that lines ought to end with words that carry particular semantic value – a noun or an action verb, for example. Ending a line with a preposition, a prefix, or an ampersand is somewhat unusual. The combination of short lines, seemingly random line breaks, and pervasive enjambment produces a poem that seems (though is surely not) erratically constructed, and this erratic quality (at least for this reader) is mimetic of the subject matter. Of course, one needs to be slightly cautious in directing students to see form as contributing to the overall semantic effect of a poem. It surely does this, but it is easy for students to confuse cause and effect. One would not find Creeley's idiosyncratic line breaks to be suggestive of wild driving if the idea were not already present in the poem, and similar formal choices might be used to very different effect elsewhere. It is important to keep in mind that poetic forms are not mimetic in any simple or predictable way, particularly if we try to think about them as existing independently of subject matter.

Denise Levertov, another poet associated with the postmodern Black Mountain School, also used stanzas and line breaks as formal accents to the subject matter of her poems. For example, "The Jacob's Ladder," which describes a stairway to heaven, employs stanzas that look to varying degrees like steps or staircases. Here are the first two stanzas:

> The stairway is not
> a thing of gleaming strands
> a radiant evanescence
> for angels' feet that only glance in their tread, and need not
> touch the stone.
>
> It is of stone.
> a rosy stone that takes
> a glowing tone of softness
> only because behind it the sky is a doubtful, a doubting
> night gray. (25)

The poem both revises and expands upon the biblical story of Jacob's ladder. The biblical text is not particularly concerned with the physical properties of the ladder, but in her revision of the story, Levertov literalizes the metaphorical ascent to Yahweh by imagining how exactly one would go about climbing the ladder. In the first stanza (which, like the rest of the stanzas, is composed of five lines), Levertov practices a bit of apophastic evocation. Although "[t]he stairway is not / a thing of gleaming strands / a radiant evanescence," Levertov's sibilant, polysyllabic language still conjures this elegant image. This Latinate vocabulary contrasts markedly with our first glimpse of what the stairway actually looks like: "It is of stone." While the first stanza is composed of a single sentence of twenty-seven words, with each of the first four lines enjambed, the second stanza begins with a blunt, four-word, four-syllable sentence contained on the first line. The emphasis, of course, is on the material: stone. Moreover, the placement of the word "stone" on the final line of the first stanza and then again on the first and second lines of the second stanza creates a sort of concrete (pun intended) poem in miniature, a visual representation of stone steps using the word "stone." This stacking up of "stone" is not something that I would expect students to notice on their own, but it is certainly a formal effect that they can appreciate if it is shown to them. The third stanza contains another word arrangement that is mimetic of the subject matter:

> A stairway of sharp
> angles, solidly built.
> One sees that the angels must spring
> down from one step to the next, giving a little
> lift of the wings: (25)

The third line of this stanza ends with an image of angels springing, and as one reads this line one's eyes must 'spring' from the word "spring" to the word "down," as if in emulation of the angels. It is a strange and – to this reader – delightful moment in which the language of the poem suddenly seems to become unusually active, as though a still picture had suddenly become animated. The seeming vitality of the language is augmented as well by an anagrammatic juxtaposition: "angles" on the second line of this stanza and "angels" on the third. The mere reversal of two letters turns geometry into mythology. Although the presence of an anagrammatic word pair is not an obviously formal issue, it calls attention to language at the material level – the level of letters arranged into words, of words as shapes and sounds, and of words printed in ink upon a page. When we pay attention to poetic language at the material level, we are reminded that this language is shaped, constructed, arranged, and, ultimately, formed.

In order to help students understand form in postmodern free verse, we have to appreciate the importance of structures and patterns, but we also need to move beyond them to describe how a particular arrangement of words works to make meaning. A discussion of form in "The Jacob's Ladder" might very well begin with the five-line by four-stanza pattern, but it would be an impoverished discussion indeed if it did not progress beyond this basic pattern to discuss the more subtle poetic effects that the form makes possible. In the case of Levertov's poem, as we have seen, the stanza patterns allow individual words like "stone," "spring," and "down" to make semantic connections vertically as well as horizontally. In prose (and often in poetry as well), meaning accumulates horizontally, from left to right. But the form of "The Jacob's Ladder" opens a second dimension within which readers can make meaning. Like angels on the ladder, words – when activated by the attentive reader – move up and down the page. And in the last stanza, it suddenly seems that the poem itself is moving upward as well:

> and a man climbing
> must scrape his knees, and bring
> the grip of his hands into play. The cut stone
> consoles his groping feet. Wings brush past him.
> The poem ascends. (25)

In conjunction with the final line of the poem, the word "cut" in the third line of this last stanza seems particularly important. In fact, I would argue that the word suggests that the stone stairway itself functions as something of an allegory for poetic form. The poem (a formed object, an artefact) describes a "cut" stairway (i.e., a stairway that has been made, has been formed). And in the final line we have the poem itself climbing this stairway, perhaps to deliver its message. It does so by means of this formed object, which the third stanza refers to as "[a] stairway of sharp angles, solidly built." One suspects that Levertov would think of her poetic structures as "solidly built" as well.

While Creeley and Levertov work with flexible, non-traditional forms, their work remains easily recognizable as poetry. This is not necessarily the case with the work of other postmodern innovators. Take, for example, David Antin. His work in the 1960s, '70s, and '80s became increasingly experimental and procedural until at last he seemed to be as much performance artist as poet. In the early '60s, Antin explains, he "began to work with prefabricated and readymade materials, recycling texts and fragments of texts, enclosing valuable and used up talk and thought and feeling, hoping to save what was worth saving, liberate it and throw the rest away" (*Selected* 14-15). To compose "Novel Poem," for example, Antin used the popular novels he was reading as source material:

> Then I put some paper in the typewriter and I began typing what I was reading, and it became a little game – no more than one line from a page. Sometimes only a phrase. Sometimes nothing. And I never went back. I read and typed relentlessly forward, quickly making up these little songs, till I was through.

Antin's description of this procedural method of composition as "a little game" has particular pedagogical relevance, for reading and composing postmodern poetry can be (dare I say it?) fun for students. It is a mistake, I think, to take poetry that was composed in a spirit of playfulness and then ask students to read or emulate it with the utmost seriousness. The experience of exploring postmodern poetry ought to be qualitatively different from reading, for example, William Wordsworth's *The Prelude* (though I am not trying to pick on Wordsworth here). But a procedural form like the one Antin employs to construct "Novel Poem" limits the extent to which language will be construed as intentional. There is a certain distance between poet and language, in that the poet can never say quite exactly what he means when his materials are always readymade. Elements of chance and indeterminacy enter the critical equation. Of course, this does not mean that any reading of a poem is as good as any other; Antin's poems are not nonsense, after all. But reading a poem constructed of recycled fragments more or less obviates the need for students to hunt down (and instructors to lecture on) arcane symbols and recondite allusions. This is a different kind of reading. For example, part six of the first section of "Novel Poem" reads, "will you do it Tom / will i do what / will you leave" (122). Though the lines are unpunctuated and lack capitalization, the tone of this conversation is easy to pick up. I hear in these lines the rapid, emotionally charged exchange of lovers in a cheap romance novel or soap opera. The next section, also only three lines long, seems as though it must have been derived from a more serious novel: "she said it without self pity / what would she do in Israel this frail old lady of seventy / Israel was for all the land that would flow with milk and honey" (122). One can easily invent a context for these lines, and this invention of narrative is part of the pleasure of reading "Novel Poem." At times, the lack of context even seems somehow fitting to the subject matter. Part nine of the first section features a narrative fragment that apparently takes place in the aftermath of World War II. In light of the cataclysmic violence and destruction of the conflict, the war might be said to produce a moment of historical and personal rupture for those who lived through it. If we think of the war as a trauma that has been felt across an entire society, then the anonymity of the characters in the following decontextualized narrative fragment – an anonymity produced by the lack of context itself – seems fitting:

> she had dozed a little after Avignon
> it was ridiculous she knew
> France was at peace
> the Germans had gone
> Vichy was a thing of the past
>
> on the train no one had spoken
> and he couldn't have cared less
> she had passed no checkpoint
> there had been no search
> no eruption of men in uniform
>
> no look of suspicion in anyone's eyes
> on the platform she put her bag down

In this post-war setting, the "she" and "he" have no names, as though their link to a world before the war has been severed. The feeling of paranoia that pervades these lines is perhaps also attributable to the trauma of the war. Yet it is also possible to see the slightest hint of a Cold War espionage narrative in the final couplet. Why would anyone be suspicious of the female character? What does she have in her bag that could arouse suspicion? It is as though we have a spy novel in miniature, and we as readers are free to construct the rest of it.

Antin used variations on the "Novel Poem" procedure in order to construct other works as well. To write *Meditations* he employed, among other sources, "lists of words high school students found difficult to spell" (18). To produce "The Separation Meditations" he worked with footnotes from a scholarly edition of the writing of Epictetus: "[...] I read through the book much as in Novel Poem, reading and writing quickly through the footnotes and continuing forward, taking a phrase here and a phrase, sometimes a word, there, working swiftly to make my kind of sense" (19). In teaching Antin's work, it may be useful to provide students with Antin's own descriptions of his writing process. The very fact that he thinks of "sense" as individual invites a sort of democratization of the entire critical process. If he can make his "kind of sense," why can we not all make our own kind of sense through poetry? By suggesting that sense – meaning – is unstable and individual, one probably runs the risk of having a precocious student ask why Antin's (or any other poet's work) is not simply nonsense, then. (Last semester, whenever my American literature class read difficult poetry that did not readily lend itself to final and determinate interpretation, an exceptionally bright computer science student referred to it as "word salad.") Yet it is relatively easy to demonstrate to students that it is nearly impossible to produce nonsense. Class discussion usually leads to some degree of critical consensus on the meaning of a poem. In any event, questions about sense, nonsense, interpretation, and indeterminacy are relatively difficult to avoid in the teaching of postmodern poetry. Just as teachers of modern art will inevitably have to explain (and perhaps defend) abstraction, teachers of postmodern poetry will inevitably have to explain the fragmentary, agrammatical, periphrastic, and indeterminate writing styles that constitute postmodernism. In doing so, I try to acknowledge the difficulty and ambiguity of many postmodern poems while stressing the fact that signal can indeed be identified amid the noise.

Antin's "The November Exercises" also employs recycled language, but it adds another procedural variable: time. Here is Antin's description of the composition process:

> But in November of 1971 I had been feeling very spent, and as usual when I feel that way I tend to experiment with short quick works. So I had started a set of exercises in which I had to write something down at least once during the day. I was working with a little book that was designed to teach English to foreigners and it had a lot of phrases I liked; and sometimes I worked with them and sometimes with the newspapers, because I'm a compulsive news reader, and sometimes with both, but always quickly and usually several times a day. I got into the habit of putting down the times of the day when I wrote them, mainly to indicate the quickness and lightness of the writing. And as I was thinking of them as something of a cross between mental calisthenics and spiritual exercise, and because I completed them in November, I called them the November exercises. (20)

The result of this procedure is a series of prose writings that – because they are organized by date and time – approximate the form of a journal. But instead of description and self-reflection, we encounter narrative fragments and aphoristic commentary on language itself. Moreover, this commentary, which sometimes seems to follow the form of a Zen Buddhist koan, reveals an intentional misunderstanding of the English language. For example, the entry for November 2nd at 12:15 p.m. plays with the meaning of the idiomatic expression "to lose one's head": "She kept her head and he lost his. She telephoned the fire department and he drove up over the curb into a tree. Otherwise the whole house might have burnt down" (262). In light of the alarming imagery (particularly the unexplained act of driving the car into a tree), one almost wonders if the male figure who has "lost" his head has done so in the literal sense. The entry for 12:20 p.m. on this same day also plays with definition: "When you blow up a building you make it smaller" (262). The sentence seems to be explaining the expression "to blow up." When one blows up a balloon, one makes it bigger. Thus, someone learning the English language would want to know that the expression has other meanings as well. To say that blowing up a building makes it smaller is true, and it gestures toward the paradoxical nature of the expression itself: Sometimes "to blow up" makes something bigger; sometimes it makes something smaller. But there is something absurd in this definition as well. The trite language mutes the shattering violence of such an act. And in thinking about the ways that language might reveal or conceal the actual effects of actions – in other words, to think about the ways that language might be ideologically inflected – one begins to see the inherently political nature of Antin's formal experimentation. Antin readily acknowledges the link between "[l]anguage and politics" when he notes that "language is the cultural matrix in which the value systems that determine politics are held" (13-14). This is an important connection to keep in mind, particularly when it comes to the teaching of postmodern form. I have been emphasizing the pleasures of reading postmodern poetry and the playfulness implicit in the act of employing postmodern forms. Such an emphasis seems useful to me, because it is not always easy to interest students in this difficult poetry. But it is also worth pointing out to students the political or ideological ramifications of postmodern forms that defamiliarize language. To the extent that a given form removes us from a commonplace, common-sense, utilitarian view of language, it provides an opportunity to describe the world and to think about the world in unpredictable new ways. It is probably naïve to expect that the revolution will begin in the poetry classroom, but one does want to do one's part.

    Few postmodern American poets have aligned political commitment and poetic form (particularly procedural form) more closely than the Language poets. Silliman, one of the most successful and prolific of this group, went so far as to structure his book-length prose poem *Tjanting* on his understanding of Marx's theory of class struggle. Using the Fibonacci number series as an organizational principal, Silliman created two parallel series of paragraphs of increasing length. The Fibonacci series, which begins with two ones, proceeds by adding each number in the series to the subsequent number to produce yet another subsequent number. Thus, the series proceeds as follows: 1, 1, 2, 3, 5, 8, 13, 21, etc. Each paragraph in *Tjanting* contains the number of sentences dictated by the Fibonacci series. The first paragraph contains one sentence, as does the second. The third paragraph contains two; the fourth contains three; the fifth contains five; the sixth contains eight, and so forth. The final paragraphs of the book contain thousands of sentences each. The parallelism of the form emerges from the fact that the Fibonacci series may be considered as two separate series each beginning with the number one. Thus, one series contains paragraphs in which the number of sentences proceeds as follows: 1, 2, 5, 13, etc. The second series contains paragraphs in which the number of sentences increases thus: 1, 3, 8, 21, etc. To complicate this mathematical procedure, Silliman decided to reuse (usually in revised or syntactically scrambled form) the sentences from a given paragraph in the next paragraph of the given series. How exactly this form allegorizes class struggle is a complicated question, and we need not consider it too closely here. The short answer is that the two series of paragraphs increase in length at uneven rates, thereby suggesting the class competition between the proletariat and the bourgeoisie. (For Silliman's explanation of this class allegory and his rationale for the use of Fibonacci form in *Tjanting*, see his interview with Tom Beckett in *The Difficulties* 2.2 [1985].) In fact, for teaching purposes it is not even necessary to discuss the class allegory enacted by the form. Rather, one can simply present the first paragraphs of the poem and allow students to come to their own conclusions. Here are the first six paragraphs of *Tjanting*:

> Not this.
> What then?
> I started over & over. Not this.
> Last week I wrote "the muscles in my palm so sore from halving the rump roast I cld barely grip the pen." What then? This morning my lip is blisterd.

> Of about to within which. Again & again I began. The gray light of day fills the yellow room in a way wch is somber. Not this. Hot grease had spilld on the stove top.
>   Nor that either. Last week I wrote "the muscle at thumb's root so taut from carving that beef I thought it wld cramp." Not so. What then? Wld I begin? This morning my lip is tender, disfigurd. I sat in an old chair out behind the anise. I cld have gone about this some other way. (15)

The number of sentences per paragraph is what we would expect (1, 1, 2, 3, 5, 8), and the expected repetition of material occurs as well. The first sentence ("Not this") is repeated in the third and fifth paragraphs, while the second sentence ("What then?") reappears in the fourth and sixth paragraphs. One can point all of this out to students, but such a didactic gesture does little to encourage the attentive, receptive reading that postmodern forms reward. To begin a classroom discussion of *Tjanting*, one might instead ask students to reread these first six paragraphs carefully and note whatever patterns or repetitions they find. Such a question might also encompass repeated themes. Students may notice that the poem frequently returns to the depiction of quotidian urban details, and that it is unusually reflexive about the writing process itself. By the time one arrives at the final sentence of the sixth paragraph ("I cld have gone about this some other way"), it is difficult not to read the statement as a meta-comment on the writing of *Tjanting*. That is, Silliman could have utilized something other than his recursive Fibonacci form to produce the subject matter.

Though *Tjanting*'s form is complex, in terms of teaching it does not strike me as the most problematic aspect of the poem. More challenging still is finding an adequate answer to a simple question that students may very well ask: Why is this poetry? One can certainly begin by noting the Language poets' fondness for the prose poem form, but that is not really the end of the issue. In the classical prose poem (think Charles Baudelaire's *Spleen de Paris*), the content is easily recognizable as poetry (Baudelaire's prose poems resemble his verse poems in subject matter, imagery, symbolism, etc.). But when the prose poem extends to more than two hundred pages and contains sentences such as "Of about to within which" (15) and "A bit a part a like" (15), we have clearly entered nontraditional territory. There is probably no answer to the genre question (*Why is this poetry?*) that is at once short, simple, and adequate. One could certainly undertake a broad discussion of genre as it is constructed across literary history, but in my own teaching I have tried for something more modest. I have paired Silliman with other poets in order to create an interpretive context. Silliman's sentences composed entirely of particles seem less strange when compared to the work of Gertrude Stein, a modernist antecedent who influenced the Language poets with her abstract and grammatically contorted prose poems. Likewise, a book-length prose poem structured by numerical constraint seems less foreign when contextualized by similar numerical forms. Hejinian (also a Language poet) organized *My Life*, a poetic autobiography treating her life up to the age of forty-five, into forty-five sections of forty-five sentences each. Taught together, *Tjanting* and *My Life* can give students a sense of how the San Francisco Language poets (another group established itself in New York) combined the prose poem form with numerical constraints in order to create a new mode of poetic realism. For like *Tjanting*, *My Life* offers a fragmentary, metonymic account of everyday life using sentences (the Language poets have called them "new sentences") that unfold paratactically, often without obvious connection to previous or subsequent sentences. Here, for example, are the first six sentences of the twenty-sixth section of Hejinian's poem:

> Last night, in my dreams, I swam to the bottom of a lake, pushed off in the mud, and rising rapidly to the surface shot eight or ten feet out of the water into the air. I couldn't join the demonstration because I was pregnant, and so I had revolutionary experience without taking revolutionary action. History hugs the world. The Muses are little female fellows. To some extent, each sentence has to be the whole story. It is hard to turn away from moving water, where the tiny pebbles are left along the shore. (*My Life* 93)

Here grammar and syntax are more normative than in the first paragraphs of Silliman's poem. But we see important similarities as well: the prose form, the narrative discontinuity, and the metatextual commentary ("To some extent, each sentence has to be the whole story").

Studied in conjunction, Silliman's and Hejinian's poems are mutually illuminating, particularly at the level of form. And there is a larger lesson to be drawn from this fact: Postmodern form comprises a number of divergent praxes, and to teach it effectively one has to present an array of examples. In a survey of English poetry, one might successfully present *Beowulf* as the single representative artefact of the Anglo-Saxon period. But there is no *Beowulf* of postmodern American poetry (or not yet, at any rate). The various forms used by various poets add up to a field that is too incoherent to be easily summarized. Thus, if we want students to develop an accurate sense of postmodern American poetry as it developed (and perhaps continues to develop), we need to provide them with a generous sampling of the forms with which these poets worked. In doing so, we can help students to develop not only a base of literary-historical knowledge, but also more sensitive and attentive reading skills. And these skills may surely be applied in other contexts. As I sometimes tell my students: If you can read difficult modern and postmodern poetry and read it well, you can probably read just about anything.

Bibliography

Altieri, Charles. "Modernism and Postmodernism." *The New Princeton Encyclopedia of Poetry and Poetics*. Ed. Alex Preminger and T.V.F. Brogan. Princeton: Princeton University Press, 1993. 792-96

Antin, David. *Selected Poems: 1963-1973*. Los Angeles: Sun & Moon Press, 1991.

Carroll, Robert, and Stephen Prickett, eds. *The Bible*. Oxford: Oxford University Press, 1997.

Creeley, Robert. *Selected Poems*. Berkeley: University of California, 1991.

Hejinian, Lyn. *The Language of Inquiry*. Berkeley: University of California, 2000.

---. *My Life*. Los Angeles: Green Integer, 2002.

Hoover, Paul, ed. Introduction. *Postmodern American Poetry: A Norton Anthology*. New York: Norton & Co, 1994. xxv-xxxix.

Levertov, Denise. *Selected Poems*. New York: New Directions, 2002.

Mayer, Bernadette, et al. "Experiments." *In the American Tree: Language, Realism, Poetry*. Ed. Ron Silliman. Orono: National Poetry Foundation, 2002. 531-34.

Silliman, Ron. *Tjanting*. Applecross: Salt, 2002.

Walter Grünzweig and Julia Sattler (Dortmund)

People's Poetry:
Translation as a Collective Experience

In the last two decades, translation has become a significant topic in literary and cultural studies as well as in the humanities at large. Following the disappearance of the hugely limiting Cold War bipolar division of the world, the emerging multi-polarity has provided a fresh impetus to not only engage in translation far beyond the traditional classical Eurocentric perspective but also to think *about* translation as a mode of acting in this new world. Following Emily Apter's fascinating metaphor of the "translation zone," the significance of translation and translation studies has been described as growing "in importance as the material and social structures of our world became more global; with the spread of financial, information, and military networks; with an increasing migration of peoples; and with war [...]" (Berman 83n).

The Modern Language Association's 2009 Presidential Forum in Philadelphia brought forth many important contributions which were subsequently widely disseminated through MLA's *Profession 2010*. Significantly, the case was made not only for translation as an important area of literary practice and academic inquiry but also as an important dimension of teaching. In the words of Jonathan Culler, "the presence of linguistically challenged students and the introduction of translation into the discursive space of the classroom can actually be pedagogically beneficial" (92).

In this essay, we will extend these ideas to the EFL classroom where the "linguistic challenge" is much less of a problem than in "world literature" courses, where students operate without (or with very limited) knowledge of the source language and culture. The argument becomes then not one of implicit or explicit loss – Marjorie Perloff warns us in her article on bilingual poetry teaching that we should never pretend "that a translation is more than a good reproduction of a painting; it is not the painting itself" (Perloff 105) – but of gain.

By translating poetry, we address central dimensions of the poetic experience and thus also of the teaching of this particular genre. Translation forces readers and translators of poetry to deal with all levels of a text in a most detailed and intimate way. As a mode of reception, translation is textual interpretation which combines a normative tendency towards adequacy and even 'correctness' with the freedom to recognize subjective meanings encountered by individual readers. As a creative endeavor, translation has a strong affinity with the processes generating poetry. As an eminently political activity, it provides access to socially relevant dimensions of literature, and of poetry in particular, not only thematically but also aesthetically. Poetry translation, then, is highly suitable for group work in the EFL classroom and it is also applicable for larger, collective group projects in the classroom and beyond, as we will demonstrate using the example of projects that were devoted to translating the poetry of Jimmy Carter and June Jordan.

Our model of translating poetry in the EFL classroom has been developed in the course of a decade within the Dortmund American Studies program. This program has a strong transatlantic, comparatist and intercultural focus and brings together international and German students for shared intercultural learning projects. We are interested in the dialogues American cultures enter into with cultures elsewhere, inside and outside of Europe. Literary translation as a primary mode of mediation between languages and culture of course has an important place in such a program.

In the late 1990s, a group of instructors and students in the Dortmund Department of English and American Studies started a project translating the poetry of former U.S. president Jimmy Carter. This project emerged from a class on the Carter presidency that examined the political cultures informing Carter's domestic and foreign policies as well as his highly successful activities after his presidency. When students read Carter's poetry, they were surprised that a politician – and an American president at that – was writing poetry, and they were disappointed that Carter's poetry was not available in German.

It was decided to translate Carter's only volume of poetry to date and to publish it in a bilingual edition. A special translation class was devoted to the project. Altogether, some 40 individuals, students and instructors, participated in this translation endeavor. Usually, two or three students collaborated on several poems; together they worked out a German version of each poem that was then discussed in class. Two 'editors,' who eventually figured as translators on the title page of the book, polished the finished product together with the publisher Stefan Weidle, himself a distinguished translator.

Some problems arose from Carter's elevated political position. First, students found it very difficult to abstract their reading of the poetry from their knowledge of Carter as a public persona and a politician. In their translations, they tended to use a 'public' voice, disregarding the often very different voices in Carter's poetry. This was especially true with regard to his nature poetry, poems relating not only to hunting but also to the natural sciences and to the existential questions that they raise.

Secondly, political issues oftentimes overshadowed questions of style in the process of translating. Environmental concerns, racism, the Middle East – each of these topics tended to drown out aesthetic complexities. The decision to present Carter's frequently rhymed poetry in unrhymed German is a clear expression of this political focus, as a 'literal' rendering required less regard for the poems' formal aspects. The specific epistemological mode of poetry was not fully brought out.

Nevertheless, the translation was successfully completed and eventually published by Weidle Verlag in Bonn, a quality publisher specializing in texts located between cultures. What participants learned from the Carter project was the importance of collective work on these translations, a strategy that was developed more fully in the Jordan translation, a project undertaken between 2008 and 2011.

Several reasons favored the selection of June Jordan (1936-2002). First of all, she had not previously been translated into German, even though her poetry has global appeal. Second, as a poet in the tradition of Walt Whitman, some of Jordan's poems had been taught before in several classes and were thus known to a number of students already. Finally, her poetry is very readable and lends itself to performance – which suited our plans for a public presentation of the results of the project.

June Jordan herself divides modern poetry into two classes. The first includes the work of poets who engage in formal experiments and place aesthetics above political message. In Jordan's view these writers, intentionally or not, prevent easy access to their poetic work for a larger, democratically conceived reading public. Aesthetic sophistication replaces or drives out the political message and obscures literature for the ordinary reader. A second group of poets, however, including "Father Walt Whitman" at the beginning and, by implication, June Jordan herself, make up a canon of "people's poetry" which is about, for and maybe even by the culturally deprived working masses:

> I too am a descendent of Walt Whitman. And I am not by myself struggling to tell the truth about this history of so much land and so much blood, of so much that should be sacred and so much that has been desecrated and annihilated boastfully. [...]
> We do not apologize because we are not Emily Dickinson, Ezra Pound, T.S. Eliot, Wallace Stevens, Robert Lowell, or Elizabeth Bishop. If we are nothing to them, to those who love them, they are nothing to us! Or, as Whitman exclaimed: "I exist as I am, that is enough."
>
> New World poetry moves into and beyond the light of the lives of Walt Whitman, Pablo Neruda, Agostinho Neto, Gabriela Mistral, Langston Hughes, Margaret Walker, and Edward Brathwaite.
>
> I follow this movement with my own life. I am calm and I am smiling as we go. (Jordan 1980, 78)

As Americanists, of course, we do not accept this rather one-dimensional differentiation, firstly because it unfairly negates the enormous political force of the experimental, mostly 'modernist,' poets, especially in their refusal to be explicitly political and accessible. Secondly, it ignores the aesthetic sophistication and complexity of the "people's poets" – foremost June Jordan herself. One can, however, identify collective voices in this "people's poetry," which imply a "mass" audience and a poet who is speaking for all. Whitman's poetry has been globally celebrated as addressing readers directly and a multitude of writers internationally and nationally have responded to Whitman in their own creative works.

June Jordan stands precisely in this tradition of appealing to the masses and she makes this appeal international in her work. If there is a contemporary poet with a world-wide perspective, encompassing the global South, American urban settings, and European crisis areas such as Bosnia and Northern Ireland, it is this African American woman lyricist who clearly transcends – and seeks to transcend – the limitations of her own immediate context. This transcendence also becomes clear when considering the styles and genres Jordan utilizes in her poetry: among others, she makes use of forms stemming from Asian contexts, such as haiku and tanka, and mixes African American dialects with Standard English.

As a "people's poet," Jordan, throughout her work, gives a voice to those who have been silenced by history: in her texts, she not only lends this voice to victims of war or crimes against humanity across the world (e.g. "Lebanon, Lebanon," "The Bombing of Baghdad"), she also addresses the LGBT community (e.g. "Kissing God Goodbye") as well as other groups in society who have traditionally been suppressed or neglected. In this manner, June Jordan can be read directly in line with such authors as Toni Morrison, who also lends a voice to those who have been silenced and who also uncovers the remains of repressed guilt and hidden racism. It was important that this multitude of voices and multitude of stories, even if they might be only whispers in the background, would be heard in the final translation. Starting from these notions, our translation project took into consideration both the "people's poet" quality of June Jordan's poetry as well as its transnational appeal.

In three seminars dedicated to Jordan's poetry in three different semesters, two at Dortmund and one at Karl-Franzens-Universität Graz in Austria, altogether 60 students participated in the translation project. The majority of students who took part were not familiar with Jordan's work before taking the class; however, they had for the most part read other "people's poets" such as Walt Whitman and were familiar with some of the political dimensions of poetry through, for example, their study of the writers of the Harlem Renaissance in their introductory classes. While this type of prior knowledge may not always be necessary for cross-cultural translation projects, it was very helpful in this case because it enabled students from the start to understand June Jordan's global outreach as well as her specific rootedness in a particular context. Other specific ideas and knowledge students brought into the classroom, such as about women's poetry and literature, African American culture and expression, and the political conflicts Jordan addresses in her work, were a helpful starting point for discussion in the classroom and ensured that while everyone brought in something different, students would support and learn from each others' contributions and questions instead of pushing their individual agendas.

The final text as prepared for publication, currently being edited by two instructors, will truly be a collective product. The input of individual translators or groups of translators will not be traceable due to the heterogeneous workings and reworkings of so many individuals in three classes. Just as importantly, the seminar groups consisted of students of different national and ethnic backgrounds, with a multiplicity of voices and viewpoints. In addition to German-speaking (German and Austrian) students, students came from Hungary, Croatia, Bosnia, and Turkey. U.S. exchange students, including African Americans, also contributed to the outcome as partners in the "intercultural classrooms."

The collection chosen for the translation project was *Kissing God Good-Bye*, one of Jordan's more recent volumes, containing poetry from 1991-1997. It was selected because of its relative contemporaneousness and thus its chronological proximity to the students' own life-span, its mix of the personal and the political (sometimes in one and the same poem), its experimentation with various challenging lyrical forms including haikus and tankas, and its nexus of American perspectives with a global vision. Finally, it seemed easier to obtain translation rights for a single volume rather than for a compilation.

The plan to publish the translation emphasized the seriousness of the endeavor from the very beginning of the classes and created a shared commitment on the part of students and instructors alike that was very different from classes without a well-defined, and ultimately published, product. The plan for a bilingual edition not only reflected the positive experience with the Carter project but also resulted from the insight that, as Perloff put it, "[w]hat bilingual study does is precisely expose the gap between the original and the translation, a gap that testifies to the poet's subtlety and skill" (103). While we do not share Perloff's preferential treatment of the source text, we do agree with the opportunities bilingual studies – and editions – provide in making the translation process transparent.

The theoretical preparation for the students' own venture in translation was essentially provided by two texts, Lawrence

Venuti's *The Translator's Invisibility* (1995) and Peter France's "The Rhetoric of Translation" (2005), especially with a view to the concepts of *foreignizing* and *domestication*. For the majority of students, the June Jordan translation project was their first encounter with poetry translation and, moreover, with translating from English into German. Dortmund's curriculum for future English teachers includes translation classes from German into English with the major goal of improving students' grammar skills and rhetorical abilities. Since these classes not only have a different goal but also a very different focus – the materials for translation are usually not poetry but rather newspaper articles or excerpts from short stories – students needed to be familiarized with the field of literary translation.

As instructors we felt that the concepts used in the two introductory texts mentioned above would not only provide a highly useful yardstick allowing participants to evaluate their own work but would also help them understand the political nature of the undertaking. Whereas we continue to emphasize the dialogical and thus humanistic dimension of translation and the teaching of literature and poetry as a whole, we did want students to realize the "violent effects of translation […] felt at home as well as abroad" (Venuti 14). This insight into the political consequences of translation was complemented by an article by Peter France that compares the activities of translator and orator. He highlights the "mediation" (255) quality of translation, "negotiating between author and readers, between source culture and target culture (or cultures, since translations are not confined to a particular cultural moment)" (261).

Venuti distinguishes between "domesticating" and "foreignizing" translations. The former attempt to make the text palatable to the target audience by using familiar language, style and form; the latter emphasize its foreignness by making it appear "strange." In discussing the theoretical texts, students originally took a mildly domesticating position, hoping to be able to provide a German *equivalent* to the American original. When translating, however, faced with the question of alterity and cultural difference, they were eventually more inclined towards foreignization if only, to quote one student, "to make readers realize the strong demand this author makes on her readers to understand the enormity of her thinking."

Indeed, students became so interested in the concept of foreignization that they had to be reminded, in the words of Venuti, that the

> "foreign" in foreignizing translation is not a transparent representation of an essence that resides in the foreign text and is valuable in itself, but a strange construction whose value is contingent on the current situation in the receiving culture. Foreignizing translation signifies the differences of the foreign text, yet only by disrupting the cultural codes in the translating language. (15)

In other words, foreignization does not ensure "faithfulness" to the original text but, at best, reminds us of the enormous cultural difference between source and target culture.

Following the methodological/theoretical introduction in each of the three classes, groups of two or three students, ideally of mixed ethnic and national origins, possibly also with different second majors, were assigned a series of poems, usually approximately five pages. In two of the three classes, two different groups were assigned the same set of poems so as to allow a comparison of the translations and to receive a pool out of which an eventual final version could be drawn.

Essentially student groups were given three tasks. First, they had to provide a translation containing all significant variations that the members of the group could think of. Secondly, they had to come up with a 'clean' version of a translation of each poem, meaning they had to reach a conclusion in each case where they differed significantly through a process of disagreement, debate and eventually compromise. Finally, they had to present central difficulties (including critical points of discussion and disagreement) along with their translations and explain how they dealt with these difficulties and what they taught them about the text.

The first task was solved in very different ways. Some pairs/groups decided to work separately at first and then compare the results of their work. Some decided to subdivide the allotted poems and then look at each others' results. Others, however, worked together throughout and produced texts which were the result of vivid interaction and dialogue. Of course, the third approach was the most time-consuming but it also seemed to be the most rewarding as it generated solutions for translations derived from an interactive process rather than a "monological" reflection.

The second task, the attempt to provide a 'final' version, in a way seemed to go against the whole strategy of the project. Having turned translation into a process including multiple voices, ultimately norms or principles had to be found according to which one opted for one or the other (or the third) translation variant. In pedagogic strategy, we strongly agree with Jonathan Culler's experience in the Baudelaire classroom:

> Translations can also generate disagreement more easily than discussion about the poem itself. If these days students are less inclined to disagree with one another in class than they used to be, disagreeing about a translation seems to involve less of a challenge to the other person. (92)

This whole process of negotiation had to be made transparent in the third, and most complex, task of the process, namely the explanation of central problems of translation. Whereas the instructors' original idea was to elucidate the provisional "workshop" quality of any translation and to provide insight into the creative process of both poetry writing and poetry translation, the first seminar quickly made it very apparent that what was explained here was not just a series of translation preferences and arguments that led to one decision and not to another, but that the *reading of poetry itself* was at stake.

What we had at best surmised in the first class became quickly the central tasks of the other two and also the argument we are making in this paper, namely that translation, as a version of reception, is central to the interpretative process that needs to be a part of the teaching of any literature, and especially poetry:

> Attempting to put a poem into another language helps us to get inside literature; it forces us to consider meaning in a new way, producing an "interliminal" space of possible meanings: attempting a translation helps us discover what the source text might mean [...]. (Culler 95)

We found out in the first seminar – and then strategically used this insight in the subsequent ones – that the central difficulties students experienced in the course of translation actually turned out to be critical for the interpretation of poems. In this way, the tasks of translation, analysis and teaching converged.

In the beginning of this article, we have stressed that translation combines both 'normative' aspects (adequacy and correctness) and subjective decisions of the translator. In bringing together translation and textual interpretation, normativity and correctness, which are oftentimes considered to be the *sine qua non* in translation, represent guiding lights rather than prescriptive standards. In a textbook on teaching German literature for native speakers of German, Ulf Abraham and Matthis Kesper stress the usefulness, but also the dangers, of using translation in the teaching of literature:

> [Comparing translations with the original] is a method of teaching literature which has hardly been used so far although it is very well suited for interdisciplinary work [...]. It does not seem reasonable to leave such comparisons completely to the teaching of foreign languages where German language translations are often used in order to demonstrate their deficit and to promote the reading of the foreign language originals. We do not want to discredit this strategy. This method, however, is reminiscent of those literature pedagogues who attempt to promote the printed book by way of denigrating the movie – and this is no coincidence. In this case as well as the other, we are dealing with a question of adaptation which should only be evaluated in the context of the linguistic, aesthetic and, in the case of translation, also cultural characteristics. (245, our translation)

Using translation in teaching poetry – and thus, in one way or another, in the interpretation of poetry – means to understand the complexity of contexts and their interactions and not to use notions of correctness or superiority to criticize students' work. Rather, students – by creating an imaginative text of their own – are empowered vis-à-vis the authority of the author (or the lyrical voice), the overpowering foreign language of the text, and the seeming professional advantage of the instructor. Literary translation, then, facilitates an emancipatory teaching of literature. In fact, the intercultural hermeneutics – as the German pioneer of teaching foreign literature in an intercultural framework, Lothar Bredella, has taught us in so many of his excellent contributions – facilitates an understanding of literature: literary and intercultural understanding thus go hand in hand (cf. Bredella 13-25).

In the process of translating June Jordan's poetry, the students in some cases had to create or extend their information base; it provided an opportunity to discuss and often reassess the meaning of contemporary global political events from the standpoint of

American Studies. In dealing with June Jordan's lyrical responses to the bloody conflicts in the Middle East or the Balkans, students not only had the opportunity to understand the contemporaneousness and lingering effects of events that happened in the past. They also came to appreciate the literary – and particularly lyrical – expression of such experiences as trauma, death, and fear as well as love and trust, and their meaning for the translation experience as such. In the process of translating, the students frequently had to open up to each other and to each others' ideas in ways that are rather uncommon in the German university classroom. They not only had to speak about the text, but also about their own, very individual readings and renderings of each passage – or each word, even – making them on the one hand more vulnerable but on the other hand much more open-minded about encountering what they might originally have perceived as the Other.

Literary translation in multinational groups, with speakers of different languages, often with neither English nor German as mother tongue, is a manifestation of intercultural dialogue. Since it will not be apparent, in the final product, who has participated in the translation of a certain text or passage, the translation becomes a truly intercultural and shared undertaking in which students and instructors have to learn to rely on each other and trust each other in the face of cultural and linguistic differences, even barriers. In the case of June Jordan, the global, but rooted African American poet, it was a special opportunity for students and instructors alike to engage in this form of encounter with each other and her poems, to open them up for an audience that may neither be familiar with poetry nor with the creative forces of translation.

As becomes evident through the many choices for each word, line, and paragraph, the translation of Jordan's poetry is a creative act in itself: through the translation, a new poem is created by the translators, in this case the students. In one of the three classes involved in the translation project, a public presentation of the poetry in English and in German was included as an additional mode to relate to the poems. All classes also included in-class readings and recitals to help the students to understand the texts by recognizing their rhythms, the manifold voices, and the sound, but the public performance of the translation following the first class at the Dortmund American Studies Department was a unique student project in itself.

The student groups each performed one or two Jordan poems in English, in German, or even in bilingual versions. They chose or developed their own mode of performance: some of the poetry was rendered with (quiet) music in the background, some was accompanied by a photo slideshow, or there were drums playing. While June Jordan's poetry is very performative in itself and many of the poems lend themselves easily to reading aloud, a performance for other students as well as friends, the university community and even parents, was a special challenge for the students. The performance did not only have to convey the texts to an audience largely unfamiliar with the poet and much of the content of the poetry, but it also had to carry the voice of Jordan's writing, a voice that is definitely political and reaches far beyond the scope of an individual speaker. After the intensive study of the texts and the numerous debates about their rendering into German, the students managed not only to express the multitude of voices Jordan incorporates into her poetry but also to find a way to realize the specific mood of each individual poem that was read to a larger audience.

In the process of translation, special problems emerged in instances where the German language does not have an equivalent for an English word or phrase and where feelings or perceptions had to be circumscribed. Poems that make use of African American Vernacular English, a variety of American English for which there is no counterpart in German, were also challenging. Another kind of difficulty arose from formal restrictions as, for instance, when Jordan had used fixed poetic forms such as haiku. Moreover, sometimes ethical decisions had to be made in the translation process. Since Jordan addresses wars and massacres in her work – some of her poems can be read as attempts to make an aesthetic approximation of the unspeakable – instructors and participants had to debate and decide on the linguistic representation of dead bodies, or of the hungry and the defeated, which would enable the readers to grasp the mood while also giving dignity to the victims thus presented. Moreover, and as the title of the poetry collection *Kissing God Goodbye* already indicates, several of the poems have a religious undertone – and they are not in favor of Christianity or institutionalized religions as such. It was frequently hard to translate such texts, especially in cases where the students would personally strongly disagree with particular attitudes of the author.

In order to provide a better idea of the translation process itself and in order to point out some of the difficulties that emerged during the discussion of the texts and their translation into German, we will use two specific excerpts from Jordan's poetry to show how decisions that impact the reading of a poem were made in the classroom by means of a dialogic transaction among students and between students and instructors. We will on the one hand be focusing in detail on translation problems that emerge out of actual problems with the wording or with the multiplicity of meanings and possible translations for a word or phrase, and on the other hand on translation problems resulting from structural and grammatical differences between the original and the target language. There are certainly also some translation problems that result simply from lack of knowledge or background information, which can be confronted by extending one's insight into a subject or field. In the case of Jordan's poetry, the students were able, for example, to work better with a text such as "Argument with the Buddha" after familiarizing themselves with some of the ideas of Buddhism which play into the poem. These kinds of problems will be neglected at this point.

We will start with an example of a translation problem that clearly had to do with semantics: one line that posed significant difficulties for the students occurred in the poem "Ghaflah." It was not so much the concept of *ghaflah* itself that was hard to understand, because once the students had read up on the concept itself ("the sin of forgetfulness," Jordan, 1980, 25), they could relate the poem to it. Rather, it was the line "I acknowledge nothing" (25) that caused a lot of discussion, because its meaning – and therefore also its translation – strongly determines the reading of the mother-daughter relationship that is at the heart of the poem.

The word "acknowledge" can be rendered in many different words in the German language. It could, for example, be translated as "billigen" (to endorse), "zugeben" (more along the line of "to confess"), as "eingestehen" (to admit), "bekennen" (to profess), "anerkennen" (to recognize), "zustimmen" (to approve) and several others. While every interpretation has to emerge through a process of careful and intensive reading, in cases such as this one we found ourselves debating whether one specific term would *sound* better in the translated version as a whole or whether we should move away from the verbal construction altogether and translate "I acknowledge nothing" as "kein Eingeständnis" (literally "no confession" or "no admission"), or whether to convert the statement into a denial of responsibility which is implicit but not explicit in the original line: "Ich war's nicht" ("It wasn't me").

Here it becomes evident that literary translation is not only an act that gives much power to the translators, but that it requires very careful reading, analytical skills and an understanding of the meaning of sound and rhythm – for the poem in the original as well as in the translated version. Sometimes double meanings have to be compromised for greater clarity or to make a poem "readable" in a different culture. However, in this case we attempted to hold on to double meanings wherever possible – and thus decided to stick to the verbal construction by translating the line "I acknowledge nothing" as "Ich bekenne nichts" ("I admit/profess nothing").

As already indicated above, other specific problems we encountered in the EFL classroom were of a more grammatical nature. We will give a more detailed example here because we believe that this is a specific problem of translation work in the context of the EFL classroom that can be solved creatively. Sometimes the interpretation of a poem forced us to stick to rather unusual constructions in German. In the classroom, we had vivid discussions about the poem "Kissing God Goodbye." This poem is one of Jordan's strongest poems, but it also brings along specific challenges that had to be addressed in the process of translation. "Kissing God Goodbye" is largely textual patchwork; it includes verses from the Bible alongside critical comments on Christianity. It points out the cruelty of the Christian God and his supposed rejection of women and everything "female," and it argues that He is for these reasons a God the (female) voice rejects and who does not hold any power over her. It also contrasts passages from the Bible that appear to condemn homosexuality with biblical verses praising love between same-sex partners, and the name of a vengeful patriarchal God with the names of those "who love." The passage that provoked most discussion was actually not from the Bible, where the translators had the option to choose between many of the existing translations and their specific subtexts, connotations and statuses, but rather a passage that follows Jordan's naming of those "who love" and establishes a voice that opposes the male-dominated Bible:

> our names become
> the names of the iniquitous
> the names of the accursed
> the names of the tribes of the abomination
> because
> my name is not Abraham
> my name is not Moses/Leviticus/Solomon/Cain or Abel
> my name is not Matthew/Luke/Saul or Paul
> My name is not Adam
> My name is female
> my name is freedom
> my name is the one who lives outside the tent of the father
> my name is the one who is dark
> my name is the one who fights for the end of the kingdom
> my name is the one at home
> my name is the one who bleeds
> my name is the one with the womb
> my name is female
> my name is freedom
> my name is the one the bible despised
> my name is the one astrology cannot predict
> my name is the name the law cannot invalidate
> my name is the one who loves
>
> and that guy
> and that guy
> you never even seen upclose (98)

There are several possibilities to translate this passage into German that come fairly close to the original text, but in fact, the translation that would be the most exact requires speakers of German to use a rather unusual grammatical construction which is nevertheless possible and on which we decided after some debate.

In the part of the section that identifies what the speaker is *not*, the German language can work with a common negation, as the original text does as well. However, as soon as we get to the affirmative part, the ways the speaker describes herself, the translation – almost unexpectedly – becomes complicated. Statements such as "My name is female" or "my name is freedom" can be translated word-for-word, but the specifications starting with "my name is the one who" are rather complicated to translate into German.

"My name is the one who lives outside the tent of the father" could be translated as "Die meinen Namen trägt, wohnt außerhalb des Zeltes des Vaters" (literally "The one who bears my name lives outside the tent of the father"). This would render the statement in unblemished German syntactically; however, it is not as effective stylistically, especially when reading it out loud, and it also interrupts the anaphoric structure ("my name"). It would cause a break in the enumeration and would thus not be a good fit. The line could also be translated as "mein Name ist die(jenige), die außerhalb des Zeltes des Vaters wohnt" (literally "my name is the one who lives outside the tent of the father"), which, even if it corresponds to the original text, as a statement sounds rather odd and convoluted to a speaker of German. It is difficult – even silently – to read because of its length as well as because of its sound structure. The third possible construction, the one which we eventually decided on, is "Mein Name ist die außerhalb des Zeltes des Vaters wohnt" (literally "My name is: she who lives outside the tent of the father").

As this example shows, in order to reach the goal of the translation, unusual patterns are sometimes preferable. As the variety of possibilities also shows, there is always more than one way to state something, but in some cases one version works better than another. Many different aspects have to be taken into account when deciding on a final version. The translation not only has to be understandable to a native speaker of German who is not familiar with Jordan's work, it also has to sound good and each line on its own has to fit the surrounding lines, i.e. the poem's translation as a whole.

One factor that greatly contributed to the success of the translation project, which is to be published in a bilingual edition in 2012, is the fact that Jordan's work was interpreted, discussed and translated by a group of people who were very diverse in themselves. This – the multilingualism of the students and their very different backgrounds – was not only a constructive challenge for the group and for the instructors, but a benefit to the outcome of the project as a whole. It gave rise to more voices, and a greater variety of voices; and it thus provided a nice analogy to the original poetry. Moreover, the multiplicity of backgrounds helped the translation in that it was often the students who were non-native speakers of German who came up with more unusual ideas for expressing or stating something – there seemed to be less hesitancy to get creative with the usage of the German language.

Our argument for translation in teaching literature and the various ways of organizing this work collectively belong together. This does not mean that we always have to have the type of "people's translations" projects inspired by June Jordan's "people's poetry". Translation can also serve very well as a purely cognitive strategy for dealing with literary texts. However, as Sandra Berman emphasizes, also reacting to the institutional crises in the humanities (no longer confined to the United States):

> On the macro level of institutional planning, translation can elicit very practical efforts of collaboration – bringing the dialogue intrinsic to the language of translation to an interpersonal, interinstitutional, and at times international level. Increasingly, collaboration affects our teaching. Using translations to reach different cultures and disciplines in our courses, we collaborate with colleagues, and often with students, of different linguistic and cultural expertise. (86)

We believe that we have shown that this macro design works very well on the level of the individual classroom. By sharing and discussing translations of the same text, by promoting dialogue between students with different backgrounds (different traditions in language and culture being of course only one dimension), we are highlighting translation as an interactive, dialogical process – which nevertheless yields significant and personally exhilarating results. It is the intercultural classroom as its best because it deals with and reflects the linguistic and cultural material of this dialogue. And, following June Jordan's political impetus, it provides students with an awareness of the necessity of action in understanding the collective struggles ahead – also, and especially, in the realms of literature and culture.

Bibliography

Abraham, Ulf and Matthis Kasper. *Literaturdidaktik Deutsch. Eine Einführung*, third revised and expanded edition, Berlin: Schmidt, 2009.
Allen, Gay Wilson and Ed Folsom. *Walt Whitman and the World*. Iowa City: University of Iowa Press, 1995.
Apter, Emily. *The Translation Zone: A New Comparative Literature*. Princeton: Princeton University Press, 2006.

Bermann, Sandra. "Teaching in—and about—Translation," *Profession* (2010): 82-90.

Bredella, Lothar. *Literarisches und interkulturelles Verstehen.* Tübingen: Narr, 2002.

Carter, Jimmy. *Angesichts der Leere. Gedichte Englisch/Deutsch.* Trans. Walter Grünzweig and Wolfgang Niehues. Bonn: Weidle, 2005.

Culler, Jonathan. "Teaching Beaudelaire, Teaching Translation." *Profession* (2010): 91-98.

France, Peter. "The Rhetoric of Translation." *The Modern Language Review* 100 (2005): 255-268.

Jordan, June. "For the Sake of a People's Poetry: Walt Whitman and the Rest of Us." *Lyrical Campaigns: Selected Poems,* London: Virago, 1980. 69-79. [1979].

---. *Kissing God Goodbye: Poems 1991-1997.* New York: Anchor Books, 1997.

Perlman, Jim. Ed Folsom and Dan Campion. *Walt Whitman: The Measure of His Song.* Minneapolis: Holy Cow! Press, 1981.

Perloff, Marjorie. "Teaching Poetry in Translation: The Case for Bilingualism." *Profession* (2010): 99-106.

Venuti, Lawrence. *The Translator's Invisibility: A History of Translation.* London and New York: Routledge, 1995.

Kornelia Freitag (Bochum)

Contemporary Indian-American Poetry: At the Crossroads of Cultures

The U.S.A. has always been a country of immigrants. As President Barack Obama put it in his inaugural address in 2008, the nation itself was "carried [...] up the long, rugged path to prosperity and freedom" by people who "packed up their few worldly possessions and traveled across oceans in search of a new life" (1). Various metaphors have been used to characterize the resulting make-up of a country consisting of immigrants. The melting pot, the salad bowl, and the pizza are meant to symbolize the (changing) ways in which ever new, ethnically and nationally vastly different immigrants have merged, mixed, and connected with earlier immigrants to become "the people" of the United States.

A problem with all these metaphors is that they take the U.S. to be a very neatly circumscribed spot in the world, and its more or less integrated citizens to be safely contained, just like iron ore in a crucible, salad in a bowl, or pizza topping within a ring of crust. Let us hold this image against the vision of the United States that Reetika Vazirani (1962-2003) conjures up in her poem "It's a Young Country" (116-117). The poet was born in India, yet came with her parents as a preschooler to the U.S. and resided there until her death.

> It's a Young Country
>
> and we cannot bear to grow old
> ...
> We say *America you are*
> *magnificent*   and we mean
> we are heartbroken
> ... (116)

Vazirani captures the fast pace and the contradictory dynamics of the "young" United States in short unpunctuated lines, rampant enjambment, and unexpected caesuras within verses. She does not even allow one to take a breath after the title, which turns into the first clause of the poem. The contradiction between the American dream ("*America you are / magnificent*") and the reality ("we are heartbroken") is condensed into three lines.

While this may not really be new, the next stanza introduces a reality that looks at what happens in the U.S. from the point of view of immigrants who came from outside the United States: "We leave for a better job / cross the frontier   wish you / were here in this hotel   Two of us one" (116). Thereby the "we" of the poem – which initially wavered between an official "We, the people" from the U.S. Constitution (declaring "*America you are / magnificent*") and a private, "heartbroken" "we" – is transformed into an immigrant "we" from another country, who "cross[ed] the frontier." "Two of us one" might thus be an immigrant's sigh thinking of a loved one at home, but it plays also on the motto that has graced the seal of the United States since 1776: "Out of many, one." "*E pluribus unum*" referred originally to the original thirteen colonies, yet has since then changed its meaning to address also and in particular the ways in which different immigrants become one people.

The last stanza continues to confront and blend private and public discourses on the American nation. It starts: "We grow old   look at this // country its worn dungarees" (117). The reference to the aging of individuals ("We grow old") turns into a statement on America's coming of age, which contradicts the initial declaration of national youth. Finally, after reciting and immediately curtailing the famous preamble of the Constitution – "We the People of the United States, in Order to form a more perfect Union" – the poem rushes to its end:

> in order to form a more perfect
> some step forward some step back
> …
> through orange portals lit tunnels
> over bridges Brooklyn Golden Gate
> …
> pack lightly we move so fast (116)

While these lines indicate that migrants are participating in shaping the country and "perfect[ing]" it, the poem stops short of suggesting that what is perfected was a "Union," not to mention any such clearly circumscribed things as melting pots, salad bowls, or pizzas. What the admonition to "pack lightly we move so fast" and the metaphors of underground and surface crossings in the East and the West ("portals," "tunnels," "bridges;" "Brooklyn," "Golden Gate") suggest, is not at all that the migrant, or America, is about to reach a final destination or form but rather that s/he keeps moving and changing: "some step forward, some step back."

This is a vision of the United States that takes into account that it is not only a destination but a crossroads of migration, or as Shelley Fisher Fishkin puts it:

> The United States is and has always been a transnational crossroads of cultures. And that crossroads of cultures that we refer to as "American culture" has itself generated a host of other crossroads of cultures as it has crossed borders. (43)

At first, this insight might strike one as almost trivial – of course we know that we live in an age of globalization. Yet this is not how we normally conceptualize – and teach – English, or the history, geography, and literature of the regions in which it is spoken. Against all evidence, there the national approach still reigns. Yet when we talk, as in this article, about contemporary American poetry we should begin

> to focus less on the United States as a static and stable territory and population whose most characteristic traits it [is] our job to divine, and more on the nation as a participant in a global flow of people, ideas, texts, and products – albeit a participant who often tries to impede those flows. (Fisher Fishkin 24)

The role of the United States as one powerful node in a wide transnational network and its specific function as a "crossroads of cultures" is evident in texts as canonical and arch-American as Herman Melville's *Moby Dick* (with its international crew and harpooneers) or Walt Whitman's *Leaves of Grass* (inspired, among other sources, by Indian epics such as the *Ramayana* and *Mahabharata*). Yet while in many texts transnational connections are deeply buried and sometimes marred by exoticism or xenophobia, literature by Indian-American writers commonly explicitly invites the new perspective:

> these texts at their best move the reader to consider why understanding the interconnectedness among nations and peoples matters, and how such understanding can be transported from the realm of literature into the material realm of politics and civic behavior. (Srikanth 3)

Hence, the transnational dynamics of "It's a Young Country" are not an exception but exemplify the tendency of Indian-American writing to "challenge rigid constructions of citizenship and overly narrow perspectives of location" (Srikanth 3). In this article I will show the ways in which a number of Indian-American poets challenge nationally circumscribed perspectives in their poems and demonstrate the great variety of poetic techniques of "transnationalizing" citizenship and location (for overviews on Indian, including Indian-American writing see King *Modern* and Biswas; a good anthology of the field is Banerjee et al.).

As there are historical and cultural reasons for the strong cross-cultural sensitivity of members of the Indian diaspora in America, I will start by sketching some of the facts that explain the current economic and cultural accomplishment of immigrants of Indian descent. The first wave of Indian immigrants to the United States dates back to the beginning of the twentieth century. It consisted mostly of Punjabi farmers and laborers, who left no literary traces in English, and it was stopped abruptly by a ban on Asian immigration in 1917. The second wave of immigrants from the Indian subcontinent to the Unites States followed the lifting of this ban in 1965. They were often well trained, highly educated, and had a middle- or upper-class background. "[T]he economic status of these immigrants remains the highest in the United States" (R. Sharma 19; cf. also Ong, Cheng, and Evans; Xie and Goyette). They are, moreover, on account of India's colonial heritage, not only well versed in British and other Western literature but also speak and write 'the King's English' to perfection. These immigrants to the United States face no linguistic barrier to U.S. culture, and Indian-American writers are also part of a community of Indians writing in English who live in India, Great Britain, Canada, and other, mainly metropolitan centers of the world. The increasing convenience of air travel, new means of communication and entertainment, and the global literary market allow the U.S. based person and writer of Indian descent an increasingly cosmopolitan life without losing touch with his or her country of birth. The career of Nobel Prize winner Salman Rushdie is the most famous case in point. This means neither that all Indian immigrants are well-to-do nor that any of them are exempt from racism or the difficulties of migration. In fact, the worries of migration and the hardships of having to grapple with two very different cultures characterize the poems of the first generation of Indian-American writers, like Chitra Banerjee Divakaruni, A. K. Ramanujan, Agha Shahid Ali, and Meena Alexander. All of them negotiate home, exile, and diaspora in poems that are often autobiographical and use first-person speakers.

Chitra Banerjee Divakaruni (b. 1957), an Indian-born poet and successful fiction writer, devotes a number of highly narrative poems to the poor Indian immigrants who settled at the beginning of the twentieth century in rural California and – without the benefit of a high caste British education or knowledge of the English language – shared the plight of other Asians in America at the time. "Yuba City School" (104-106), for instance, is written in the anguished voice of a mother who readies herself to see her son's teacher, knowing full well that her tongue will be "a stiff embarrassment in [her] mouth" with the "few / English phrases" that she can muster, and hence her "son will keep sitting / in the last row / among the red words that drink his voice" (lines 56-61). Divakaruni's "Indian Movies: New Jersey" (113-114), on the other hand, captures the mood of a modern-day, globally connected immigrant community whose affluent members are enjoying the idyllic world of a Bollywood movie, where "the flickering movie-light / wipes from our faces years of America, sons / who want mohawks and refuse to run / the family store, daughters who date on the sly" (113). Globalized entertainment, in which India has become a main player, grants Indians worldwide a connection to their homeland, if only a fake and superficial one, as the irony of the quoted lines suggests. And yet, the end of the poem reverses too harsh judgements of the well-to-do immigrants' obvious escapism. The fake Indian movie world is shown to offer relief from the constant threat of racist atrocities (police terror and race-related violence), and it turns out to be just a slight variant of the American

Dream: "we can trust / in movie truth: sacrifice, success, love and luck, / the America that was supposed to be" (114).

The first-generation Indian-American poet is, of course, neither as helpless as the Yuba mother nor as superficial as the New Jersey movie goers. As Divakaruni's poems show, the poet works often as an observer of and reporter on both cultures – acutely aware of the shortcomings and advantages of each as s/he straddles both. A. K. Ramanujan (1929-1993), who moved to the United States at the age of 31 and became one of the most sophisticated Indian-American poets, refers to himself "as the hyphen in Indian-American" (King, "To Be" 144). In this way Ramanujan positions himself as negotiating both cultures while being at home in neither. His writings reflect (upon) the general impossibility of a 'pure,' 'authentic' culture. He observes, "[n]o culture we know is innocent of 'encounter' with another" ("Parables" 138).

This insight finds its poetic expression in the striking and witty transnational moments of poems like "Chicago Zen" from *Second Sight* (83-85), where the speaker relates his momentary transport from a Chicago city street to a Himalayan visionary scene:

> Watch your step. Sight may strike you
> blind in unexpected places.
>
> The traffic light turns orange
> on 57th and Dorchester, and you stumble,
>
> you fall into a vision of forest fires,
> enter a frothing Himalayan river (83)

This transnational transcendence, or rather "cultural encounter" (Ramanujan, "Parables" 142), is carefully set off from the misleading superficial connectivity effected by modern means of transportation and migration:

> the country cannot be reached
>
> by jet. Nor by boat on a jungle river
> ...
>
>   Nor by any
> other means of transport,
>
> migrating with a clean, valid passport (83-84)

Meaningful transnational cultural encounters, the poem suggests, do not result from simply 'going there.' An approximation has to be reached by blending both cultures, as is done here not just by rendering the epiphany of the Himalayan river in the middle of Chicago traffic, but by fusing in it modernist poetic technique with Sanskrit poetics. That the 'passage to India' occurs at the moment of crossing a street is no coincidence but part of Ramanujan's carefully prepared poetics "at the crossroads of cultures."

Agha Shahid Ali (1949-2001), who immigrated to the United States in the 1980s, was acutely aware "that multiculturalism, change, exile, difference, loss and nostalgia are common to the human condition" (King, *Modern* 258) and his lyrical texts consciously reach out over borders, connecting continents, histories, traditions, and fates. The powerful poem "Eurydice" (107-109), which opens and sets the tone for his *Nostalgist's Map of America* (1991), is a monologue spoken by a character from Greek mythology and is set in Bergen-Belsen. Through the haunting perspective of a victim, Ali thematizes the vexing situation of the artist as reporter but also helpless witness of life and history. The title figure, "a woman / brought limping to Hell" (a concentration camp inmate), relates how "he who ... / could dissolve bombs" (Orpheus/the artist) has entered the camp and she now hopes for freedom. "But a guard hands him papers, [...] he is pushed into the van. / His gaze runs through my tears" (108), and she dies. She is killed not only, the mythical undertones suggest, by "mustard twilight" (gas) but also by Orpheus's gaze, which here comes to symbolize the poet's inability to change history, rescue the victim, and prevent death. Speculations about the potentials and limits of poetry and the poet characterize Ali's intensely lyrical and nostalgic poetry, which is instantly gripping and deeply speculative, and in his many meta-textual moves even distancing, all at the same time.

Other poems are written in a lighter tone, in an autobiographical and highly self-reflexive mode. "When on Route 80 in Ohio / I came across an exit / to Calcutta," a poem in the series "In Search for Evanescence" (121-136) begins,

> the temptation to write a poem
> led me past the exit
> so I could say

> India always exists
> off the turnpikes
> of America (123)

Through the following nine stanzas, imaginary encounters with daily Indian life are related: crossing from "Howrah," the twin city of Calcutta, over "the Ganges," meeting overcrowded "trains," hungry "children," "vendors [...] bargaining," feeling the "monsoon." After a colon, the only punctuation mark in the whole poem, the regular three-line stanzas change to four final couplets. Each of them merges and transforms the two heretofore separately rendered realities of the exit to small-town American Calcutta on Route 80 and the Indian megalopolis Calcutta – in a quasi-imagist move – into a vivid image of loss that carries a variety of regional, trans/national, and personal connotations:

> The warm rains have left
> many dead on the pavements
>
> The signs on Route 80
> have all disappeared
>
> And now the road is a river
> polished silver by cars
>
> The cars are urns
> carrying ashes to the sea (124-125)

Only these concluding lines hint at the fact that the poem, like the whole series, commemorates the death of a close friend of Ali's.

The series was inspired by the nineteenth century poet Emily Dickinson's riddle poem about a hummingbird: "A Route of Evanescence / With a delusive wheel / [...] / The Mail from Tunis – probably – / An easy morning's ride" (Number 1489, 1305). Dickinson, "the very poet of loss" (Oates 806), finds cheerful and mundane poetic metaphors of "evanescence" in her occasional text. Ali, who "traces a journey of loss" (Katrak 203) in his own right, appropriates Dickinson's "Route of Evanescence" to tease out at least three "routes," or "crossroads": first, between ordinary life and its transience (in an update of Dickinson's idea); second, between the U.S. and India (in an acquisition of Dickinson's vision of

Tunis); third, between his own poetic endeavors and the U.S. poetic tradition (into which he squarely inscribes himself).

Meena Alexander (b. 1951) writes also about exile. Born in India, she was raised there and in Sudan, earned her Ph.D. in England, and came to the United States at the age of 28. She explores in her texts exile and diaspora without much nostalgia, as daily lived and embodied experience that necessitates constant cultural interaction and solidarity. She writes that "the old notions of exile [...] are gone; smashed underfoot in the transit lounges, the supermarkets, the video parlors of the world. [...] No homeland here." Yet she balances this blunt negation of the big obsession of exiles with the loss of their homeland with the insight that

> over and over you fabricate a homeland, a sheltering space in the head. You can never escape into the ceaseless present that surrounds you. What you need, in Frank O'Hara's words, is "Grace / to be borne and live as variously as possible." (*Poetics* 193)

Hence, her poems stay clear of nostalgia but engage with emotional intensity and an acute attention to "variousness" (cf. O'Hara) with the places, spaces, languages, nations, and people she grew up with, keeps coming back to, and encounters anew.

A poem published after her move to the United States is aptly named "Relocation" (*River and Bridge* 3). The surreal and strongly meta-poetical text starts with the announcement of a rethinking of old and routine ways of "composition" (which might refer to her own strategies of composing, to poetic traditions, or to more general ways of understanding and outlining the world):

> Scraping it all back:
>
> A species of composition
> Routine as crossing streets
> Or taking out the garbage

After continuing to characterize the described compositional technique as one that charts ordinary local life ("Broadway thicken[ing] with bicycles," "magnolias lift[ing] petals / from abandoned traffic islands"), the two last stanzas turn to and rewrite William Carlos Williams's famous "Spring and All" (183). In his poem, Williams writes about the beauty and importance of ordinary

183

American life, nature, and people. For him, a practicing pediatrician, this also includes the life of the body and its pains. His poem starts with the line "By the Road to the Contagious Hospital," and tells about "the stark dignity of / entrance," which refers to new life in spring and to new-born life at birth. In Alexander's rereading it comes also to include new immigrants. Her last but one stanza begins "The road to the hospital / is contagious already," for nowadays even on the backroads of America, the reverberations of migration, of "the questions of / travel scored by icy borders," have become palpable. Thereby the immigrant from India carefully relocates texts and ideas of an American poet, whose focus on the ordinary and embodied she treasures and whose local perspective she widens for her global concerns.

Alexander's poem "Art of Pariahs" (*River* 35) is written more in the tradition of feminist U.S. poet Adrienne Rich. It is freely associative and inspired by Alexander's familiarity with Indian and Sudanese culture. The speaker introduces Draupadi (a central female figure from the *Mahabharata*), the Rani of Jhansi (a nineteenth century Indian queen who fought against British colonial rule), and the Queen of Nubia (a legendary queen from what is now Sudan and Egypt) who "have entered with me / into North America and share these walls." She declares that with them she will "make up an art of pariahs." A stanza in the middle of the poem reports crimes against children in New York at the time of writing and, in the face of the atrocities, the speaker calls on the legendary and historic heroines to join in the creation of an intercultural and transnational alliance that is envisioned at the end of the poem: "Outcasts all let's conjure honey scraped from stones, / an underground railroad stacked with rainbow skin, / Manhattan's mixed rivers rising." These lines connect, recontextualize, and mix metaphors and hi/stories in order to create a vision of boundary crossing and humanitarianism. The biblical metaphor of "honey from the rocks" (Psalms 81:16) is envisioned as the result of joined endeavors that "scraped [honey] from stones" and it becomes the symbol of interconnectedness. The last but one line links the poem to African American history by referring to the secret supportive system for runaway slaves, the "underground railroad," yet Alexander's phrase "rainbow skin" indicates that she refers to a common project of people of all skin colors. The emphasis on the broad alliance of "outcasts" is continued with the concluding image of

"Manhattan's mixed rivers rising." The supportive community of people that Alexander conjures up in her symbolic river unites the participants in cultural solidarity against racist exclusion and violence. The symbol she finds for this community is, of course, not one of stability (pot, bowl, or dish) but one of powerful movement and multiplicity – "mixed rivers rising."

While for Alexander exile and diaspora carry less nostalgic meanings than for Ali and stronger internationalist responsibilities than for Ramanujan, they are still the linchpin of her writing and being. This is not necessarily so for many younger Indian-American writers, who seem to live less troubled and more self-confidently "between" cultures. In the words of poet Jeet Thayil, they feel to be "post-diaspora," "absolument moderne,"

> citizens not of geographical place as much as citizens of time; [...] writers who live simultaneously in so many literary and geographical continents as to be beyond nationalism, beyond narrowness, and beyond diaspora. ("Divided" 127)

This artistic position is expressed, for instance, in the opening poem of *English* (2003). "About the Author" is a mock biography of Thayil, who was born in India, educated in Hong Kong, New York, and Bombay, and lived at the time of writing in New York:

> Born in a hamlet near the southern Him-
> alajas, the author's youth was spent in,
> and under, the twin shadows of madness
> and avalanche. (3)

Also Shailja Patel, poet, playwright, and theater artist of South Asian-Kenyan descent, who lives in Nairobi and the San Francisco Bay Area, seems not to be overly troubled by exile and diasporic existence. Her webpage shows the Indian proverb "The night is short and our garments change," which she explains to mean "don't put down roots, don't get too comfortable."

Yet her autobiographical, two-part performance piece "Shilling Love" (note the play on "chilling") strikingly illuminates the less affluent and thereby nationally very much grounded underside of Thayil's or Patel's cosmopolitan life. Set against the recital of the steadily dropping Kenyan shilling against the British pound from 1975 to 2000 (the formal device reminiscent of Theodor Fontane's dramatic countdown of miles to Buffalo), the speaker tells of the iron determination and self-denial of her family to enable her and her sister to move up socially, and eventually out of Kenya: the mother "hurls" the daughters "like cannonballs / into the all-white classrooms" of the best school in Nairobi, the father "relinquished [his own] dreams" to make enough money as a mechanic, and the daughters themselves have to be "twice as good three times as fast four times as driven" as any of their peers (121-122). Nobody is easily crossing continents or lingering in movie theaters here. If your father is a blue collar worker, better to keep your emotions in check: The parents "never said / they loved us // ... // *I love you honey* was the dribbled caramel / of Hollywood movies / Dallas / ... / where emotions had no consequences" (120). Patel highlights the class-barriers to and within migration, which are too often hidden in today's talks, texts, and images of cosmopolitanism.

Yet for many second generation Indian-American writers, exile and diaspora are no longer the main concerns. While they feel that writers like Ali or Alexander "gave [them] a platform to push issues that felt personal and political," in the words of American-born Prageeta Sharma,

> the problem is that the publishing world and writing workshops have a tendency to encourage that voice [that is explicitly personal and political – KF] and a conflict arises for the writer about authenticity. They were pioneers; we, however, may need to look around us to see what our poems are really about. ("Not Your Mother's Diaspora" 28)

The effort to find different forms to express their own concerns does not necessarily mean to give up India in writing, but for them India and its culture is just one reference point next to America and a whole variety of Western and Eastern poetic traditions. India is found in books, made out of words, and is worked into all kinds of poems, like Sharma's own, highly playful and experimental texts. In the poetry series "Finite Sheets" in her collection *The Opening Question*, she reworks different stories about origins from Hindu mythology and English colonial and newer Indian literature (for instance, the origins of Ramakrishna, the elephant's trunk, and a fictional character created by Salman Rushdie) into quirky speculations on life, thought, literature, and the meaning of nation from an Indian-American woman's perspective.

As she puts it in "Questions" (51), the introductory poem: "Into the creation, the bittersweet negation, I begin / an epistolary of sorts, the sweets of milk on my tongue." Her questions are: "How do you stay alive? How do you move to its rhythm? How can you / press down?" The first statement immediately indicates Sharma's dialectical approach, in which "creation" is always paired with "negation" and the philosophical with the mundane ("the creation" with "milk on [her] tongue"). This worldliness, together with the funny set of questions that follow the statement, highlights her texts' thoroughly postmodernist qualities. In the words of Charles Altieri (quoted by David Huntsperger in his contribution to this volume), Sharma's poetry is "ope[n] to worldly contingency" and privileges "those features of textuality that distribute the compositional forces into processes of weaving and unweaving meanings" (794). It is textuality, not logic, that leads from her first question ("How do you stay alive?") to the second ("How do you move to its rhythm?"), and on to the third. The latter question always negates the former linguistically: not to "stay alive" but "move to its [i.e. the life's] rhythm;" not to "move to its rhythm" but to "press down."

In "Finite Sheets," her postmodern poetic "weaving and unweaving meanings" (Altieri) serve a complex postcolonial trajectory that is played out, for instance, in her acquisition and transformation of Rudyard Kipling's children's parable of the much spanked Elephant's Child, who wanted (and finally won himself) a trunk (67-86). In the four parts of Sharma's "Just-So Poem," Kipling's story becomes a postcolonial parable with the Elephant's Child (roughly) in the role of India. The poetic 'mini-series' highlights unacceptable colonial self-deprecation by the Elephant Child's parents, who declare to be "a child" "[t]he merriest epoch" (54). It also shows imperialist and imperial attitudes towards a former colony by "the crocodile," who asks, "Will I catch another elephant child?" (55) and "THE EMPIRE," who complains in a three-line rant "I owned the Limpopo river, the woods," and so on (56). This is balanced by the sober account of the dis(re)putable behaviour and "stormy firelike passions" (56) of the Elephant's Child – independent India itself.

The series' final poem, "The Fantasist's Speech on the Fifteenth of August" (i.e. on India's Independence Day) is dedicated to Salman Rushdie, whose novel *Midnight's Children* (1981) ascribes special powers to the children born at midnight on 15 August 1947.

Thereby Sharma inscribes herself into the tradition of imaginative deconstructions of the implications of "Mother" India's independence. Words and phrases that in the light of the first part of the poem refer to the Indian nuclear *arms* program and the *pulling down* of the Babri Mosque in 1992 by Hindutva fanatics (which kindled riots throughout the country, leaving more than 2000 people dead) are taken up and "woven and unwoven" in the closing lines of the poem: "when the *arms* become fantastic sources / when we *pull down* books, […]. / The wonders become, / the mother surprised, // the independence eminent" (60, emphasis added). Sharma closes by remarking that "there are now children's poems about independence" – which is not free from cautionary undertones, if one thinks of the Elephant's Child's irresponsible antics.

Chicago-born poet Srikanth Reddy struggled, like Sharma, with

> the traps of identity politics, and the limitations placed on young writers by a reading public (and publishing industry) that rewards hackneyed, familiar approaches to the problem of postcolonial or otherwise marginalized forms of identity. ("Centre of Margin")

When he "ultimately […] found it impossible and disabling to avoid" the subject of his "Asian-American cultural background," he approached it "obliquely" ("Centre of Margin"). Like Sharma, he stayed away from speaking in a confessional personal voice, commenting on American-Indian culture, or enlisting the Indian literary traditions as direct models. Yet unlike Sharma and in the tradition of internationally aware language writers (like Lyn Hejinian), and modernist and postmodernist poets who use collage (such as T.S. Eliot and Rosmarie Waldrop), he developed his own kind of postmodern textuality. His thoroughly transnational poetic speculations, variations, and narratives engage with, rearrange, and update texts from American and world literature (from Henry David Thoreau as much as from Rudyard Kipling or Plato) to express a vision of life in the world.

Hence, Reddy's poem "Junglebook" (25) neither refers to a specific story by Kipling nor is a parable, while the title still suggests a setting (Kipling's Indian jungle), a generic frame (didactic tales about the law of the jungle), and a cast of characters (Mowgli the "man-cub" and his animal friends). The expectations created by these suggestions are at once met and disappointed:

> Once we scavenged in the jungle I asked my friend
> about sadness. "How will I know when it comes?"
> He was up on his haunches, pulling a leafy branch
>
> I couldn't reach. "First learn about jackfruit," he said

While the poem works as an animal tale, and while the speaker, like Mowgli, wants to be educated, the question about sadness and the further development of the 'plot' suggest as a second intertext Plato's dialogue between Socrates and Phaedrus, who, during a walk in the countryside, discuss, among other things, love, madness (note the rhyme on Reddy's "sadness"), and rhetoric.

Rhetoric's work is termed "sow[ing] . . . seeds" by Plato's Socrates and the unregulated dissemination of thoughts is one of his main concerns (107). In the *Phaedrus* much room is given to the elaboration on right and beneficial, as opposed to wrong and detrimental ways of using language in order to spread ideas. When Reddy's speaker "split[s] open a seed" he sees "a very small tree / folded up inside" that "sprang to life / & put out hundreds of jackfruit blossoms" which flew away when he "started to *speak*" (emphasis added). The last word in the poem underlines its underlying linguistic argument. Just as Derrida argued in *Dissemination*, his deconstruction of Plato's *Phaedrus*, language cannot be contained. Hence, Reddy's speaker is not able to prevent the scattering of seeds but can only look after the dispersion of what he holds in his hands. On a further level, the parable-like dialogue on the scattering of seeds proves also to be a metatextual comment on Reddy's ways of "reaping the fruits of other writers' literary seeds" by "weaving and unweaving meanings" (Altieri 794) into his texts.

All the poems of *Facts for Visitors* show Reddy's acute awareness of the necessity of positioning himself and his readers not just in America today but in the larger world and its history. 'Indian' topics are not separate but part of this project. So, still on another level, his "Junglebook" is a pun on the Indian diaspora – the word in Greek literally meaning "the scattering (of seeds)." Reddy self-confidently insists on his position as a North American writer while at the same time claiming his right to write about the world with a special relation to India:

> I'd like to be free to write about the world rather than restricted to any particular part of it, and if India enters into that exploration then I'd hope that I would be able to acknowledge the fact that I'm as much a visitor there as I would be in Europe or South America or China or Africa, albeit a visitor with a strange sort of connection to the place. ("Centre of Margin")

Both his insistence on being a U.S. American poet and his interest in more than the immediate concerns of the U.S.A. make Reddy a typical representative of the ways in which the transnational approach of the first generation of Indian-American writers is taken up and continued in the second generation. While their strategies vary from first person, autobiographical, and identity-focussed (Thayil, Patel) to postmodern, collage-based, and strongly meta-textual (Sharma, Reddy), they are united by writing decidedly American poetry that simultaneously "challenges rigid constructions of citizenship and overly narrow perspectives of location" (Srikanth 3) and shows the U.S.A. as a "crossroads" of poetic discourses and ideas from all over the world.

American-born Ravi Chandra's "Cleanup on Aisle # 3" (137-39) may serve to take us back to the beginning of this article and to national food metaphors. Unlike the previously discussed authors, this slam poet seems not to reach out across U.S. national borders to other nations and their cultures. In fact, his poem stays stuck in the aisles of a supermarket and is thereby located in the heart of U.S. culinary consumer culture. Yet even in this straightforward oral performance piece, the point is a definite diversification of the way in which ethnicity figures in the American nation. Chandra starts with the question, "Why is it that every kind of person out there / has their counterpart in food?" (137), and he tries to find out what he might be in these terms.

> ... I'm a Scrambled Egg Burrito
> in a Tomato Tortilla
> with Black Beans, Basmati Rice, Guacamole, and Sriracha,
> garnished with sweet Papaya Chutney
> with a side of Bitter Melon. (138)

While the poem never leaves the "Safeway aisles" (138) – that is the interior of an American grocery chain store – transnational connections abound in the plentiful, ethnically and culinary diverse

American-Mexican-Thai-Indian food references. If this underlines the speaker-poet's uniqueness, it also emphasizes his un-assimilability into melting pots, pizzas, or salad bowls. In the end of his poem he cleverly plays upon a well-worn slogan from the Florida Orange Juice Growers Association that advertises their product as "not just for breakfast anymore." In Chandra's re-coding, the advertisement becomes an expression of his argument for accepting the United States as "a participant in a global flow of people ... and products" (Fisher Fishkin 24). He insists on being part of this crossing of many different (culinary) cultures:

>   ... I'm
>   on
>   your
>   plate.
>
> Your eyes have never seen a dish like me before,
> and I'm not just for breakfast,
> anymore. (139)

Bibliography

Alexander, Meena. *Poetics of Dislocation*. Ann Arbor: University of Michigan Press, 2009.

---. *River and Bridge*. Delhi: Rupa, 1995.

Ali, Agha Shahid. *The Veiled Suite: The Collected Poems*. New York, NY: Norton, 2009.

Altieri, Charles. "Modernism and Postmodernism." *The New Princeton Encyclopedia of Poetry and Poetics*. Ed. Alex Preminger and T.V.F. Brogan. Princeton, NJ: Princeton University Press, 1993. 792-796.

Banerjee, Neelanjana, Summi Kaipa, and Pireni Sundaralingam, eds. *Indivisible: An Anthology of Contemporary South Asian American Poetry*. Fayetteville, NC: University of Arkansas Press, 2010.

Biswas, Mita. *Representations of a Culture in Indian English Poetry*. Shimla: Indian Institute of Advanced Studies, 2009.

Chandra, Ravi. "Cleanup on Aisle # 3." *Indivisible*. Ed. Neelanjana Banerjee, Kummi Kaipa, and Pireeni Sundaralingam. 137-139.

Dickinson, Emily. *The Poems of Emily Dickinson. Variorum Edition*. Ed. R.W. Franklin. Vol 3. Cambridge, MA: Belknap Press, 1998.

Divakaruni, Chitra Banerjee. *Leaving Yuba City*. New York: Doubleday, 1997.

Fisher Fishkin, Shelley. "The Crossroads of Cultures: The Transnational Turn in American Studies." *American Quarterly* 57.1 (March 2005): 17-57.

Katrak, Ketu H. "South Asian American Literature." *An Interethnic Companion to Asian American Literature*. Ed. King-Kok Cheung. Cambridge, MA: Cambridge University Press, 1997. 192-218.

King, Bruce. *Modern Indian Poetry in English*. Rev. ed. New Delhi: Oxford University Press, 2001.

---."To be or Not to be Diasporic: Alas, Poor India!, I knew her." *Journal of Postcolonial Writing* 42.2 (November 2006): 139-154.

Kipling, Rudyard. *Just So Stories. The Writings in Prose and Verse of Rudyard Kipling*. Vol. XX. New York, NY: Charles Scribner's Sons, 1911.

Oates, Joyce Carol. "Soul at the White Heat: The Romance of Emily Dickinson's Poetry." *Critical Inquiry* 13.4 (Summer 1987): 806-824.

Obama, Barack. "Barack Obama's Inaugural Address (transcript)." *New York Times* 20 Jan. 2009. 1-3. Web. 26 Aug. 2010.

Ong, Paul M., Lucie Cheng, and Leslie Evans. "Migration of Highly Educated Asians and Global Dynamics." *Asian and Pacific Migration Journal* 1.3-4 (1992): 543-567.

Patel, Shailja. "Shilling Love." Ed. Neelanjana Banerjee, Kummi Kaipa and Pireeni Sundaralingam. *Indivisible*. 120-125.

---. Homepage. *Shailja.com*. 26 Aug. 2010. <http://www.shailja.com/index.html>.

Plato. *The Phaedrus, Lysis, and Protagoras*. Trans. J. Wright. New York, NY: Macmillan, 1887.

Ramanujan, A. K. "Parables and Commonplaces." *Writers in East-West Encounters: New Cultural Readings*. Ed. Guy Amirthanayagam. London: MacMillan, 1982. 138-149.

---. *Second Sight*. Delhi: Oxford University Press, 1986.

Reddy, Srikanth. "Centre of Margin." Interview by Amatoritsero Ede with Srikanth Reddy. *Sentinel Poetry (Online)* 52 (April 2007). Web. <http://www.sentinelpoetry.org.uk/0407/interview.html>. August 26, 2010.

---. *Facts for Visitors*. Berkeley, CA: University of California Press, 2004.

Sharma, Rahsmi. "Crossing the Dark Waters." Introduction. *Living in America: Poetry and Fiction by South Asian American Writers*. Ed. Roshni Rustomji Kerns. Boulder, CO: Westview Press, 1995. 11-25.

Sharma, Prageeta. "Not Your Mother's Diaspora: Voices of the Asian-American Avant-Garde." Interview with Summi Kaipa. *The Women's Review of Books* 19.10-11 (July 2002): 27-28.

---. *The Opening Question*. New York, NY: Fence, 2004.

Srikanth, Rajini. *The World Next Door: South Asian American Literature and the Idea of America*. Philadelphia, PA: Temple University Press, 2004.

Thayil, Jeet. "Divided Time: India and the End of Diaspora." Introduction. *Journal of Postcolonial Writing* 42.2 (November 2006): 125-128.

---. *English*. New Delhi: Penguin, 2003.

Vazirani, Reetika. *World Hotel*. Port Townsend, WA: Copper Canyon Press, 2002.

Williams, William Carlos. *The Collected Poems of William Carlos Williams.* Vol. I. 1909-1939. Ed. Walton Litz and Christopher MacGowan. New York, NY: New Directions, 1986.

Xie, Y., and K.A. Goyette. *The American People, Census 2000: A Demographic Portrait of Asian Americans.* New York, NY: Russell Sage Foundation Press, 2004.

Martina Pfeiler (Dortmund)

No Rules But in Schools?: Teaching and Learning from Slam Poetry

Despite its initial grassroots status in the United States, slam poetry has spread globally, to urban centers and small towns, as a popular performance poetry event – one that has been taken to a professional level in both national and transnational arenas. Over the past 25 years, poetry slams have encouraged hundreds of thousands of people of all ages, ethnicities, professions, sexual orientations and literary backgrounds not only to write poetry but also to share it with fellow poets and audiences in a live situation. The performance aspect of slams can be characterized by a number of elements that are at work such as, for example, immediacy, dramatic tension, vernacular speech, humor and consequently laughter, physical and vocal control, spontaneity and improvisation. These and many more characteristics are closely related to the performative skills of the poet and place anyone who is interested in critically approaching slam poetry into quite a different mode of analysis than he or she may be used to from analyzing print poetry. Furthermore, what makes poetry slams special is that they thrive on a dynamic interaction between a slam poet and his or her audience. All of this gives an indication of how slams can be utilized in the classroom. There is, however, even more to gain from a literary, media and cultural investment in the subject.

In her book *Voicing American Poetry: Sound and Performance from the 1920s to the Present* (2008), Lesley Wheeler points out that "[l]iterary debates about voice in the 1960s and 1970s, and early 1980s, cast oral and written cultures into competitive relation within one another" (19). Even though a lot has changed since then, slam poetry has up until recently been largely ignored for educational purposes *inside* the classroom. Likewise, slam poetry itself has traditionally positioned itself critically *against* academia. I hope that my discussion of the genre will shed some light on slam's literary and cultural significance for teachers and students who may become, or may well already be, slam poets and members of responsive slam audiences themselves.

The purpose of this essay is thus threefold: (1) to provide a transatlantic introduction to the history of the genre; (2) to engage in a sample analysis of a slam poem entitled "Bi-Racial Hair" by Zora Howard from 2006; and (3) to conclude with some suggestions about how to teach the poem in order to highlight its literary and cultural relevance for the English classroom.

1. Slam Poetry: A Transatlantic Introduction to the Genre

Poetry slams were initiated by construction worker and poet Marc Kelly Smith's idea to stage poetry in a competitive form at the Green Mill Tavern in Chicago in 1987. Only four years later the first National Poetry Slam (NPS) was hosted in San Francisco and due to its success staged yearly in alternating U.S. cities (e.g. in Boston, Chicago and New York City). Among the earliest and by now the best known slam poets in the United States, one can consider Ariana Waynes, James Cagney Jr., Patricia Smith, Saul Williams, Tracie Morris, Jessica Care Moore, Beth Lisick, Suheir Hammad, Wanda Coleman, Taylor Mali, Bob Holman, Steve Marsh, Maggie Estep and Marc Kelly Smith (aka "Slam Papi") himself. Each of these poets reveals his or her distinct performance aesthetics, yet they are all connected through a creative outburst when they compete against each other with their poetic texts in front of a live audience.

Despite slam's reputation as a relatively young urban literary phenomenon, poetry slams should be seen as part of a much longer tradition of performing poetry in the United States. This tradition's early history includes, for example, Frances Ellen Watkins Harper, an early African American feminist lecturer and poet-performer and the touring poets Charles Whitcomb Riley and William Carlton from the late 19th century. In the 20th century, numerous poets from the Harlem Renaissance, the Beat Generation, feminist poets and spoken word poets, as well as rap and hip hop artists, have made performance their most lived form of poetic expression (cf. Pfeiler 2003; Wheeler 2008).

Across the Atlantic it would not take long for slam poetry to catch fire among many known and unknown writers in Europe, who were, just like their U.S. counterparts, eager to perform (and not just read) their poems and prose texts in front of an audience. In Germany it does not take a lot of effort to find a poetry slam in or near one's hometown or to get informed about upcoming performances by one's favorite slammers through *MySlam.Net*, a web portal that is supported by the European Union's Education, Audiovisual and Culture Executive Agency (cf. http://www.myslam.net). Grassroot initiatives still keep pace with official attempts to turn poetry slams into a marketable product that continues to receive considerable media coverage on public and private television in both the United States (HBO, PBS, MTV) and Germany (ARTE, WDR).

In November 2010, the 14th German International Poetry Slam was hosted in Duisburg as one of the European Cultural Capital events that went on in the Ruhr-Area that year (cf. http://www.slam2010.de). In Dortmund, where I teach U.S. American literature and culture, poetry jams and slams regularly take place both on-campus and off-campus. They have become a vital part of the city's literary landscape – one that is well connected with other slam cities including Hamburg, Hannover, Bremen, Koblenz, Kassel and Bielefeld. A very small but highly active number of my students regularly participate in slams or engage in hosting poetry events, which for them and their fellow students has taken class discussions related to performance poetry to a very tangible level. Thus, organizing a poetry slam in the classroom and attending at least one public poetry slam with students have become crucial components of my seminars.

Although poetry slams may vary considerably in particular cities, there are certain rules that the organization Poetry Slam, Inc., (PSI) has specified for the international coalition of poetry slams:

- Each poem must be of the poet's own construction;
- Each poet gets three minutes (plus a ten-second grace period) to read one poem. If the poet goes over time, points will be deducted from the total score;
- The poet may not use props, costumes or musical instruments;
- Of the scores the poet receives from the five judges, the high and low scores are dropped and the middle three are added together,

giving the poet a total score of 0-30 (cf. http://www.poetryslam. com).

If one briefly reflects on these rules, it becomes clear that in slam poetry literary authorship, as well as the "authorship" of a performance, is fundamental to the genre. In other words, it would neither be acceptable to perform a poem written by another poet (dead or alive), nor to have one's own poem staged by someone else. Interaction with the audience, facial expression, gesturing, vocal control and other components of the physical performance of the poem are solely in the hands of the composer. Writing *for* the stage is thus crucial when writing a slam poem, which can be lyric, dramatic or narrative in style or a mixture of all of these literary modes of writing. It additionally involves putting much effort into working with the sounds of spoken language as well as with body language, instead of focusing for example on the visual effect of written words on the page.

Given the intimate and social atmosphere at poetry slams where the author of a poem is physically present, there is a lot of room for speculation as to whether the material of a poem is close to the performer's life. In her chapter "I Sing the Body Authentic: Slam Poetry and the Cultural Politics of Performing Identity," Susan Somers-Willett explores Judith Butler's concept of identity being performative. The performance of identity, in Butler's terms, can be interpreted as a convincing performative citation of culturally established behavior patterns (75). Therefore, Somers-Willett calls poems that come across as an expression of the author's self "identity poems": "Inhabiting the space where the 'I' of the page translates quite seamlessly to the 'I' of the stage, the author comes to embody declarations about personal experience in performance" (69). Although an embodiment of a written self cannot directly translate into a performative self on stage, given the shift in media involved, identity poems function as cultural circuits of personal expression in live performance. These identities are performed and perceived as authentic, because they sound, feel and appear to be very close to the poet on stage as well as to the recipient's perception of the author.

However, there also many slam poems in which alternative subject positions are explored within the fictional realm of writing and performing. Oftentimes irony is achieved by creating a persona that is very different from the poet and is thus implicitly mocked.

Based upon the rules mentioned above, a slam poem can tentatively be considered confined poetry, since a performance text is restricted to a maximum of three minutes and ten seconds. This has an effect not only on the written piece, but also on the speed and style of its delivery. The rules also enforce a clear generic boundary between musical and theatrical performances and slam performance, as no props, costumes or instruments are allowed on stage. Sheets of paper can be held in one's hands or put on a sheet stand, yet most poets who perform at the National Poetry Slams recite their poems from memory and frequently reveal a high level of trained acting skills.

The competitive nature of slam poetry is guaranteed through a point system, in which five jury members assign a maximum of ten points to each poem, after which the worst and best result gets dropped. There is a deduction of 0.5 points for each ten seconds that the poet goes over time (i.e. over three minutes and ten seconds).

What remains unmentioned in the list above is that a master of ceremonies (SlamMaster; Emcee) is ultimately in charge of the event. He or she introduces the poets, counts the points and announces the ones who make it into the next round, as well as juggling the oftentimes varied emotional reactions of the audience. Much of the spirit of a poetry slam is geared towards finding compromises, so that excellence in poetic and performative style can be (but does not have to be) outdone by a great sense of humor (and vice versa). Especially in Germany, where frequently prose texts are included in slams, rather than rhymed or free-verse poetry, the question of where a poetry slam starts and stand-up comedy (or "slamedy") begins, has often been raised. Ko Bylanzky's and Rayl Patzak's *Poetry Slam. Was die Mikrophone halten*, an anthology of German and U.S. poets published in 2000, testifies to this interesting genre-bender. Several of the contributions by German writers are prose texts, such as slam veteran Jaromir Konecny's "Liebesgrüße aus der Gruft" or Laura E.'s text "ursprung," whereas only two prose texts are part of the chapter on "U.S. Slammers."

On asking Bob Holman, slam master/poet/activist and founder of the Bowery Poetry Club in NYC, whether he thinks that there is something distinctly "U.S. American" about slams, despite (or because of) slam's international commitment, he quite comprehensively explains:

> Only in that U.S. has institutionalized the rules and a sense of "ownership." Competitive and mock competitive poetry readings have occurred throughout history – oral improvised poetry battles are found in many cultures even today. The energy of U.S. Slam is undeniable, and that certainly helps to promulgate Slam. But each locale remakes slam its own way, and that's the way it should be. (Email to author, 16 January 2011)

Whereas at regular poetry slams usually individuals compete against each other, National Poetry Slams in the U.S.A. have become team slams over the past few years, in which 80 teams (consisting of four to five poets and a coach) try to win for a particular city over the course of several days. As a consequence, the Individual World Poetry Slam has been held since 2003, which brings back the spirit of individual winners of slams and connects slam poets internationally.

> The Individual World Poetry Slam, or iWPS is a performance poetry tournament much like NPS, though designed for individual competition. Poets from all over the world meet and compete in a multi-day performance poetry contest. iWPS got its start in April 2003, when Poetry Slam Inc. voted to start a new event: the Individual World Poetry Slam Championship. The idea was to pull poets from both certified poetry slam venues around the world and individual poets not affiliated with any certified venues (storm poets). These poets would compete to declare who was THE number one poet in the world. (http://www.poetryslam.com)

Since 2008 Poetry Slam Inc. has organized a yearly competition entitled Women of the World (cf. http://wow.poetryslam.com), in which twelve women who excelled in the National Poetry Slam compete against each other. The reason for this is that quite often poetry slams are dominated by men.

Furthermore, what is interesting from a youth-culture perspective is that poetry slams for teenagers have gained enormous popularity in the U.S. over the past fifteen years. *Youth Speaks*, a non-profit organization, which has been devoted to working with young people in numerous creative ways since 1996, has taken on poetry slams as one of its most thriving educational tools:

Committed to a critical, youth-centered pedagogy, Youth Speaks places young people in control of their intellectual and artistic development. We are urgently driven by the belief that literacy is a need, not a want, and that literacy comes in various forms. As we move more deeply into the 21st Century, oral poetry is helping to define the new American Voice. By making the connection between poetry, spoken word, youth development and civic engagement, Youth Speaks aims to deconstruct dominant narratives in hopes of achieving a more inclusive, and active, culture. Believing that young people have the tools to take control of their lives through language, Youth Speaks encourages youth to express themselves using their own vernacular. (http://youthspeaks.org/voice/about/what-is-youth-speaks-history)

Youth Speaks organized the first Teen Poetry Slams in the U.S.A. in 1998. Additionally, as one of its many initiatives, the first annual Unified District Poetry Slam took place in San Francisco in 2010, in which more than 60 youth poets represented 25 Bay Area high schools across eight school districts (cf. http://www.youtube.com/watch?v=YdV-DpglXZY). In 2011 the fourteenth Brave New Voices International Youth Poetry Festival was held in San Francisco. At the event more than 500 young poets from international communities in the U.S.A. and many other countries met in workshops and participated in the championship (cf. http://www.bravenewvoices.org).

On the East Coast, introducing teenagers to literary art education, building community and expressing social concerns through slam poetry are equally on the agenda of the creative mentors who work for Urban Word NYC, "a grassroots non-profit organization that provides free, safe, uncensored and ongoing writing and performance opportunities for NYC teens" (http://www.urbanwordnyc.org). The topics that high school students address in their slam poems are highly outspoken. The teenagers write about overwhelming issues such as what it means to live with the aftermath of rape, abortion, racial and sexual discrimination, police brutality or the terminal illnesses of relatives. Given the direct and creative engagement with these harsh topics, as well as lighter ones, the communal value that poetry slams have for teenagers in urban communities in the USA is highly significant.

In the next section of this paper, I will therefore provide an analysis of the poem "Bi-racial Hair" by Zora Howard based on a

YouTube clip of her performance in front of 1,500 people at the Urban Word NYC Teen Poetry Slam in 2006 – at an age of only thirteen years.

2. Slam Poetry: Analyzing "Bi-racial Hair" by Zora Howard

The poem "Bi-racial Hair" has been accessed on YouTube 525,000 times, surging by an astounding 30,000 hits in just one month between December 2010 and January 2011. Despite the controversy of making content available on YouTube or MySpace for free, it has to be considered the poem's major form of publication as well as its main source for analysis. Additionally, when interpreting slam poetry one often has to transcribe a poem based on what one hears, which is what I had to do for the poem "Bi-Racial Hair" by Zora Howard. The poem has also recently been published in *Clutch*, Howard's first collection of poetry. Moreover, in 2009 Zora Howard won New York City's first Youth Poet Laureate title at the legendary Nuyorican Poetry Café.

Bi-Racial Hair

I have bi-racial hair
Pantene Pro-V waves on the top
Easy to comb, style, rock
Until I encounter my naps.
I'm not talking about those cute detangle-with-the-spray-naps.
I'm talking about those, slave naps, like,
No comb, brush, or man can handle the mess I am naps, like,
No way you are touching my hair-naps, like,
Back ten feet up, or we can dance naps
Those naps, like,
Damn!
I have bi-racial hair,
Those smoothed side silk flats hanging long from my mane,
Until you get to the back until you encounter the jungle, in which you can
find Tarzan and Jane.
In the front you forget and relax in pleasure,
Until you reach to the back and remember pain
Baby soft baby hair slicked back with that good 4-dollar-pomade,
Get those roots and biscuits entangled,

Soaked in that same olive oil in the spaghetti sauce ma made.
I have bi-racial hair.
Combs attracted to run freely in my fine breezy, just put them combs in
the parts the most you can make,
Until it gets to the back and
Breaks.
I have bi-racial hair
Like –
Momma said all she could do with it was put in two big braids,
And sometimes that was too much,
So she left half of it free.
Hours in the mirror, hours in the mirror,
Convincing myself I look just like Alicia Keys
I have bi-racial hair,
'cause I have bi-racial blood.
I'm not talking about that cute they met and fell in love blood.
I'm talking about that slave raped six times by the master,
Birthing six mixed babies, later hung, blood.
I'm talking about that cross burning in the mud blood
And you call me a mud blood?
Slit my wrist,
my blood does not excrete in black and white.
I dream in verse and in red
Like what dripped from Emmet Till's lip when he was killed
from breaking down color lines
Bi-racial who never dares question the story told by her middle school,
Bi-racial who succumbs to the abuse of the kid in her middle school,
Because her lack of brute makes him call her an Oreo
"But her skin isn't that dark, so more like cinnamon vanilla wafer
or a mullato-that's more like it: a reverse mulatto"
I am not a fucking cookie or a berry!!
My roots are deep too
my bi-racial roots are not blind
or more than cotton soft
because my blood's from in the sun, picking cotton too
a thousand times discredited for my race
discredited from my history y'all never get
Because there are no captions about my truth in textbooks
let textbooks be your truth
and sprinkle the ashes of your history into streams
I scream for a day some place where
maybe y'all all accept me
Maybe we need to wake up again one day

And get a new point of view
Like something new or maybe it's time for me to make up my own race

> They'll love my high yellow belly, their hips, skinny fingers, no cheek
> having and biracial hair
> maybe I'll be green 'cause my people drove me there
> cause ya'll people drove me there
> with my tender heart
> tender head
> and bi-racial hair

Zora Howard, who performs her poem by heart, starts out with an affirmative statement, exclaiming the following sentence into the microphone on stage: "I have bi-racial hair." This short assertion of a first-person speaker is very characteristic of a slam poem, which frequently starts with a sentence of self-characterization or self-agonizing, which to a varying degree immediately shocks or entertains the audience (e.g. Wanda Coleman's ironic rendering of her poem "I Live for My Car," Maggie Estep's "I Am an Emotional Idiot" in Adler and Holman 1996; or Susan Ross's "White Girl Blues" and Evert Eden's "I Want to be a Woman" in Devlin 1998).

The successive, rhythmically alternating lines that follow, "Pantene Pro-V waves on the top / Easy to comb, style, rock," which end in a near rhyme, create an immediate flow – one that seems (almost) induced by the shampoo product. In addition to rhythm, meter, rhyme, tone, volume, facial expressions and gestures become crucial markers of the slam poem by Zora Howard, who right from the beginning evokes a great response from her audience. The speaker seems to be proud and relaxed about her easy-to-comb hair and gestures this, until she discovers "naps" in it. More specifically, she discovers "slave naps" at the back of her head, which takes her on a tour-the-force of self-discernment in which she negotiates what it means to her to be confronted with her "biracial heritage."

Evoking Malcolm X's autobiographical text "Hair," and many other stories of African Americans who forcefully attempted to conk their (entire) hair, the speaker shares childhood memories of straightening her hair that is not soaked with harsh chemicals, but a "good 4-dollar pomade" and "olive oil." It is the same oil with which her mother used to cook spaghetti, making her implicitly an accomplice to white beauty standards. Whenever she describes her smooth hair at the front part of her head, Zora Howard's voice, too, takes on a softened quality until she gets to her "jungle" in the back, in which her comb not gets only stuck, but even "breaks."

The speaker's dramatic self-obsession with her hair poses not simply a disappointment over the hair that she inherited, favoring her "smooth and silk" type of hair over her curly hair. Rather, the hair at the back of her head functions as a physical token through which painful collective memories surface. After a brief humorous confession that she has tried to convince herself that she looks just like the bi-racial musician Alicia Keys, she relates herself to her female black ancestors on her paternal line, who: "[were] raped six times by the master, / Birthing six mixed babies, later hung blood." The speaker's vocal performance in this part of the poem becomes increasingly aggressive and accusative, creating an emphatic response in the audience. Consequently, her description of the obstacles involved when combing her hair gains in metaphoric quality, which points to highly complex feelings that the speaker in the poem has about her ethnic identity.

In a dramatic monologue that follows, she contests racist perceptions of others who call her "a mud blood," challenging them to "Slit my wrist, / my blood does not excrete in black and white. / I dream in verse and in red / Like what dripped from Emmet Till's lip when he was killed / from breaking down color lines." The speaker counters assumptions about blood with a powerful uttering of the line "I dream in verse and in red" and equates herself metaphorically to every human being. In her identity quest, Howard makes an ardent case for the poetic fervor that pulsates through her veins.

The consecutive lines recall the murder of Emmet Louis Till, an African American fourteen-year-old boy from Chicago, who was abducted and brutally killed during his summer vacation, visiting his uncle in Alabama in 1955. Despite the fact that all evidence pointed to Carolyn and Roy Byrant, the murderers were never convicted. The couple acted out of racial hatred, which was provoked by Emmet Till's resolute attempt to ask Carolyn Bryant out for a date during her husband's absence at their grocery store in order to impress his cousins (http://www.emmetttillmurder.com).

In the final part of the poem, the speaker addresses the racism she herself has experienced at school, by vocally and mimetically slipping into the role of a classmate who likens her to Oreo cookies and analyzes her skin color in a racist way. He sarcastically demarcates color lines with the lines "But her skin isn't that dark, so more like cinnamon vanilla wafer / or a mullato – that's more like it: a reverse mulatto." After these remarks, during which she has lowered her voice to imitate her male classmate, the speaker briefly pauses, then puts one hand into the other, before her speech unexpectedly explodes with the enormously enraged and yet self-confidently shouted line "I am not a fucking cookie or a berry." At this point in the performance clip, a medium shot of an audience section, where predominately but not exclusively African Americans sit, is provided. After Howard refutes her classmate's statement, many audience members break out in acclamations and stand up from their seats to cheer her performance.

In an unswerving voice, the speaker claims her place in history, linking herself to the hardships of her ancestors by having her blood transcend time as it has "picked cotton too." In the following lines below she takes up and subverts the river and the dream as symbols that have been employed by many African American poets and politicians before her – most notably Langston Hughes in his poems "The Negro Speaks of Rivers" (1921) and "A Dream Deferred" (1951) and in particular Martin Luther King's "I Have a Dream" speech (1963):

> Because there are no captions about my truth in textbooks
> let textbooks be your truth
> and sprinkle the ashes of your history into streams
> I scream for a day some place where
> maybe y'all all accept me
> Maybe we need to wake up again one day

The tone in her voice and the content of the poem, however, do not share King's optimism. The speaker poignantly suggests that rather than continuing to dream, "maybe we need to wake up again one day." She is aggravated, outraged and exhausted by a centuries-long racial discrimination that still continues into her daily life at school in the twenty-first century.

Zora Howard closes her slam poem with what seems like a random choice at first: "maybe I'll be green cause my people drove me there / cause ya'll people drove me there / with my tender heart / tender head and bi-racial hair." Among playful associations that these lines may evoke on a content level in terms of a punk-like green hair and an unrealistic green skin color (in addition to the yellow belly in the preceding lines), the sulky and dramatic tone seems to convey that all people harassing her have a potential to push her into suicide. It is a future in which the speaker can retain her "bi-racial hair" and where she no longer has to go through a collective or personal trauma. Whereas in a silent reader reception of the final section in the poem, I would argue, one is much more tempted to interpret the content of them poem as an *ironic* stance, the tension that Howard creates in her acoustic performance renders it in a much more dramatic and confrontational way.

Having become witness to how identity is negotiated and performed in this piece by a young female teenager of African American and Caucasian American decent, the audience responds in an overwhelming way. The judges too were impressed by her performance, ultimately making her the winner of the Urban Word NYC Teen Slam in 2006.

3. Slam Poetry: Teaching "Bi-racial Hair"

A slam poem such as Zora Howard's "Bi-racial Hair" sparks many questions on a literary and cultural level that can be utilized for lively classroom discussions. It will have to remain for the teacher to decide which texts and suggestions that are mentioned below he or she would like make use of, but I hope to provide at least some vital ideas for what students can learn from slam poetry.

Reading a slam poem silently renders its acoustic quality only hypothetical, even though one can make students try to vocally mine its potential for sound without having heard the performance version. Thus, in order to make students aware of the differences between silent reader reception of a poem, hearing a spoken-word poem, watching a performance clip or writing and performing a poem themselves, I usually try to expose them to as many (re-)mediated versions as possible. Even if there is a print publication of the poem available, the performance versions of slam poems often differ from the one in print in terms of length or word choice. Analyzing the recording of a slam poem and juxtaposing it with the experience of reading print poetry raises a student's awareness of signifying practices in various media. In the course of the 20th century, poetry as a genre has seen exceptional developments through convergences with audio, audiovisual and hypermedia technologies. It has entered the World Wide Web through electronic poetry and audiovisual platforms such as YouTube. There are even live-stream broadcasts of poetry slams on the Internet such as, for example, those organized by the Bowery Club in New York City. Poetry, a first and foremost cultural phenomenon that is intertwined with media cultures on all levels, should therefore not only be seen in the context of old performance poetry traditions, but also of new ways of creating and publishing poetry (cf. Pfeiler 2010).

Zora Howard's performance is targeted at an audience that has only one chance to listen to it. However, since the poem is not all that easy to understand, I ask students to watch and listen to the clip several times before coming to class. In addition I show the poem at least once in class in its entire length and then divide it up into audiovisual sections. This way the class can focus on both the bodily performance and the vocal performance in more detail.

From a stylistic point of view, it is important to talk with the students about the fact that rather than employing complex imagery, thematic density and linguistically innovative formal features, slam poems draw from everyday speech that can be characterized by repetition, anaphora, parallelism, colloquialism, proverbs, dialect and slang. Words such as "like," "y'all," and "cause" and the phrase "I am not a fucking cookie" may not be expected in poetry, yet they become relevant markers of the speaker's youth-cultural background and performed sociolect. Moreover, the poem also contains a conspicuously high number of alliterations and an occasional internal rhyme, as for example very noticeably in the following two lines: "Soaked in that same olive oil in the spaghetti sauce ma made" and "Combs attracted to run freely in my fine breezy." Drawing one's students' awareness to these formal sound features will provide them with an idea of how the soundscape achieves its very direct and appealing quality. Introducing concepts such as phonetic intensifiers and onomatopoeia, cacophony and euphony, rhyme and repetition, rhythm and meter, tone and pitch, volume and pause provides students with a sufficient terminology to address the vocal specificities of a slam poem in addition to the images that are created on the semantic level.

The most pressing and interesting cultural issue that this poem raises is how people with a bi- or multi-ethnic heritage perceive themselves and are perceived in the U.S.A. The slam poem can thus be taught as part of a series of slam texts related to ethnicity, while also sparking discussion of expressions of ethnic identities in one's own country and, respectfully, in one's classroom. A broader (self-)reflection on racial inequality and racial discrimination and the complexities of a "bi-racial" heritage contribute to a deeper cultural understanding of the issue at hand.

As has been shown in this analysis, Zora Howard belongs to a group of slam poets who "linger on personal and political themes, the most common of them being the expression of marginalized identity" (Somers-Willett 7). A productive resource for further discussion about literary expressions of identity is Pearl Fuyo Gaskins's book *What are You? Voices of Mixed Race Young People*, which contains a diverse range of portraits and literary expressions of American teenagers with a bi- and multiracial heritage.

What Howard's poem clearly bears witness to is that a highly problematic history of slavery in the United States still plays out discursively, poetically and performatively in the life of a contemporary teenager. Zora Howard's slam poem is far from the postmodern celebration of diversity that one often encounters in TV shows or in commercials, even as her reference to the colors yellow and green instead of black & white thinking breaks up binary oppositions.

To conclude, this essay has aimed to demonstrate that slam poetry has much to teach students and instructors about social controversies. As a genre, it locates itself in the midst of very subtle clashes within contemporary literary and ethnic culture(s), while presenting one of the currently most popular forms of poetry in the U.S.A. and in Germany and many other countries in the world.

Bibliography

Adler, Bill and Bob Holman. *Grand Slam! The Best of the National Poetry Slam*. Mouth Almighty Records, 1996.
Anderson, Deverey. *Emmett Till Murder*. <http://www.emmetttillmurder.com>. Jan 2011.
Anglesey, Zoe. *Listen Up! Spoken Word Poetry*. New York: One World, 1999.
Bowery Poetry Club Website. Bowery Club. <http://www.bowerypoetry.com>. Jan 2011.
Gaskins, Pearl Fuyo. *What Are You? Voices of Mixed Race Young People*. New

York: Henry Holt, 1999.
Holman, Bob, and Mark Pellington. *The United States of Poetry*. New York: Harry N. Abrams, 1996.
Howard, Zora. "Bi-racial Hair." YouTube 18 Sept. 2006. <http://www.youtube.com/watch?v=RTnxJdxhU7o>. Jan 2011.
Howard, Zora. *Clutch*. NYC Youth Poet Laureate Series Nr. 1. New York: PenManShip Publishers Group, 2011.
Jordan, June and Adrienne Torf. *Collaboration. Selected Works (1983-2000)*. Abango Music, 2003.
MySlam.Net: Living Poets Society. MySlam. <http://www.myslam.de>. Jan 2011.
Patzak, Rayl, and Ko Blanzky. *Poetry Slam. Was die Mikrophone halten: Poesie für das Neue Jahrtausend*. Mainz: Ariel, 2000.
Pfeiler, Martina. *Sounds of Poetry: Contemporary American Performance Poets*. Tübingen: Narr, 2003.
---. *Poetry Goes Intermedia: U.S.-amerikanische Lyrik des 20. und 21. Jahrhundert aus kultur- und medienwissenschaftlicher Perspektive*. Tübingen: Francke, 2010.
Poetry Slam Inc. Website. Poetry Slam, Inc. <http://www.poetryslam.com>. Jan 2011.
SlamNation. Dir. by Paul Devlin. With Saul Williams. Devlin Pix, USA: 2005. (1998).
Somers-Willett, Susan. *The Cultural Politics of Slam Poetry: Race, Identity, and the Performance of Popular Verse in America*. Michigan: Michigan University Press, 2009.
Urban Word NYC Website. Urban Word NYC. <http://urbanwordnyc.org>. Jan 2011.
Wheeler, Lesley. *Voicing American Poetry: Sound and Performance from the 1920s to the Present*. Ithaca: Cornell, 2008.
Youth Speaks Website. Youth Speaks. <http://youthspeaks.org>. Jan 2011.

Contributors' Addresses

Prof. Dr. Kornelia Freitag, Ruhr-Universität Bochum, Fakultät für Philologie, Englisches Seminar, Universitätsstr. 150, D-44780 Bochum.

Prof. Dr. Walter Grünzweig, Technische Universität Dortmund, Fakultät für Kulturwissenschaften, Institut für Anglistik und Amerikanistik, Emil-Figge-Str. 50, D-44227 Dortmund.

Dr. David Huntsperger, Lawrence Technological University, Department of Humanities, Social Sciences, and Communication, 21000 West Ten Mile Road, Southfield, MI 48075-1058.

Prof. em. Dr. Heinz Ickstadt, Freie Universität Berlin, John-F.-Kennedy-Institut Department of Literature, Lansstr. 7-9, D-14195 Berlin.

Dr. Martina Pfeiler, Technische Universität Dortmund, Fakultät für Kulturwissenschaften, Institut für Anglistik und Amerikanistik, Emil-Figge-Str.50, D-44227 Dortmund.

Dr. Brian M. Reed, University of Washington, Department of English, Box 354330, Seattle, WA 98195-4330.

Prof. Dr. Susanne Rohr, Universität Hamburg, Institut für Anglistik und Amerikanistik,Von-Melle-Park 6, D-20146 Hamburg.

Dr. Julia Sattler, Technische Universität Dortmund, Fakultät für Kulturwissenschaften, Institut für Anglistik und Amerikanistik, Emil-Figge-Str. 50, D-44227 Dortmund.

Prof. Dr. Sabine Sielke, Rheinische Friedrich-Wilhelms-Universität Bonn, Institut für Anglistik, Amerikanistik und Keltologie, Lehrstuhl für North American Studies, Regina-Pacis-Weg 5, D-53133 Bonn.

Dr. Lisa Simon, University of Montana, Department of English, Liberal Arts 133, 32 Campus Drive, Missoula, MT.

Prof. Dr. em. Wolfgang Wicht, Universität Potsdam, Institut für Anglistik und Amerikanistik, Am Neuen Palais 10, D-14469 Potsdam.